We Are NOT Charlie Hebdo!
Free Thinkers Question the French 9/11

Edited by Kevin Barrett

Library of Congress Cataloging-in-Publication Data
We Are NOT Charlie Hebdo! Free Thinkers Question the French 9/11
edited by Kevin Barrett
ISBN 978-0-9961430-0-4

1. January 7 Terrorist Attacks, 2015. 2. War on Terrorism—Political aspects. 3. France—Politics and government, 2015. 4. Charlie Hebdo magazine, 2015.

Cover drawings by Hossein Niroumand
Cover design by Sandra Taylor, The Graphic Page

Advance Praise for
We Are Not Charlie Hebdo:
Free Thinkers Question the French 9/11

"A necessary set of challenging responses to the Islamophobic manipulation of the Charlie Hebdo incident, suggesting the urgent relevance of dissent and suspicion in response to official versions of controversial events."
–Richard Falk, Prof. Emeritus of International Law, Princeton University

"Today's Western governments and mainstream media are not trustworthy. If you want the truth, you need to read books like this."
–Paul Hellyer, former Canadian Secretary of Defense,
author of *The Money Mafia: A World in Crisis*

"Kevin Barrett is among the world's most thoughtful and provocative public intellectuals. In this important volume he has assembled an array of equally adept minds to disassemble and reassess the Western news media-intelligence complex's single most significant cavalcade of misdirection and disinformation since September 11th, 2001."
–James Tracy, Professor of Communications, Florida Atlantic University

"Read Guy Debord if you want it explained to you why you are either a knave or a dupe if you continue to participate in 'free and fair elections.' Read this book if you want it explained to you why you are either a knave or a dupe if you tolerate any form of Islamophobia for a single nano-second."
–Eric Wilson, senior lecturer of Law at Monash University,
author *The Spectacle of the False Flag: Parapolitics from JFK to Watergate*

Dear Humaira
With Best wishes
for a happy and fulfilling
life, here and in
hereafter!
Anjum Hassan
4-29-15

SIFTING & WINNOWING

"WHATEVER MAY BE THE
LIMITATIONS WHICH TRAMMEL
INQUIRY ELSEWHERE, WE BE-
LIEVE THAT THE GREAT STATE
UNIVERSITY OF WISCONSIN
SHOULD EVER ENCOURAGE
THAT CONTINUAL AND FEAR-
LESS SIFTING AND WINNOWING
BY WHICH ALONE THE TRUTH
CAN BE FOUND." TAKEN FROM A
REPORT OF THE BOARD OF REGENTS
IN 1894.
MEMORIAL, CLASS OF 1910.

BOOKS

CONTENTS

Dedicated to all of the victims of the "clash of civilizations". . . and to everyone working to end it.

A Muslim cartoonist's first reaction to the news that fellow cartoonists had been murdered in Paris:

INTRODUCTION: WHY
WE ARE **NOT** *CHARLIE HEBDO ?*

Kevin Barrett

When I heard that a group of cartoonists from the magazine *Charlie Hebdo* had been massacred in Paris, apparently by Muslim extremists, my first reaction was sorrow and anger. As a Muslim and a person of conscience, I am appalled by the destruction of innocent human life. And as a controversial satirist, I know that laughter can be a formidable weapon against power, privilege, and oppression—and that the powerful sometimes retaliate. So when satirists are targeted, my instinct is to defend them.

What's more, I am something of a francophile. I spent a very special year of my life in Paris (1989-1990). My address was on rue Henri IV, adjacent to the Jewish district of *le Marais*. I loved that neighborhood, and the city and country surrounding it. I had Jewish friends there, and Muslim friends as well. (I never dreamed I would be accepting Islam three years later.)

The senseless massacres of January 7th 2015 sickened me. As a Muslim, I felt embarrassed, since the culprits seemingly claimed they had been acting in the name of my religion.

But as I followed news reports on the *Charlie Hebdo* affair, I quickly noticed disturbing signs that something was amiss. The first discordant note was the virtually instantaneous, perfectly-choreographed blossoming of demonstrations that soon included millions of people holding virtually-identical signs displaying the exact same slogan in the exact same font: "*Je suis Charlie.*" It reminded me of the 1929 Torches of Freedom women's rights demonstrations organized by Edward Bernays, the father of modern mind-control techniques, at which thousands of women simultaneously lit and puffed cigarettes for the newsreel cameras. Those seemingly spontaneous demonstrations were covertly manufactured by Bernays. His paymaster: the tobacco companies, who were desperately seeking a way to convince women to smoke. Their problem was that most people at the time believed smoking was unladylike.

Easter Sunday, 1929: Thousands of women in the street simultaneously lit cigarettes. A social taboo disappeared overnight, and cigarette sales doubled.

Torches of Freedom was a mass mind-control operation that caused millions of people to react in exactly the same way, even though none had any conscious knowledge that they had all been brainwashed through the manipulation of their unconscious minds and emotional reactions. Bernays' triumph set a precedent for future mass brainwashing campaigns by governments and corporations.

Fast forward to January, 2015: Millions of people in the street held up the same *Je suis Charlie* sign; France was swept by a wave of anti-Islamic anger; the French underwent mass identification with the "victims," the concepts *Jews/Israel* and *freedom/secularism*; and French society was irretrievably altered. Within a few days, fifty-four people had been arrested for saying things the government didn't like, all in the name of protecting freedom.[1] As on 9/11, the official, paradoxical response to terrorists attacking freedom was to roll back freedom. It smacked of social engineering, Edward Bernays style.

On January 7th, just hours after the attack, more than 100,000 people gathered across France, many with the *Je suis Charlie* signs.[2] Four days later, on January 11th, about three million people marched in France, two million of them in Paris. The Paris march was led by French President François Hollande and several world leaders, including Benjamin Netanyahu, whose Israeli government had murdered more than two thousand Palestinians, most of them civilians, during its onslaught on Gaza the previous summer.

To dissent, to refuse to say "*Je suis Charlie*," had become an Orwellian thoughtcrime. An illusion of mass consensus had been manufactured.

But a few brave, independent, critical voices—representing a wide variety of religious and political perspectives—dared to speak out. Some were mainstream figures. Pope Francis 1st questioned whether free speech includes pornographic blasphemy: "There is a limit. Every religion has its dignity. I cannot mock a religion that respects human life and the human person. If [a close friend] says a swear word against my mother, he's going to get a punch in the nose. One cannot provoke, one cannot insult other people's faith, one cannot make fun of faith."

In the *New York Times*, the Jewish secularist liberal David Brooks published a thoughtful piece on January 8th entitled "I Am Not Charlie Hebdo": "Public reaction to the attack in Paris has revealed that there are a lot of people who are quick to lionize those who offend the views of Islamist terrorists in France but who are a lot less tolerant toward those who offend their own views at home." His conclusion: "In short, in thinking about provocateurs and insulters, we want to maintain standards of civility and respect while at the same time allowing room for those creative and challenging folks who are uninhibited by good manners and taste."[3] His point is well taken: Hardly anyone thinks all forms of obscene or blasphemous insult are okay; but the question is, where do we draw the line? Reasonable people can and do disagree.

Alongside such sensible but unsurprising remarks from the mainstream, there was also a barrage of critical reflection from more original and independent voices. Dieudonné, France's most popular and most controversial comedian, tweeted *Je me sens Charlie Coulibaly*, "I feel like Charlie Coulibaly." (Coulibaly was one of the three alleged terrorists). The dark, ironic joke's meaning was that Dieudonné has been persecuted and prosecuted so much for his political jokes that he feels like a terrorist. The tweet was also a hundred-megaton hand grenade tossed in the general direction of false unanimity and manufactured consensus. But Dieudo's irony was apparently lost on the French government, which—hilariously or tragically, depending on your sensibility—arrested him for his *bon mot*.

High-level Turkish officials also dissented from Charlie Hebdo orthodoxy. Turkey's President Recep Tayyip Erdogan suggested the Charlie Hebdo massacre was a false flag operaton along the lines of Operation Gladio: "The culprits are clear: French citizens undertook this massacre and Muslims were blamed for it." Speaking on Monday, January 12th, Ankara Mayor Melih Gokcek that "Mossad [the Israeli spy agency] is definitely behind such incidents . . . it is boosting enmity towards Islam." Gokcek said Israel staged the attacks to retaliate for French recognition of Palestine. And Ali Sahin, a parliamentarian and foreign affairs spokesman for the ruling AK Party, listed eight reasons why the Charlie Hebdo affair was a false flag.[4]

Influential Russians likewise endorsed the false-flag interpretation. Alexander Zhilin, director of the Moscow Centre for the Study of Applied Problems, said the attack was retribution for Hollande's calling for an end to anti-Russia sanctions. And another leading Russian political analyst, Alexei Martynov, head of the International Institute of New States, said: "For the last 10 years, so-called Islamist terrorism has been under the control of one of the world's leading intelligence agencies. I am sure that some American supervisors are responsible for the terror attacks in Paris, or in any case the Islamists who carried them out."[5]

Another powerful dissenting statement was Paul Craig Roberts' January 13th article "Charlie Hebdo." (A revised version of the piece is published in this book.) A former high-level presidential advisor and Wall Street Journal editor, Roberts points out that the Charlie Hebdo affair "has many of the characteristics of a false flag operation." Two days before Roberts' article, on January 11th, French philosopher-activist Alain Soral had already given a video lecture that prefigured much of what we have learned since. I believe Soral's talk, the transcript of which is included in this book, will stand as a masterpiece of speaking truth to power in the heat of the moment, when it matters most.

As I followed the unequal battle between Charlie Hebdo orthodoxy (Goliath) and Charlie Hebdo dissidence (David), it occurred to me that someone should put together a collection of articles questioning "Charlie orthodoxy" from a variety of perspectives. After all, if the evil terrorists hate nothing more than freedom of thought and expression, our best revenge is to think and write freely, is it not? On the other hand, if if it was, as so many observers suggest, a likely false flag operation, designed to produce the kind of mythic consensus that followed 9/11 and Pearl Harbor, would not our best response *also* be to think critically and freely?

So I began seeking out alternative perspectives. I contacted Dr. Roberts and other notable free thinkers of my acquaintance and solicited the essays and cartoons in this book.

Obligatory disclaimer: The views expressed by each contributor are his or her own. Some like and/or respect some of the slain Charlie Hebdo cartoonists' work; others not so much. Some are deeply offended by certain things published by Charlie Hebdo, while others are not. Some think it was a false flag, others that it *may* have been a false flag; while still others choose not to pursue such lines of inquiry.

This book will ruffle almost everyone's feathers. While each reader will find many things to agree with, he or she will undoubtedly also find portions of the book disagreeable or even offensive. Even I, the editor, am offended by portions of some of the contributions. For example, my friend and colleague Webster Tarpley has outraged me by attacking Alain Soral and Dieudonné, both of whom I admire tremendously. I am equally outraged by Webster's favorable comments on Ataturk and Gen. al-Sisi, whom I view as among the worst genocidal dictators in history. My feelings about those comments of Webster's are probably not unlike the feelings of a Jewish editor facing a contributor who makes admiring remarks about Hitler and Mussolini. But my emotional reactions and personal opinions are not the point. Webster is a brilliant historian, and his contribution to this volume is one of the most important alternative analyses of the Charlie Hebdo affair.

Even people who marched for Charlie Hebdo may find something congenial in these pages. For, ironically, this book is a tribute to the values the high priests of the Church of the Charlie Hebdo Martyrs claim to promote: genuine diversity, respectful dialogue between people with opposing opinions, and the freedom to think and speak in ways that may challenge or offend.

So, at the risk of challenging or offending you, dear reader, I return to my personal narrative to explain from whence the fire-in-the-belly that drove me to make this book happen.

By January 11th, 2015, the day of the gigantic demonstrations, I was no longer identifying with Charlie. I had seen the French government preposterously claim that it would not have caught the killers but for the serendipitous fact that one of them conveniently dropped his ID card in an abandoned getaway car.[6] I had read about the suspicious "suicide" of Helric Frédou, the police investigator who had discovered a hot lead . . .

and then, shortly after refusing an order to drop the case, was found dead with a bullet in the head.[7] I had seen the video purportedly showing the killing of the police officer Frédéric Boisseau with a point-blank AK-47 shot to the head—except that it appears that Boisseau was not shot at all, but rather than the "terrorist" fired a blank round whose cotton or paper wad struck the pavement a few feet away from Boisseau's head, revealing that the "killing" had been staged.[8] I had seen credible news reports that the Rothschilds bought the money-hemorrhaging *Charlie Hebdo* a month before the killings . . . and, thanks to the killings, made a killing.[9] A few weeks later, I saw French political leader Jean Marie LePen call the event a false flag by French intelligence agencies[10]—and then get beat up, and have his house burned down, in apparent retribution.[11]

In short, I suspected I had been duped. My emotions, and the emotions of millions of people around the world, had been manipulated. The Charlie Hebdo affair appeared to have been yet another bloody public relations stunt orchestrated by the forces of what Peter Dale Scott calls "the deep state."[12] It looked like more Operation Gladio, NATO's false flag terror program that butchered hundreds of Europeans in attacks falsely attributed to leftists during the Cold War. With the disappearance of the Communist enemy in 1990, Operation Gladio morphed into Gladio B, a false-flag wave of terror designed to demonize Islam and accomplish various geo-strategic objectives.[13] I thought it likely that Gladio B, perhaps aided and abetted by elements of Israeli intelligence, had struck France. The brilliant, careful, detailed investigative journalism of Hicham Hamza at Panamza.com supplied evidence confirming those impressions.

But whether or not I am right, Charlie Hebdo Orthodoxy needs to be questioned. The purpose of this book is to seek the truth, whatever it may be, in the company of critical, independent thinkers from a variety of national, ethnic, religious, and political backgrounds and perspectives. I respectfully invite you, the reader, to join in the dialogue.

PART 1: BACKGROUND: HISTORICAL PERSPECTIVES

TOWARD A CIVIL GLOBAL DIALOGUE ON BLASPHEMY VS. FREE SPEECH: A MUSLIM VIEW

Kevin Barrett

On January 7th 2015 around 11:30 a.m. local time, a shooting took place at the Paris offices of the French satirical weekly *Charlie Hebdo*. Twelve people were reported dead, including eight *Charlie Hebdo* employees and two national police officers.

Two days later, in an apparently related incident, hostages were taken and five people (including the gunman) were killed at a Hypercasher (Hyper Kosher) supermarket.

The two shootings, which left a total of nineteen people dead, were followed by an orchestrated campaign of mass outrage. The phrase "je suis Charlie" (I am Charlie) became a worldwide advertising brand name vaunting support for free speech and opposition to violence.

Regardless of how, why, and by whom the attacks may have been orchestrated, and regardless of how they were manipulated by politicians and the media, they underlined the need for a global dialogue on issues of blasphemy and free speech. Many Muslims, and some Christians, feel their sacred symbols have been targeted by forces that aim to exterminate their religious communities. (These feelings parallel those of Jews who fear that certain kinds of anti-Jewish speech betray genocidal intent.) Such sensitivities, and insensitivities, create a climate in which violence can flourish.

How can these issues be sorted out? As French philosopher Alain Soral so eloquently states in his contribution to this book, what is needed is a critical historical perspective to counter the mythic, ahistorical discourse of the mass media.

A natural way to begin the dialogue is with a Muslim perspective on the history of blasphemous attacks on the Prophet Muhammad. These "verbal, symbolic attacks" have long been wielded as a weapon of war against the religion of Islam and the community of believers. They did not begin with Charlie Hebdo, or the Danish cartoons, or Salman Rushdie's *Satanic Verses*. They have been occurring for more than one thousand years.

Historical Overview

Throughout the history of the Christian West, discourse on Islam has been marred by periodic bouts of incivility. The West's attitude toward Islam and its prophet—unlike the Muslim world's attitude toward Christianity and its savior—has tended toward visceral hostility and ad hominem attack. This asymmetry of attitudes has sparked conflicts, inflamed hatreds, and contributed to the outbreak of violence.

Medieval Christians did occasionally engage in reasoned or even friendly debate with Muslims. When Saint Francis decided he wanted to become a martyr, he marched into Islamdom clutching a cross, fully expecting that his vigorous defense of Christianity and lack of respect for Islam would inevitably lead to his execution. Instead, he discovered that the Muslims he met, including Sultan Malik al-Kamil, treated him kindly, even reverently, and enjoyed discussing and debating religious issues with a Christian holy man.[14]

But the gentle Saint Francis was the exception that proves the rule. For most medieval Christians, Islam was a diabolical heresy and its prophet a demonic deceiver or false god. Such assumptions prevented Western Christians from rationally assessing Islam or engaging in reasoned dialogue with Muslims.

Dominating early Western perceptions of Islam was the myth of Mahound, an agglomeration of religious writings, legends, and popular beliefs denigrating Islam's prophet. Karen Armstrong describes the mythic figure Mahound as "the enemy and shadow self of Christendom." She describes some of these bizarre slanders:

To explain Muhammad's success, the legends claimed that he had been a magician who had concocted false "miracles" to take in the credulous Arabs and destroy the Church in Africa and the Middle East. One tale spoke of a white bull which had terrorized the population and which finally appeared with the Qur'an, the scripture that Muhammad had brought to the Arabs, floating miraculously between its horns. Muhammad was also said to have trained a dove to peck peas from his ears so that it looked as though the Holy Spirit were whispering into them. His mystical experiences were explained away by the claim that he was an epileptic, which at that time was tantamount to saying that he was possessed by demons. His sexual life was dwelt on in prurient detail: he was credited with every perversion known to men and was said to have attracted people into the religion by encouraging them to indulge their basest instincts.[15]

This medieval hate propaganda, though outlandish and absurd, was remarkably effective. Throughout most of the history of Western Christendom, Christians misunderstood Islam and generally did not tolerate Muslim communities in their midst, despite the fact that most

Muslim lands did tolerate and protect Christians. This "tolerance gap" may be explained by the two groups' respective attitudes toward the other religion's prophet and message. Whereas Christians loathed and slandered Muhammad and his message, Muslims revered and honored Jesus and regarded the Gospels as a divinely revealed (though imperfectly preserved) religion.

Muslims, given their love of Jesus, cannot understand why any Christian would disparage the Prophet Muhammad. Insulting any prophet, whether Moses, Jesus, Muhammad, or any of the 124,000 prophets, seems to Muslims to be in criminally bad taste and tantamount to blasphemy. So while Muslim authorities and populations have been relatively lenient in allowing the expression of heterodox views—Islam has never experienced anything like the Christian Inquisition, witch hunts, and wars of religion—they have tended to draw the line at insults to prophets, especially their own.

A little over 1100 years ago, when Andalusian Islamic civilization was on the rise, and young Christians vied with each other in expressing themselves in polished Arabic, a few Christian extremist malcontents discovered that they could garner attention, and provoke repression from the Muslim authorities, by insulting the Prophet of Islam. Maria Menocal explains:

> In 855, a small number of the most radical opponents of the conversion of their Christian and Latin world openly sought martyrdom. One by one, they indulged in conspicuous public declarations of the deceits of Islam and the perfidies of the Prophet; and although Islam was elastic in matters of doctrine, particularly when it had to do with Christians, they had zero tolerance for disparagement of their Prophet. The would-be martyrs thus knew for a certainty that they were forcing the hands of the authorities of the city by expressly choosing to vilify Muhammad. Leaders on both sides made every attempt to head off such radical behavior and its fatal consequences—in vain. The virulent public attacks continued and the offending Christians were beheaded in public. After about fifty of these gory executions, a spectacle that horrified and enthralled Cordobans of all religions, it was over. The passions of the moment passed and life went on as it had before in this city of thriving religious coexistence. The widespread civil unrest feared by both the Muslim and Christian hierarchies as the violent events were unfolding did not come to pass.[16]

But centuries later, a virulently assertive West began to remember these Christian extremists as the "Mozarab martyrs." In place of the historical truth described by Menocal, Western collective memory invented a false version in which the foul-mouthed provocateurs were remembered as heroes who had chosen death rather than sword-point conversion to Islam. In fact, at the time, the provocateurs "were viewed as wild-eyed, out-of-control radicals by other Cordobans, both Christians and Muslims."[17] Yet later these wild-eyed zealots, whose Christian religion was fully tolerated and protected by the Cordoban Muslim authorities, were remembered by the West as heroes who had resisted the mythical practice of forced conversion to the faith of Mahound. Perhaps those who invented the mendacious myth of the Mozarab martyrs were projecting their own religious intolerance upon their more tolerant Muslim counterparts—exemplifying Armstrong's previously-mentioned interpretation of Mahound as "the shadow self of Christendom."

Though the "tolerance gap" between Muslims and Christians only began to close during 18th century Enlightenment, some Westerners from earlier centuries had already expressed enlightened views, preferring civil dialogue to passionate confrontation. Erasmus, for example, had argued for dispassionate religious dialogue "because in this way the truth, which is often lost amidst too much wrangling may be more surely perceived." Montaigne, another early humanist, had argued for toleration by applying corrosive skepticism to all human opinions: "We should remember, whatever we receive into our understanding, that we often receive false things there, and by these same tools that are often contradictory or deceived."[18] His views recall the way traditional Islamic scholars habitually list the extant opinions about a given topic, sometimes explaining which view they find the most persuasive and why, yet always end with the stipulation: "But God knows best."

The Enlightenment raised Montaigne's corrosive skepticism—and the religious toleration that grew out of it—to the level of official dogma, at least for a growing segment of the Western elite. Such Enlightened intellectuals as Goethe felt free to sing the praises of Islam: "Ob der Koran von Ewigkeit sei? Darnach frag ich nicht! Ob der Koran geschaffen sei? Das weiß ich nicht! Daß er das Buch der Bücher sei, Glaub ich aus Mosleminen-Pflicht." ("Whether the Koran is of eternity? I don't question that! Whether it is created? I don't know that either. That it is the book of books I believe out of the Muslim's duty.")[19]

Goethe's lines reflect the West's growing knowledge about Islam. The great German poet, unlike many of his medieval predecessors, was relatively well-versed in Islamic doctrine and history, thanks to the rise of Orientalist scholarship, whose leading centers were France and Germany. Goethe knew that one of the great debates in Islamic intellectual history concerned the question of whether the Qur'an is created or uncreated—a controversy central to the rise and fall of the Mu'tazilites, a rationalist school that left its mark on Islamic thought more than 1000 years ago.

Goethe's sympathetic, erudite view of Islam would have been unimaginable anywhere in the West only a few centuries earlier.

While the Enlightenment and Orientalist scholarship permitted a freer and better-informed discussion of Islam in the West, the industrial revolution of the 19th century and subsequent imperial conquests created an asymmetry of power that obstructed the prospects for dialogue on the basis of equality. In his famous book *Orientalism*, Edward Said argues that Western knowledge of Islamic cultures was incorporated into the power structures and ideologies of empire, warping that knowledge into a discourse whose internal consistency masked its lack of correspondence with reality.[20]

Today, the West's political, economic, and military domination of the world is in sharp decline. A 2012 study by the Organization of Economic Cooperation and Development (OECD) forecasts that "China, India and the rest of the developing world will eclipse the west in a dramatic shift in the balance of economic power over the next 50 years."[21] The study found that the US and the Eurozone, which currently account for about 40% of global GDP, will decline to 24% of global GDP by 2060, while the total output of China, India and the rest of the developing world will rise from less than 30% to around 60% of total global output.

Perhaps as a reaction to the West's impending relative decline—and to the subsequent fragility of Israel's long-term prospects—a strident discourse of civilizational chauvinism emerged at the beginning of the 21st century. And the primary target of that discourse has been Islam and Muslims. When, after the events of September 11th 2001, US President Bush let slip the word *crusade* and stated "you're either with us or you're with the terrorists," he was not drawing a distinction between those who use the military tactic of terrorism (attacks on civilians) versus those who do not. On the contrary, his barely veiled meaning was to draw a stark line between the West and the Islamic world. This official adoption of the Bernard Lewis/Samuel Huntington "clash of civilizations" has not been conducive to civility in West-Islam dialogue.

The post-9/11 US-led wars on the Muslim-majority nations of Iraq and Afghanistan, and the US-led targeting of such Muslim countries as Syria, Libya, Somalia, Egypt, Lebanon, Sudan, and Iran for violent regime change, has polarized the relevant Western and Muslim publics and contributed to an accelerating breakdown of civility.[22] The catalyst was media coverage of the attacks on New York and Washington; American television networks immediately began broadcasting footage allegedly showing Palestinians celebrating the destruction of the World Trade Center and the attack on the Pentagon. In fact, the supposed images of Palestinians celebrating 9/11 were fabricated, according to an investigation by Annette Krüger Spitta of the German public television service ARD.[23]

But enraged American television viewers would be permanently imprinted with hostility towards Muslims, Middle Easterners, and Palestinians; few would realize that they had been manipulated by a carefully-orchestrated mind-control operation. The repeated statements by Osama Bin Laden deploring the "un-Islamic" attacks and denying any involvement were censored by most US media, and downplayed by the few outlets that did report them.[24] Likewise, the American FBI's confirmation that Osama Bin Laden has never been wanted for 9/11 because there is "no hard evidence" of his involvement was censored by the media, and is therefore unknown to most Americans.[25]

The 9/11-triggered campaign to incite American anger against Israel's enemies was not limited to fake "Palestinian celebration" footage. Its goal was expressed by Sivan Kurzberg, one of four Israeli spies who were caught filming and celebrating the destruction of the World Trade Center: "We are Israeli. We are not your problem. Your problems are our problems. The Palestinians are the problem."[26] The campaign to convince Americans that Israel's problem was America's problem continued with the anthrax attack of September and October 2001, which the US government has implicitly admitted was a false-flag attack from an American germ warfare lab designed to incite hatred of Muslims and solidarity with Israel. Scrawled on the anthrax letters was the message: "Death to America. Death to Israel. Allah is great." The islamophobic pro-Israel propagandist(s) who mailed these letters succeeded in killing four Americans and infecting another seventeen—and convincing Americans that Muslims could deliver WMD to anyone with a mailbox.

The 9/11-anthrax operation polarized global opinion to a degree unprecedented in history. The majority of Westerners were led to believe that anti-imperialist Muslims were behind the attacks, which triggered a vast outpouring of hatred toward Islam and Muslims that has not yet abated, and may not even have peaked. The vast majority of the world's Muslims, by contrast, immediately believed and still believes that 9/11-anthrax was an inside job. According to a 2007 poll of leading Muslim-majority countries: "On average less than one in four (Muslims worldwide) believes al Qaeda was responsible for September 11th attacks. Pakistanis are the most skeptical—only 3 percent think al Qaeda did it."[27]

This polarization of beliefs about 9/11-anthrax has profound consequences for dialogue between Muslims and non-Muslim Westerners; the divergence of opinions leads each side to believe that the other side's civilization is seriously flawed. Non-Muslim Westerners think there must be something very deeply wrong with Islamic civilization to have produced such a cataclysmic act of apparent suicide terrorism. Muslims, for their part, obviously do not share the American exceptionalist viewpoint that the USA's government is benign and well-intentioned. On the contrary, the belief that 9/11 was an inside job implies that the whole Western official discourse emanating from governments, universities, and the mainstream media is dubious at best, and that the civilization ruled by such mendacious mass murderers appears to be in a terminal state of decline.

Given such conflicting worldviews, Muslims and non-Muslim Westerners are vulnerable to misunderstandings and communications breakdowns that can lead to shouting matches, exchanges of ad-hominem insults, refusals to listen thoughtfully to the other side's arguments, and other forms of uncivil dialogue. The Westerner whose emotional image of Islam is governed by hatred imprinted on his subconscious by 9/11-anthrax may transfer that hatred onto the founder of the religion, and imagine Muhammad as a caricatural suicide terrorist.

Terrorist Caricatures

Since 9/11, Muslims have been widely caricatured as terrorists, and Islam as a terrorist religion. A substantial proportion of the Islamophobic political cartoons analyzed by Gottschalk and Greenberg in *Islamophobia: Making Muslims the Enemy* invoke or allude to the terrorist caricature.[28] This kind of distorted and stereotyped pejorative image, both in specific cartoons and other images as well as in the Western collective imagination, functions as a rhetorical framing device. Such devices were ably analyzed by George Lakoff in his book *Don't Think of an Elephant.*[29] According to Lakoff, frames (such as the Islam-terrorism equation) are typically designed by political operatives to constrict and direct the public's thoughts and actions. The effect of the ubiquitous *terror* trope is to delegitimize the exercise of power by Muslims, and to legitimize the exercise of power against them. Above all, it delegitimizes any Muslim resort to violence—even in self-defense—while offering carte-blanche legitimacy to violent aggression against Muslims.

The reality of terrorism is quite different from the stereotype. The standard definition of terrorism is as follows: "Violence against civilians to achieve political or ideological objectives by creating fear." Since all major modern wars feature such violence, it would seem that war and terrorism are virtually synonymous. Some military forces do kill and maim civilians more ruthlessly and/or in greater quantity than others. So though all militaries (regular and irregular) are terrorists, it is possible to speak of relative degrees of terrorism.

Ironically, it is the major Western powers, beginning with the United States, that lead the world in terrorism. The US has killed about 55 million people, mostly civilians, in its wars and interventions since World War II, which puts it far ahead of any other nation or group.[30]

But the truth about terrorism—that the US and its allies are the world's worst terrorists—is generally ignored in the Western media. The words "terrorism" and "terrorist" are used without regard to historical or contemporary reality. These terms are caricatural labels, weaponized words, whose purpose is to denigrate and dehumanize.

In his book *On Killing*, Lt. Col. Dave Grossman explains how the dehumanization of enemies through the use of denigrating labels, slurs, and epithets became an integral part of the US military's basic training program starting around 1950.[31] Murderous racism became official military doctrine after World War II due to the studies of Brigadier General S.L.A. Marshall, who discovered that 80 to 85% of US soldiers in World War II deliberately avoided killing the enemy: "Those who would not fire did not run or hide (in many cases they were willing to risk great danger to rescue comrades, get ammunition, or run messages), but they simply would not fire their weapons at the enemy, even when faced with repeated waves of banzai charges."[32] Archeological studies of historical battlefields showed that this was not an anomaly: ". . . throughout history the majority of men on the battlefield would *not* attempt to kill the enemy, even to save their own lives or the lives of their friends."[33]

Marshall discovered that throughout history, the vast majority of battlefield killing has been done by the roughly 2% of the male population that is clinically psychopathic, with the 10 to 15% that would test fairly high on a psychopathy exam doing virtually all the rest. The vast majority of men in battle has always consisted of de facto conscientious objectors . . . at least until around 1950.

That was when the US military responded to Marshall's research by imposing aggressive programs of Pavlovian homicidal conditioning on recruits. Trainees were forced to repeatedly practice the act of killing, in the most realistic possible way, until it became second nature. While turning homicide into a conditioned reflex, they were taught to loathe the ethnic group of the enemy du jour, and inculcated with racist hate words: Koreans were *biscuit heads, bucket heads, kinks*; Vietnamese were *gooks, dinks, vinks*, and *slants*. Today, Muslims targeted for murder in Iraq, Afghanistan, and elsewhere are *ragheads, hajjis, sand niggers, sand monkeys, sand nazis, camel humpers*, and *mos*. The latter term "mo" is short for Mohammad, the name of the prophet of Islam.

The American program to turn ordinary, non-psychopathic men into functionally-psychopathic killers was a brilliant success. Grossman notes that in the Korean War (1950-1953) roughly 50% of American troops attempted to kill the enemy—a vast increase from the 15% World War II figure. By the Vietnam era (1964 - 1974) the firing rate of US troops had raised to over 90%, where it presumably remains today.[34]

Such increased military efficiency came at a terrible price. Grossman explains that non-psychopathic soldiers conditioned to become temporary battlefield psychopaths suffer almost unimaginable psychological damage. When they return home, they experience extremely high rates of depression, drug and alcohol addiction, and suicide, due to their horrific memories of killing their fellow human beings. As of early 2014, roughly twenty-two American veterans commit suicide every day, and the rates are skyrocketing, especially for younger men and women.[35]

What is the relevance of Grossman's "killology" research to the spread of the *terrorist* meme post-9/11?

The word *terrorist* functions in the American media in the same way that such words as *raghead, hajji, sand nigger, sand monkey, sand nazi, camel humper,* and *mo* function in US military conditioning programs. *Terrorist,* like other terms of abuse directed mainly at Muslims, is a weaponized term designed to legitimize ethnically-specific mass murder.

Obviously one cannot fight a war against an abstract noun; the term *war on terror* makes no sense except as part of a homicidal conditioning program. The bizarre notion of a "war on terror" is a euphemism for "mass murdering Muslims" who are the main recipients of the *terrorist* label.

The word *terrorist* is designed to produce a caricatural enemy image. A person who has been labeled a *terrorist* is no longer a real human being, but a sort of subhuman vermin who deserves to be murdered. The key to this process is *othering*: Reducing the target human being to subhuman status by imagining that he or she is "not like us." If we can think of someone as a bizarre caricature of physical or cultural traits very different from our own, murdering that person becomes much easier. Grossman explains: "In combat against Japan (during World War II) we had an enemy so different and alien that we were able to effectively implement cultural distance . . . Thus, according to Stouffer's research, 44 percent of American soldiers in World War II said they would 'really like to kill a Japanese soldier,' but only six percent expressed that degree of enthusiasm for killing Germans."

Perhaps the leading cultural trait that made the Japanese seem "other" to Americans was the military tactic of kamikaze suicide attacks. Most Americans could not imagine themselves deliberately crashing an airplane into an enemy ship and thereby sacrificing their own lives for the war effort. The suicidal ferocity of the kamikazes terrified Americans, who imagined that Japanese people must be fanatical, brainwashed monsters. How, otherwise, could they be capable of such outlandish acts?

Today's caricature of the *suicide terrorist* is an updated version of the World War II kamikaze image. Americans imagine that Muslims, colored by association with the *terrorist* label, are crazed fanatics eager to blow themselves up on a crowded street or crash a plane into a building. This slur on Muslims has no factual basis. University of Chicago professor Robert Pape explains, "The data shows that there is little connection between suicide terrorism and Islamic fundamentalism, or any one of the world's religions."[36] Pape explains, based on his exhaustive study of every suicide attack between 1980 and 2003, that people of any religion or no religion often choose to use the military tactic of suicide attacks when resisting occupation. The caricatural image of Muslims who blow themselves up in order to earn a ticket to a paradise full of virgins is a blood libel, like the notion of oversexed black men raping white women that justified lynching, or the notion of Jews drinking Christian babies' blood that justified pogroms.

So much for the caricature. What is the reality?

All available statistics, evidence, and academic research prove that the fear of "Islamic terrorism" that swept the US after 9/11 is wildly exaggerated. A 2010 study by by researchers at Duke University and the University of North Carolina at Chapel Hill looked at every attack, arrest, or incident involving alleged Muslim terrorism since 9/11—which turned out to be a surprisingly easy task, since there was so little to look at. The study showed that radical Muslims are responsible for a minuscule fraction of the violence in American society. According to one of the authors, Charles Kurzman, "Muslim-American communities have been active in preventing radicalization. This is one reason that Muslim-American terrorism has resulted in fewer than three dozen of the 136,000 murders committed in the United States since 9/11."[37] Kurzman, who had begun his research believing that Islamic terrorism was a significant threat, was surprised to discover that he—and the society around him—had been wrong. He explores the reasons for the shocking lack of Islamic terrorism in his book *The Missing Martyrs: Why There Are So Few Muslim Terrorists*.[38]

A 2013 follow-up study by Kurzman showed that what little Muslim-American terrorism exists has continued to decline. Entitled "Muslim-American Terrorism in 2013," it found that despite the high-profile Boston Marathon bombings (which have been attributed to Muslim extremists despite evidence suggesting a possible false flag set-up)[39] there was still very little Muslim terrorism in America.[40] The study did note one relatively new area of concern: "The scale of Muslim American involvement with terrorist groups in Syria is still unclear." Any such involvement, of course, would put the terrorists on the same side of the conflict as the American government—hardly the first time that US policy makers and Islamic extremists have found common cause.

The FBI has compiled a database of all terrorist attacks in America from 1980 to 2005. According to this document, Muslim extremists account for 6% of terrorist attacks, putting Islamic extremism between communism (5%) and Jewish extremism (7%) as a terror threat.[41] The shocking lack of Islamic terrorism is even more extreme in Europe, where a Europol database of terror attacks from 2007 through 2009 shows that 99.6% of attacks in Europe were perpetrated by non-Muslim groups, while Muslim extremists accounted for only 0.4% of attacks.[42] The same general trend seems to have continued through 2013 according to the most recent Europol report.[43]

The above statistics, which show that Muslims commit only a minuscule fraction of such terrorism as actually exists, fail to convey the extent to which Americans and Europeans have been deceived by the great terror scare. To understand just how insignificant the so-called Islamic extremist terror threat really is, it is essential to understand that terrorism itself—including the 95%-plus that has nothing to do with Muslims—is a non-threat. In the USA, even counting the freak occurrence of 9/11, citizens are more than ten times as likely to be hit by lightning or drown in their bathtubs than be killed by terrorists of any kind.[44]

The ineluctable conclusion is that while many stereotypes are based, however loosely, on reality, the notion of an Islamic terror threat is not. It is a caricature without a real subject, a hate-mongering hallucination.

The promulgation of the "Islamic terrorism" trope might usefully be viewed not as a caricature of terrorism or a discourse on terrorism, but as a form of terrorism. Those who spread the baseless "Islamic terrorism" meme are terrorizing whole societies. Above all, they are terrorizing Muslims, who are being surveilled, infiltrated, entrapped, vandalized, kidnapped, tortured, and murdered in very large numbers for no reason at all.

Psychological War on Islam

As we have seen, the Christian-dominated West has a history of attacking Islam by defaming its Prophet. In Cordoba in the year 855, the Christian extremists who courted martyrdom by insulting the Prophet Muhammad felt themselves a disempowered, endangered minority. For them, insulting the dominant religion was a way to express their sense of frustration and powerlessness—an act of symbolic violence reminiscent of the way small-scale terrorism often serves as a weapon of the weak. (The large-scale terrorists, of course, are always the strong.)

Today, Western civilization is globally dominant. But recent high-profile attacks on the Prophet Muhammad that have strained relations between the West and the Islamic world, like the provocations of the so-called Mozarab Martyrs more than 1,000 years ago, betray the insecurity of those who sense that Islam is on the rise—while fearing that their own civilization may be in decline.[45]

11

Because they target a people's sacred symbols, blasphemous attacks on the Prophet may be considered a form of terrorism in service to genocide. When a culture cannot defend what it holds most sacred, that culture effectively no longer exists. That is why the Cordoban authorities, after a seemingly endless series of sacrilegious provocations, finally felt they had no choice but to execute the Mozarab Martyrs. Semiotic terrorism like that of the Mozarabs, which aims at desecrating its victims' sacred symbols, amounts to an existential threat to the victims' culture; if it is not answered, and the sacred symbols are not defended, the cultural system based on those sacred symbols is annihilated. Successfully desecrating sacred symbols with impunity is tantamount to cultural genocide.[46]

Many in the West claim not to understand this. They advocate a world where anyone can insult anything, a world in which nothing is sacred. They campaign for the repeal of blasphemy laws, cheer for obscene performances by intruders in Russian churches, and complain that the prosecution of such blasphemers is a violation of human rights. These people believe that insulting the sacred symbols of Islam, including the person of the Prophet, is a form of free expression that must be protected. Yet many such free-expression extremists have no qualms about laws shielding the received narrative of the Nazi holocaust from critical historical inquiry. They wish to protect the crudest and most obscene insults against religions and religious figures, yet support sending historians to prison for the crime of conducting careful, dispassionate historical inquiry and expressing controversial conclusions in carefully measured terms. The apparent contradiction is odd to say the least.

Are the attacks on the Prophet part of a cultural genocide attempt aimed at annihilating the religion and culture of Islam? Many Muslims think so. According to a 2007 poll of four Muslim-majority countries by World Public Opinion, four out of five Muslims believe the United States seeks to weaken and divide the Islamic world.[47]

The notion that elements of the West are waging war on Islam is not limited to Muslims. US President George W. Bush announced on September 16th, 2001: "This crusade, this war on terrorism is going to take a while. And the American people must be patient. I'm going to be patient."[48] By announcing a long-term "crusade" (holy war against Islam) just five days after the September 11th incident, a "crusade" that would be hidden beneath the euphemism "war on terrorism," Bush seemingly let slip the real agenda.

But Bush's slip of the tongue was too subtle for some, who would have preferred a more unambiguous announcement that the West was declaring a long-term war against the religion and culture of Islam. James Schall, then a Professor of Government at Georgetown University and a

Hoover Institution associate, explained: "I always thought it was a mistake not to say what Iraq really was, that is, a war against an expanding Islam."[49]

At first glance, Schall's assertion that the US invasion of Iraq was "a war against an expanding Islam" seems questionable. After all, the American invaders overthrew Saddam Hussein's Ba'ath Party, a secularist regime dominated by such high-profile Iraqi Christians as Tariq Aziz, and opened the door to a more religiously-oriented Islamic government. How could overthrowing secularists and replacing them with more explicitly Islamic rulers be part of a war on Islam?

The likely answer: The Iraq war was intended as a psychological blow against the Islamic world. The penetration and desecration of Mesopotamia, historically near the heart of the Islamic nation or *ummah*, by non-Muslim aggressors from halfway around the world was designed to deliver a message to the world's 1.5 billion Muslims: "We Westerners can invade, occupy, and destroy you at will. There is nothing you can do to defend yourself, your women, your family, your community, or your religion." Like the Zionist annihilation of Palestine, the American destruction of Iraq—the most technologically, scientifically, and educationally advanced Arab country—was intended to induce in Muslims a sense of learned helplessness, by convincing them that they cannot protect what they value the most.[50]

Any doubts about whether the US attack on Iraq was a psychological war of desecration and desolation aimed at the whole Islamic world were laid to rest by the Abu Ghraib scandal. The leaked pictures of sexual abuse of prisoners, and the news that innumerable far worse photos existed, were a calculated psychological attack on the religion and culture of Islam. The strategists behind this operation appear to have been Israelis. According to Robert Fisk, writing in the London Independent:

> The actual interrogators accused of encouraging U.S. troops to abuse Iraqi prisoners at Abu Ghraib jail were working for at least one company with extensive military and commercial contacts with Israel. The head of an American company whose personnel are implicated in the Iraqi tortures, it now turns out, attended an 'anti-terror' training camp in Israel and, earlier this year, was presented with an award by Shaul Mofaz, the right-wing Israeli defense minister...[51]

The BBC confirmed this, adding: "Allegations are increasing that Israelis had a major role in both instructing and participating in torture of Iraqi prisoners at Abu Ghraib in Baghdad. Gen. Janis Karpinski who managed the prison said, 'Israelis were there' and third nation nationals have been identified, including a John Israel who is alleged to be an Israeli Mossad operative."[52]

13

Seymour Hersh, America's best-known investigative journalist, helps us understand the Abu Ghraib incident (including the planned revelation of the photos and unveiling of the scandal) as an neoconservative-Israeli psychological warfare operation. Hersh cites the Israeli anthropologist and psychological warfare expert Raphael Patai:

> The notion that Arabs are particularly vulnerable to sexual humiliation became a talking point among pro-war Washington conservatives in the months before the March 2003 invasion of Iraq. One book that was frequently cited was *The Arab Mind*, a study of Arab culture and psychology, first published in 1973, by Raphael Patai, a cultural anthropologist who taught at, among other universities, Columbia and Princeton, and who died in 1996. The book includes a twenty-five-page chapter on Arabs and sex, depicting sex as a taboo vested with shame and repression.... The Patai book, an academic told me, was "the bible of the neocons on Arab behavior." In their discussions, he said, two themes emerged—"one, that Arabs only understand force and, two, that the biggest weakness of Arabs is shame and humiliation."

The Israelis have a century of experience destroying Palestinian identity by desecrating its most sacred symbols, including Islam (via repeated desecrations of the al-Aqsa mosque, the Islamic world's third-holiest shrine and greatest architectural and historical monument) and sexual honor (violated by Israel's policy of routine sexual torture of Palestinians). The US war on Iraq, a neocon-Zionist project, borrowed from the Israeli strategy of sexual torture, desecration of holy symbols including mosques, shrines, and Qur'ans, and other methods of cultural genocide.

It has been argued that the war on Islam is primarily the product of the Zionist invasion and occupation of the Islamic holy land of Palestine. According to this line of analysis, the Zionist destruction of Islam's heartland necessarily entails a clash between Zionism, an aggressively expansionist Jewish nationalism, and the basically defensive (though sometimes militant) Islamic nationalism that has arisen in response.[53] The post-September 11th wars, in any case, are the creations of a small group of hard-line Zionist neoconservatives, as has been proven by scholars including James Petras and Stephen Sniegoski, whose book *The Transparent Cabal* explained: "The origins of the American war on Iraq revolve around the United States' adoption of a war agenda whose basic format was conceived in Israel to advance Israeli interests and was ardently pushed by the influential pro-Israeli American neoconservatives, both inside and outside the Bush administration."[54] James Petras, a leading American sociologist and commentator, agrees:

The most important political force (behind the Iraq war) was also the least openly discussed. The Zionist Power Configuration (ZPC), which includes the prominent role of long-time, hard-line unconditional Jewish supporters of the State of Israel appointed to top positions in the Bush Pentagon (Douglas Feith and Paul Wolfowitz), key operative in the Office of the Vice President (Irving (Scooter) Libby), the Treasury Department (Stuart Levey), the National Security Council (Elliot Abrams) and a phalanx of consultants, Presidential speechwriters (David Frum), secondary officials and policy advisers to the State Department.

It is important to note that the West's war on Islam is neither fully-conscious nor unanimous. Very few Westerners are even aware of the existence of such a war, and even fewer are well-informed about it. Only a handful, such as the aforementioned James Schall, are willing and able to express themselves clearly and directly and "say what it really is." Yet despite the inarguable reality of the war on Islam, we will see that there is some question about "what it really is"—whether we are dealing with mere geostrategic struggles for money and power, or whether there is a larger philosophical and/or demonic agenda at war not only with Islam, but with all the revealed religions.

Attacks on the Prophet

As we have seen, Western attacks on the Prophet of Islam have a deep-rooted history. Given the current "clash of civilizations" in which Islam has replaced communism as the West's designated arch-enemy, it is unsurprising (though dismaying) that the Prophet Muhammad has been targeted by practitioners of hate speech in the US and Europe. These libelous assaults are a form of terrorism in service to cultural genocide. Their aim is to terrorize Muslims into resignation and learned helplessness, in order to weaken and ultimately destroy the religion of Islam and the community (ummah) based on it.

The internet-driven communications revolution of the past two decades has coincided with Western leaders' decision to make Islam their new civilizational enemy. As a result, it is now much more difficult for Muslims to simply ignore scurrilous attacks on their Prophet, since they are exposed to so many such incidents; and it is also much more difficult to take action against individual acts of hate speech, likewise because there are so many of them. This creates a terrible dilemma for Muslims, who cannot ignore the accelerating onslaught of opprobrium, yet find it very difficult to take meaningful action to stop it. These attacks are felt as personal violations; they desecrate the sanctity of the targeted individual's home via the internet and other mass media, and can follow the victim wherever he or she goes by showing up on cell phones, smart phones, tablets, and laptops.

Since it is very difficult to either avoid or put a stop to these acts of hate speech, Muslims find themselves in a classic position of "learned helplessness." The phrase was coined by American psychologist Martin Seligman, who discovered that animals exposed to sustained attacks of unpleasant stimuli that they are unable to avoid become depressed and incapable of action. Even when the situation changes and an avenue of escape from the painful stimuli opens up, the animal will not take it; it has ceased to care, and no longer bothers to act in its own best interests.

Inducing a state of depressed apathy in a human community via learned helplessness amounts to an attempt to destroy that community. Learned helplessness is a weapon of genocide, like gas chambers, nuclear bombs, or race-specific biological agents. It just works more slowly.

The results of centuries of weaponized learned helplessness may be observed on Native American reservations facing epidemics of alcoholism, depression, suicide, drug abuse and family breakdown. Dr. Maria Yellow Horse Braveheart coined the term "historical trauma" to account for these symptoms of intergenerational learned helplessness:

> What is historical trauma? Historical trauma is cumulative emotional and psychological wounding over the lifespan and across generations, emanating from massive group trauma. Native Americans have, for over 500 years, endured physical, emotional, social, and spiritual genocide from European and American colonialist policy . . . brave Native leaders who did everything humanly possible in the face of the ongoing march of European-American colonists across their land to protect their people and their way of life, but sadly to little or no avail. They eventually saw countless violent acts perpetrated on their people and lands. Descendants of these early leaders to this day suffer the adverse effects of historical trauma grief that is displayed into the present day . . . The effects of historical trauma include: unsettled emotional trauma, depression, high mortality rates, high rates of alcohol abuse, significant problems of child abuse and domestic violence.[55]

The war on Native Americans, like the war on Islam, has been a disguised religious war—a sort of stealth crusade. In *Pagans in the Promised Land*, Steven T. Newcomb exhaustively documents "that Old Testament religious concepts form a significant part of the backdrop of federal Indian law and policy."[56] Specifically, the notion of a chosen people authorized (indeed ordered) by God to invade another group's territory, exterminate the inhabitants, and claim the land was taken (or mis-taken) from the Old Testament and applied to the Americas—as it has also been applied to Southern Africa and Palestine. Americans, like Zionists and apartheid-era Afrikaaners, have misinterpreted the Old Testament in order to imagine themselves an exceptional nation, a chosen people, with the divinely-anointed right to invade other lands and destroy other cultures. Anthony Hall notes that the crusade against Native Americans has melded seamlessly into the War on Islam; today's "merciless heathen savages," the world's Muslims, are mowed down by helicopter gunships named after genocided Native American leaders (Black Hawk) and tribes (Apache).[57]

Fortunately the global Muslim community has not fared as badly as Native American communities. Unlike them, it has survived the worst of the colonialist onslaught with the core of its culture—the religion of Islam—relatively intact. As Dr. Javed Jamil's exhaustive study shows, Muslims are actually performing better than non-Muslims on a wide variety of social indicators: They have significantly lower rates of alcohol and drug abuse, divorce, suicide, and violent crime than non-Muslims.[58] But the internet-enabled barrage of attacks on everything Muslims hold sacred (alongside the mass murder of Muslims in invasions, occupations, and destabilizations of Muslim-majority countries) has only been happening for two decades, unlike the centuries-long abuse of Native Americans. There are worrisome signs that divorce rates and other negative social indicators are rising among at least some Muslim communities. For example, sociologist Dr. Ilyas Ba-Yunus at State University of New York recently discovered that divorce rates among North American Muslims have been rising and now stand at an alarming 31%—despite the widespread Islamic teaching that of all non-forbidden things, the most hateful to God is divorce.[59] The post-9/11 acceleration of the psychological war on Islam, and North American Muslims' feeling of helplessness in the face of the onslaught against their religion, is undoubtedly responsible, at least in part, for the rising divorce rate—and probably also for increasing drug and alcohol problems, violence, and suicide.

The global Muslim ummah needs to recognize that it is under assault and take vigorous and effective counter-measures. That is the only way to avoid being sapped and eventually destroyed by learned helplessness and eventual cultural-civilizational collapse. In the remainder of this chapter I will contemplate strategies for effectively responding to—or better yet, pre-empting—blasphemous attacks on the Prophet of Islam, by briefly examining the three best-known cases: The Salman Rushdie affair, the Danish cartoon controversy, and the *Innocence of Muslims* film.

The Salman Rushdie Satanic Verses incident

The controversy surrounding Salman Rushdie's book *The Satanic Verses* brought the issue of blasphemy against the Prophet of Islam to the

17

attention of the global public. As is well-known, the book and its author were condemned by the Ayatollah Ruhollah Khomeini, the father of Iran's Islamic Revolution and the man most responsible for helping spark the global Islamic Awakening of the past half-century. The case drew tremendous attention worldwide. It marked the first time that Muslims all over the world had responded so strongly against a symbolic attack on Islam, and put the world on notice that Islamic values would be strongly defended. And it seemingly pitted two values—sanctity of religion and freedom of expression—against each other.

The Rushdie case was far more complex, in terms of the allegedly blasphemous content, than the Danish cartoons and the *Innocence of Muslims* and Charlie Hebdo affairs. The latter cases involved blasphemous images in works that obviously were created for no other reason than to insult and provoke Muslims, had no evident artistic or expressive value, and left little room for interpretation. But Salman Rushdie's novel *The Satanic Verses* is not a simple, straightforward case of hate speech or verbal aggression; it is a maddeningly complex maze of ambivalence that, while it arguably shows blasphemous intent, requires a fair amount of interpretation to decipher. Even after a lifetime of therapy, it is doubtful whether Rushdie or his psychoanalyst could ever really understand what motivated the writing of such a book.

Normally, it would probably serve Muslims better to let a book like Rushdie's suffer the fate of virtually all such obnoxiously pretentious efforts: Well-earned obscurity and eventual oblivion. But in the context of the times, the tremendous publicity surrounding the Rushdie affair—which had the unfortunate effect of turning an egotistical second-rate novelist into a global celebrity and bestselling author—served as an announcement to the world that the religion and culture of Islam were alive and well, and that Muslims would respond vigorously to attacks on their sacred values.

Faisal Devji has observed:

> The controversy marked the first demonstration of Islam's globalization, allowing Muslims from around the world to imitate one another's protests as seen on TV, without any organizational links. Whatever the local politics involved at each site of Muslim protest, it was the global arena emerging with the end of the cold war that gave the Rushdie affair its meaning. The author and his book were incidental to this mobilisation, which is why so few of its Muslim critics had read the novel.[60]

If Rushdie's book was incidental to the protests against it, what were those protests really about? Devji argues that in Britain, the main object of the protestors' ire was the double-standard in British blasphemy laws, which protected Christianity but not Islam. Indeed, Britain's parliament repealed the nation's blasphemy laws in 2008 rather than give Islam equal protection to Christianity: "Great Britain's reluctance to concede to Muslim demands for equality under the law was due primarily to British fear of losing its identity and traditional Christian roots if it protected all religions equally and became a secular society."[61] But the Christianity-only blasphemy law was only one of many double standards, formal as well as informal, that have made Muslims feel like second-class citizens both of Western nations like Britain and of the larger global community.

The issue of double-standards is simply one manifestation of a larger problem: The Western imperial-colonial conquest of most of the Islamic world, which included attempts to eliminate Islam as the basis of society —an effort that has not yet abated even in the ostensibly post-colonial era. In virtually all colonized Islamic lands, the European colonialists substituted European-dominated secular systems for the indigenous Islamic codes. Secular education was instituted, secularism was promoted, and secularized indigenous people became the local satraps—a role they continued to hold even after nominal independence, when comprador classes became the local faces of neo-imperialism. It was the rising global reaction against this worldwide disempowerment of Islam—not a narrowly focused argument about an individual case of blasphemy—that drove the anti-Rushdie protests.

Today, the Western media is almost unanimous in its portrayal of the *Satanic Verses* controversy as a barbaric Muslim onslaught against freedom of expression. By framing the debate in these terms, the dominant Western discourse (led by Zionists) scores cheap propaganda points against Islam. But the implied argument in favor of absolute freedom of expression makes little sense. Even those societies most strongly committed to freedom of expression do limit speech based on criteria that would seem to apply to the publication of Rushdie's book. To take one example: If a speech act creates "a clear and present danger" then it may be restricted. Justice Holmes, voicing a unanimous Supreme Court decision, wrote: "The question in every case is whether the words used are used in such circumstances and are of such a nature as to create a clear and present danger that they will bring about the substantive evils that Congress has a right to prevent."[62] Due to its provocative and hurtful attack on what Muslims hold sacred, Rushdie's novel might have been expected to create a clear and present danger of potentially violent conflict.

Another limitation on the free speech enshrined by the First Amendment of the United States Constitution is the government's right to ban "fighting words." According to the Supreme Court decision *Chaplinsky v. New Hampshire:* "The English language has a number of words and expressions which by general consent [are] 'fighting words' when said without a disarming smile. ... Such words, as ordinary men know, are likely to cause a fight." Rushdie's novel, which included descriptions that seemed designed to profoundly shock and anger Muslims, could be considered "fighting words"—as the global fight that broke out after the novel's publication would suggest.

A third generally-accepted limitation on free speech that might apply to *The Satanic Verses* is the restriction on libel and slander. Certain passages of Rushdie's novel appear to libel the Prophet Muhammad and his family. If ordinary people are protected against libel and slander, it can be argued that the founders of great religions should enjoy the same protection.

A fourth limitation on free speech that has been upheld by US courts involves obscenity, the offensive depiction of sexuality or bodily functions in a manner that violates "community standards." Whether such a depiction is offensive obviously depends on its context. Certain passages of *The Satanic Verses* are clearly obscene in the context of Muslim community standards.

And finally, a fifth limitation on free speech involves blasphemy, offensive attacks on sacred symbols or personages. Though the now largely post-religious West has substituted the rather similar categories of hate speech, vilification of religion, or religious insult for blasphemy, the result is similar: Rushdie's novel arguably presents itself as an act of hate speech that vilifies and insults a religion and its adherents.

Rushdie's attorney Geoffrey Robertson defended *The Satanic Verses* against a British blasphemy lawsuit. He defends the book against the charge *"The book grossly insults the wives of the Prophet by having whores use their names"* by claiming: "This is the point. The wives are expressly said to be chaste, and the adoption of their names by whores in a brothel symbolizes the perversion and decadence into which the city had fallen before it surrendered to Islam." This argument seems disingenuous at best. As a trained literary scholar and long-time teacher of literature at the university level, I would give a student who proposed this interpretation a high grade for imagination, but a low grade for plausibility. (And yes, I have read the novel.) If this is the best available defense against the charge that *The Satanic Verses* is blasphemous, then the book stands convicted by its own defense attorney.

Yet most of the Western intelligentsia still seems clueless. As author and literary editor Blake Morrison put it: "The novel was bold and imaginative, yes. But blasphemous? How could a late-20th-century novel be that?"[63]

Morrison is implicitly referring to the mid-20th-century controversies over novels by such authors as James Joyce, D.H. Lawrence, Henry Miller, and William S. Burroughs, which resulted in the legalization of virtually anything in novelistic form. Joyce's *Ulysses* was the object of a famous 1933 trial in New York that began opening the floodgates of the West to obscene and/or blasphemous literature when the book was acquitted on both charges, largely due to Judge John M. Woolsey's recognition that the book was a sincere and accomplished literary effort, not simply an attempt to shock or titillate. This doctrine was later applied to another 1920s literary figure, D.H. Lawrence, whose *Lady Chatterly's Lover* was the subject of decades-long censorship controversies. The shift towards a doctrine of "anything goes as long as it's literature" led to the proliferation of indecent "literary" efforts issued by such publishers as Maurice Girodas. Henry Miller, whose *Tropic of Cancer* was more shocking to established morality than Joyce's *Ulysses* had been, saw his works unbanned in 1961 and officially legitimized by the US Supreme Court in 1964. The even more grossly offensive William S. Burroughs novel *Naked Lunch* was banned in 1962 but legalized in 1966 on the grounds that despite its unbelievably disgusting content it was not without social or literary value. The upshot of this capsule history is that by the mid-1960s, the West had arrived at a consensus that novels ought never to be banned on the grounds of blasphemy, obscenity, or indecency.

Despite this anything-goes consensus, there is an obvious answer to Blake Morrison's question, "How could a late-20th-century novel be blasphemous?" A contemporary novel might be deemed blasphemous if it attacked the sacred narrative of the Nazi holocaust. A European author who wrote such a novel, and publicly admitted that he doubted the new holy trinity of "extermination order, gas chambers, and six million Jewish murder victims" might be prosecuted for what is, in essence, a new form of blasphemy. Such a prosecution would transfer the protections formerly offered to the great religions to Holocaustianity, the new Holocaust religion, which Israeli intellectual Yeshayahu Leibowitz argues has partially usurped the place of traditional religion in today's world.[64]

So the implied claim that the West offers absolute, blanket protection to all forms of expression is obviously false. And the fact that the West regularly prosecuted books far less extreme than Rushdie's for blasphemy, obscenity and indecency just a few generations ago suggests that the current obsession with absolute freedom of expression for blasphemers and pornographers is a passing fad, not an ineluctable feature of the West's values or identity. Yet discussions of the *Satanic Verses* scandal in the Euro-American media tend to gloss over these details, and instead frame the issue as one of Western free expression versus Islamic repression. This unbalanced portrayal is the product of the unbalanced power relations between the West and the Islamic world, and between the powerful non-Muslim majority in Western countries and the less-powerful Muslim minority. The discussion, as so often happens, is framed by the powerful. The viewpoint of the less-powerful party is downplayed or ignored. And it is precisely this asymmetry of power, and the double-standards that come with it, that feed Muslim anger and outrage. Thus the West's response to the Rushdie affair has contributed to the larger problem that created the affair in the first place, setting off a sort of self-perpetuating feedback loop in which Muslim anger and Western chauvinism kept reinforcing each other and eliciting ever-more-intense responses from the other side.

The Islamic world and the West have not yet managed to extricate themselves from the feedback loop of mutual antagonism instigated by the Rushdie affair. This vicious circle of recrimination contributed to the ideological foundations of the so-called war on terror, which was drafted by Western strategists as a replacement for the Cold War at the Jerusalem Conference on International Terrorism (JCIT) in 1979.[65]

The war on terror did not get its official product launch until 2001—when 9/11, "the most successful and most perverse publicity stunt in the history of public relations" according to National Medal of Science winner Lynn Margulis, inaugurated a new age in Western ideology.[66] Following this official Western declaration of hostilities against the Islamic world, symbolic attacks on Islam and the Prophet Muhammad increased exponentially in frequency and intensity. The internet-based communications revolution further polarized the situation, by allowing each side to retreat into pockets of partisanship while simultaneously being more frequently exposed to the other side's attacks.[67]

The Danish Cartoon Scandal

September 2005 witnessed the birth of a second worldwide scandal triggered by Western blasphemy against the Prophet Muhammad. The issue arose when the Danish newspaper *Jyllands-Posten* published twelve cartoons featuring insulting images of the Prophet. As in the case of the *Satanic Verses* affair, Muslim outrage spread around the world. The globalized dimension of the protests was widely noted:

> No longer is the issue merely that of belittling an immigrant group," wrote Jürgen Gottschlich, a German journalist based in Istanbul. "Just as there are heroes of free speech in Denmark, there are also heroes from the Arabian peninsula to North Africa to Indonesia who are ready to take to the barricades to defend their prophet's dignity." Ibrahim Magdy, 39, an Egyptian Coptic Christian with a florist business in Rome, said,

"The problem now is that when you say something or do something, you are not just talking to the Egyptians or to the Syrians or to the Saudis, but you are talking to the entire Muslim world."[68]

As with the case of *The Satanic Verses* and Britain's Christianity-only blasphemy laws, and the later Charlie Hebdo affair, Western double-standards were exposed by the Danish cartoon controversy. The British newspaper the *Guardian* reported:

Jyllands-Posten, the Danish newspaper that first published the cartoons of the prophet Muhammad that have caused a storm of protest throughout the Islamic world, refused to run drawings lampooning Jesus Christ, it has emerged today. The Danish daily turned down the cartoons of Christ three years ago, on the grounds that they could be offensive to readers and were not funny.[69]

Not funny? Offensive to readers? Terms like these obviously could equally apply to cartoons attacking the founder of any great religion. But the editors of Jyllands-Posten seemingly do not agree. Are they blind to their own hypocrisy? Or were they fully aware of the controversy they were provoking—perhaps in service to some larger agenda?

Investigative journalist Christopher Bollyn offers evidence that neoconservative Zionists orchestrated the Danish cartoon incident to fuel the fires of the so-called clash of civilizations:

The fact that the editors behind the anti-Islamic images claim to be exercising free speech while refusing to address Europe's strict censorship laws regarding discussion of the Holocaust and the ongoing imprisonment of historical revisionists reveals the existence of a more sinister agenda behind the provocative cartoons. "Agents of a certain persuasion" are behind the egregious affront to Islam in order to provoke Muslims, Professor Mikael Rothstein of the University of Copenhagen told the BBC. The key "agent" is Flemming Rose, the cultural editor of JP, who commissioned cartoonists to produce the blasphemous images and then published them in Denmark's leading morning paper last September.[70]

Bollyn posits a conspiracy involving Rose; the dean of American Islamophobia, Daniel Pipes; and other Zionist agents in the media:

Rose traveled to Philadelphia in October 2004 to visit Daniel Pipes, the Neo-Con ideologue who says the only path to Middle East peace will come through a total Israeli military victory. Rose then penned a positive article about Pipes, who compares 'militant Islam' with fascism and communism . . .The dangerous "game" that was started by the Danish editor has now been picked up by at least seven newspapers across Europe. Supposedly in support of the Danes, papers in France, Germany, Italy, the Netherlands, Spain and Switzerland simultaneously reprinted the cartoons on February 1. The timing suggests that this response was coordinated by a hidden hand. In Paris, for example, Arnaud Levy, editor-in-chief of the financially-strapped France-Soir, chose to print all 12 of the offensive cartoons. Asked if there had been coordination between European editors about the simultaneous publication of the cartoons, Levy said, "Absolutely not."

One of the cartoons portrayed the Prophet of Islam wearing a turban shaped as a bomb with a burning fuse, according to the International Herald Tribune.[71] This traded on the offensive stereotype of Islam as a violent religion that insists on converting non-Muslims at sword-point—the centuries-old blood libel at the basis of the defamatory Mahound and Mozarab Martyrs legends, and current genocidal "killologies," discussed earlier. Such psychological attacks are designed to put Muslims in an impossible position: If they vigorously defend themselves, they are cast as fanatics whose reaction confirms the charge that their religion is inherently violent; while if they do not defend themselves, they are seen as acquiescing and pleading "no contest" to the charge of belonging to a religion with a propensity for violence.

Unfortunately, some of the worldwide demonstrations against the Danish cartoons erupted in violence, allowing the Western media to reinforce the blood libel on Islam. According to the *New York Times*, more than 200 people have died in violent incidents related to the cartoons.[72] This kind of unfocussed violent reaction is morally abhorrent, since the victims are unlucky innocents. It does not serve the cause of defending Islam from rhetorical attacks. And it is not conducive to the kind of civil dialogue that could discourage such incidents.

A more effective Muslim response to the Danish cartoons was mounted from Iran. There, Supreme Leader Ayatollah Seyyed Ali Khamenei argued (backed by some evidence, as we have seen) that the cartoon scandal was a Zionist provocation.[73] The newspaper Hamshahri co-sponsored a Holocaust cartoon contest that exposed Western double-standards on free speech; the winner was Moroccan cartoonist Abdollah Derkaoui, who depicted Israel's apartheid wall, featuring a picture of the Auschwitz concentration camp, growing taller and obscuring the al-Aqsa Mosque—a clever reference not only to the oppression of Palestinians by Israeli apartheid, but also the replacement of traditional religion by the new holocaust religion which has been used to legitimize Zionist atrocities. The cartoon, like the statement from Ayatollah Khamenei, highlighted truths that Western media and governments ignore or suppress. Such courageous and forceful truth-telling opens the path to genuine dialogue, which can only occur between equals who are not afraid of frankly expressing their real views.

Hamshahri's cartoon contest exemplified the kind of symmetrical, proportionate response that promotes peaceful and respectful dialogue. By contrast, disproportionate responses to provocations are unjust and counterproductive; Muslims who rioted or engaged in violence against persons or property in response to the Danish cartoons were responding asymmetrically and disproportionately. Such responses not only portray Muslims in a bad light, but also risk further asymmetrical and disproportionate escalations that could lead to further damage—to human life and property as well as to interfaith relations.

The opposite kind of asymmetrical, disproportionate response— defensive apologetics—is equally damaging. When one is forcefully insulted, a response of roughly equal forcefulness is called for; when a sadistic bully attacks, one must fight back, not whimper apologies, or the bully will escalate his bullying. As we have seen, the attacks on the Prophet are part of a genocidal war on Islam, a sort of bullying-writ-large.

The above-discussed Iranian responses to the Danish cartoons were symmetrical in the sense that they were, like the offending cartoons, intense symbolic messages calculated to cause offense to some recipients and evoke scandal—in this case, by raising the subject of Zionist conspiracy and displaying skeptical irreverence toward the sacred holocaust narrative, both taboo topics in the West. But they were not *merely* symmetrical. They were also asymmetrical in a positive sense, in the same way that asymmetrical warfare by a less-powerful party can neutralize the weapons of a more-powerful opponent.

This positive asymmetry was made possible by the asymmetries of knowledge and power between the West and the Muslim world. It is often said that knowledge is power; but it is less often realized that in power relationships, the less-powerful party often knows more than the powerful party. The British drama *Upstairs-Downstairs* dramatized the well-attested fact that servants generally know more about their masters than the masters know about the servants. This is partly because masters tend to be arrogant. They have a hard time recognizing or taking seriously the fact that the servants are human beings like themselves. So they do not bother to get to know them, and feel no shame about revealing things to them that they would never reveal to "equals."

The servants, by contrast, are often privy to their masters' secrets and blind spots. The masters' egotistical behavior can be nakedly revealing, and the servants become experts at psychoanalyzing the masters.

Applying this knowledge-power asymmetry to the West-Islam clash over the Danish cartoons: The West and the Muslims both know that

Muslims are sensitive to insults to their Prophet, because both parties understand that Islam is a religion and that religious objects and personages are held sacred. But Muslims know something about what the West holds sacred that the West itself does not know—or, more accurately, does not allow itself to know: The extent of clandestine Zionist power[74]; and the fact that the Holocaust story has become the most sacred narrative of the West, despite the questionable factual basis of some of its most important details, doubts about which have apparently inspired the powerful social and legal prohibitions against examining the story too closely.[75]

Muslims understand the West's neurotic repression of its knowledge of Zionist power and the irrational basis of the new holocaust religion. This gives Muslims an advantage in "asymmetrical verbal warfare" over such issues as the Danish cartoons. By responding symmetrically (with their own cartoons) they take advantage of the above-noted asymmetry, calling attention to something the West does not want to see: that it has turned Zionism and the holocaust into sacred cows. The West's neurotic attachment to Zionism is one of the root causes, perhaps the most important cause, of the attacks on the Prophet Muhammad; by exposing this repressed truth, Muslims reduce the level of neurotic energy that drives Western sacrilegious attacks on Islam. By revealing truths about the West that the West itself cannot face, Muslims can, to some extent at least, level the discursive playing field and remedy the power imbalance.

Innocence of Muslims and the Benghazi incident

In September 2012, an obscure, badly made YouTube video purporting to be a trailer for a film entitled *Innocence of Muslims* was translated into Arabic and promoted heavily on the internet. The short film was given widespread publicity in the Muslim world after a segment was broadcast on Egypt's Al-Nas television by Sheikh Khalad Abdalla on September 9th.

The blasphemous film was an even more obviously orchestrated provocation than the Danish cartoon scandal. It was designed to trigger a wave of Muslim outrage on September 11th, which has become something of an annual Islamophobic holiday in the USA. And that outrage appears to have provided cover for a sophisticated pre-planned attack on the American diplomatic mission in Benghazi, Libya that killed four Americans: Ambassador Chris Stevens, Information Officer Sean Smith, and former Navy SEALS Tyrone Woods and Glen Doherty.

Gordon Duff, a leading alternative journalist and reputed US intelligence insider, has pointed out that since both the blasphemous film provocation and the Benghazi attack were highly professional pre-planned operations coordinated to coincide on September 11th, they appear to have been staged by the same group.[76]   Duff argues that neoconservative Zionists connected to the US military-intelligence apparatus (roughly the same group that planned and executed 9/11) seem to have also been behind the Benghazi operation, which was designed to promote the "war on terror/ war on Islam" concept while providing ammunition for neocon-supported Republican presidential candidate Mitt Romney to attack President Obama as soft on Islam/terror.

Mainstream journalist David Brock agrees that there was something strange about the Romney campaign's lightning-fast, extremely well-prepared reaction to the Benghazi attack.[77] At 10:24 Eastern Time on September 11th, as the first, confused reports of the attack were filtering in, Romney's campaign was already on-message:

> "I'm outraged by the attacks on American diplomatic missions in Libya and Egypt and by the death of an American consulate worker in Benghazi," (Romney's) statement read. "It's disgraceful that the Obama administration's first response was not to condemn attacks on our diplomatic missions, but to sympathize with those who waged the attacks."[78]

Brock points out that this talking point had been worked out much earlier by the Romney campaign, which wanted to cast Obama as overly sympathetic to Muslims/terrorists, but had lacked an opportunity to do so until the Benghazi incident miraculously appeared as if on cue:

> Had the Benghazi attack not occurred at this unique moment—on a day when the Republican candidate for the presidency and his promoters in the conservative media were desperate for a new storyline, especially one that would undercut the popular effect of the raid that killed Osama bin Laden the year before—this tragedy might not have been converted into a political scandal.[79]

Duff argues that the timing of the *Innocence of Muslims* outrage together with the Benghazi raid "at this unique moment" (September 11th) was no coincidence. Duff cites evidence that the notorious Qur'an-burning minister Terry Jones, an alleged Operation Gladio agent-provocateur, was part of the neoconservative operation behind the *Innocence of Muslims* film trailer and the Benghazi attack. According to Duff, Terry Jones, whose church has only 25 members, put on a heavily-funded anti-Muslim telethon in the run-up to September 11th 2012 as part of a coordinated operation with the *Innocence of Muslims* film promotors. The purported fear of a Muslim response to the provocations was used as an excuse to send an Operation Gladio black operations team to Benghazi, which then coordinated the attack: "Studies now reveal as many as 15 separate teams involved, from surveillance to traffic management, to perimeter security to fire support and communications, not to mention 'infil' and 'exfil' teams along with logistical support."[80]

Regardless of what may have really happened at Benghazi, the *Innocence of Muslims* affair (like the Danish cartoon scandal) illustrates how blasphemous attacks on the Prophet Muhammad have become a political weapon in the West. Right-wing groups that profit from Islamophobia have a clear motive to manufacture such scandals and give them maximum publicity; while no matter how much Muslim leaders try to educate their communities, there will always be a percentage of Muslims, however small, that will respond violently to a sufficiently offensive provocation.

For all of these reasons, it was entirely predictable that the Charlie Hebdo incident, or something like it, would occur. And it seems equally inevitable that another such incident will arise. When (not if) it does, how should people of good will, including both Muslims and non-Muslims, respond?

Responding to the next attack on the Prophet

The Romney campaign was able to obscure the facts about the September 11th, 2012 Benghazi incident, and successfully promote its deceptive message, because it had prepared a carefully-thought-out response in advance of the events. The Obama campaign, by contrast, was caught by surprise and unable to respond effectively. In the same way, the neoconservatives were prepared to unleash their message within seconds after the 9/11/2001 attacks; while those who would have favored a more measured response were caught by surprise and unable to react with speed and efficacy. The result was a de facto neocon coup d'état. But one does not have to be part of a conspiracy to commit mass murder in service to a Big Lie to recognize that pre-emptive preparation for an event that one knows is coming is a good idea.

We all know that another scandalous attack on the Prophet Muhammad is likely, whether tomorrow, next year, or sometime in the next decade. All people of good will, both Muslims and non-Muslims, should prepare to respond to the coming attack in such a way as to discourage future attacks, while simultaneously promoting civil dialogue and coexistence between people from different religious backgrounds.

But how can these two seemingly very different goals be accomplished? Will not strong actions intended to discourage such blasphemies—such as the Ayatollah Ruhollah Khomeini's fatwa against Salman Rushdie, or Pakistani cabinet minister Ghulam Ahmed Bilour's $100,000 bounty on *Innocence of Muslims* maker Nakoula Basseley Nakoula[81] —push the discussion of these issues, and inter-civilizational discussion in general, away from civil dialogue and toward a vicious spiral of incivility and violence? Yet on the contrary, will not dispassionate pleas for discussion and dialogue fail to dissuade the blasphemers, but rather encourage them by seemingly offering them impunity for their crimes against the dignity of religion? And even if every Muslim on earth fails to respond violently to a given level of provocation, will not the provocateurs simply offer something even more obscene, even more blasphemous, until they trigger the desired response? And if even that does not work, will they not simply orchestrate a false flag attack to be blamed on Muslims?

Given the momentum of historical forces, there is no simple or short-term solution to this problem. Nothing that people of goodwill can say or do will prevent the next Islamophobic idiot, be he a lone nut or a political operative, from staging Muslim-baiting provocations. Nor is there any practical way to prevent angry Muslims from responding intemperately. Even less can we stop Western propagandists and publics from condemning intemperate Muslim responses, whether out of principle or for political advantage.

But we can begin working on a long-term solution by addressing the problem in terms that the larger global public can understand. Simply defending the Prophet Muhammad, without framing that defense in terms of universal moral principles, risks alienating the non-Muslim global public by making it appear as though Muslims are trying to impose their specific religious sensibilities on non-Muslims.

Islam has a long and venerable history of respecting and protecting other religions. Blaspheming against any established religion or religious figure is anathema to Muslims. This long-standing Islamic tradition of respecting all established religions, not just ones own, harmonizes with universal moral principles that form the basis of international law and human rights initiatives. Both to remain true to their tradition, and to mount the most effective defense of their own religion in an increasingly interconnected world, Muslims ought to continue to broaden their defense of the Prophet Muhammad and forge a coalition to protect all prophets, major religious figures, and sacred symbols.

Specifically, Muslims ought to unite with Christians to oppose blasphemies against Jesus, who is known as the Prophet Issa (pbuh) in Islam. There have been a number of high-profile cases of blasphemy against Jesus, yet Muslims have been conspicuously absent from efforts to protect the founder of Christianity and beloved prophet of Islam from the blasphemers. A recent example is the controversy that erupted when a clearly blasphemous so-called art work entitled "Piss Christ" was put on display at the Edward Tyler Nahem Gallery in New York shortly after the Benghazi incident of September 11th, 2012. The neoconservative propaganda channel Fox News used the incident as an excuse to attack US

President Obama for allegedly trying to protect Islam—by pressuring Youtube to remove the film *Innocence of Muslims*—while ignoring an equally ugly blasphemous attack on Christianity.[82] This would have been a perfect moment for Muslims to step forward, join forces with their Christian brothers and sisters, and demand that the blasphemous object be banned or destroyed. Such an effort could have helped convince Christians to support the mostly Muslim-sponsored initiatives to get protection of religious figures written into international law and human rights agreements.

Many Christians, like Muslims, believe their religion is under attack. We have already seen that Muslims, who have borne the onslaught of Western imperialism and colonialism, and who have been the prime targets of the so-called war on terror, have good reasons to feel that way. But Christianity, too, is beleaguered—both in the Middle East, where the Christian population is fleeing the war zone, and especially in the West, where an anything-goes policy toward attacks on religion has contributed to the progressive loss of the sense that anything is sacred (except perhaps the received version of the Nazi holocaust narrative).

Today, the East may be rising up against the West's war on traditional religion. Russia's Eastern Orthodox Christian President Vladimir Putin has come to the defense of traditional religion both in his speeches and by signing into law bills that criminalize homosexual propaganda and blasphemy.[83] The Islamic world, too, is resisting being dragged into a brave new world in which nothing is sacred. It stands to reason that Muslims and Christians should work together to resist the blasphemous attacks that appear to be part of the New World Order's assault on all traditional religions.[84] One of the world's notable Islamic scholars, Shaykh Imran Hosein—who is well-known for his expertise on international affairs— argues that Muslims will unite with Eastern Orthodox Christians to defeat the New World Order.[85] Some traditional Catholics have also expressed interest in joining this kind of alliance.[86]

As they make common cause with Christians, Muslims also need to unite among themselves to argue effectively that blasphemy is not a protected form of free expression. The Organization of Islamic Cooperation (OIC) is the leading international forum for such efforts. The OIC needs to renew its efforts to mount effective arguments in favor of generally-accepted Islamic positions on such issues as the non-protected status of blasphemy. It needs to be proactive, rather than simply responding to each crisis after it occurs.

The OIC's response to the Danish cartoon incident illustrates the ineffectiveness of ad hoc responses to each new crisis. Its letter of protest to the Danish government over the offensive cartoons was received in mid-October, 2005, just a few weeks after the cartoons' publication, and several months before the outbreak of worldwide demonstrations. The Danish government refused to take any action on the grounds that the cartoons were protected free speech, and did not disclose that it had received the OIC protest letter until March 2006.[87]

Alongside such short-term reactive measures, the OIC has also mounted a long-term effort to convince the international community to condemn defamation of religion—but then seemingly backed down in 2011. This issue was first brought before the UN by Pakistan in 1999 on behalf of the OIC as a campaign against defamation of Islam. When non-Muslim members of the UN Human Rights Commission suggested broadening the resolution to include all religions, the sponsors agreed. Since then, both the Human Rights Commission and the General Assembly have repeatedly passed UN resolutions condemning the defamation of religion. These measures were opposed by the US and EU but supported by most of the rest of the world.

Then on March 24th, 2011, under pressure from anti-religion forces, the OIC retreated. Reuters reported: "Islamic countries set aside their 12-year campaign to have religions protected from 'defamation', allowing the U.N. Human Rights Council to approve a plan to promote religious tolerance...." The new HRC resolution seemingly surrendered to the Western countries' argument, defeated in all previous votes, that human rights law "should not protect belief systems" as the French EU representative Jean-Baptise Mattei argued in 2009.[88] Instead the new resolution "condemns any advocacy of religious hatred that amounts to incitement to hostility or violence against believers and calls on governments to act to prevent it" but rejects the concept of defamation of religion.[89] Another 2009 UN document calls it "impermissible" for laws to discriminate in favor of religious believers over non-believers and affirms the "right to blaspheme."[90]

At issue is whether religion has any special status or deserves any special protection. The Western position is that it does not and must not. In other words, the West—representing a small minority of humanity—claims the right to eradicate religion as the basis of society worldwide, based on a virulent anti-religious shift in Western beliefs and behavior that is less than a half-century old.

When I was born a little over 50 years ago, few Americans doubted that religion deserved special protection, and that religious beliefs about the sanctity of life and property were a major source, if not *the* major source, of both legislation and social convention. Religiously-based legislation of sexual morality and decency, the prohibition of blasphemy, and tax breaks for churches were taken for granted; divorce and childbirth out of wedlock were stigmatized and very rare, with the result that violent crime, suicide, drug abuse, and child poverty rates were very low; abortion was everywhere illegal and almost universally despised; and drugs and alcohol were regulated in accord with religious belief (for example, by prohibitions of the sale of alcohol on Sunday, the Christian holy day). Today, all of the above features of pre-1960s American society would be decried by the radical secularists who have seized power in the West as symptoms of massive and systematic discrimination in favor of religious believers against non-believers.

While Western elites may have lost their religious faith as early as the 19th century,[91] it was not until the so-called sexual revolution of the 1960s that Western populations began to follow suit in large numbers. This gradual loss of religion in the West has been seen as a symptom of civilizational decline by many observers, including leading American conservative commentator Patrick Buchanan.[92] Others, including Eustace Mullins, Mujahid Kamran and Henry Makow, have argued that freemasonic secret societies funded by the world's wealthiest international banking families have mounted an intergenerational conspiracy to debase religion and morality in service to the New World Order (NWO).

I have argued that the term New World Order means several things at once. It is *new* in the senses that it would be the first-ever world order to be (a) planetary, (b) not based on religion, and (c) built primarily by usury and only secondarily by military might, as "economic hit man" John Perkins has noted.[93] It is also a "New World" order in the sense that its headquarters are in the New World—in New York and Washington, DC. (It is inherently difficult to dominate the world from a base in the Western Hemisphere, as Zbigniew Brzezinski argues in *The Grand Chessboard*, which may partly explain the extremist tactics to which the NWO-dominated West has resorted.)[94]

So the debate about whether religions deserve special protection such as anti-blasphemy laws is really just one facet of a larger debate: Should (some) human civilization(s) continue to be based on religion, as all known civilizations have been until very recently? Or should religion be eradicated —or relegated to the status of just another "lifestyle choice" (which amounts to the same thing)?

On one side of the debate are those who argue that human communities, whether supranational (the Islamic Ummah, Christendom), national, or sub-national, have the right to choose to continue to ground themselves in religion. In their view, communities may, if they wish, regulate members' behavior by religious standards and base their legislation on religion. This camp believes that the community's collective right to uphold religious standards and maintain religious traditions trumps the individual's right to blaspheme or to otherwise claim immunity from religiously-based strictures.

On the other side of the debate, the partisans of the New World Order argue that religion deserves no special rights—meaning that no society on earth should be allowed to ground itself in its religious tradition. By making religion the basis of legislation, in this view, a tradition-based society would be discriminating against non-believers. According to the NWO, such discrimination is a violation of human rights and an affront to "freedom of conscience"—the freedom to ignore and flaunt religiously-based morality.

Ironically, it is the self-styled promoters of "tolerance"—the NWO anti-religion crusaders—who want to impose their own peculiar vision on the entire world. They are out to destroy all religion and all religious morality, everywhere; while their opponents, the defenders of religion, are not advocating any such totalitarian monoculture. Pro-religion advocates simply want to allow particular communities to remain free to choose how to govern themselves; they support a pluralistic world in which different communities would have self-determination according to each community's own religious tradition. They are not trying to force their own views on the whole world; all they are asking for is a world in which all established religions merit at least a modicum of respect—a pluralistic world in which different religions can thrive.

Will we have a pluralistic religious world or an irreligious McWorld of ruthlessly-enforced and globally-uniform "totalitarian tolerance"? That is the real question underlying the debate about human rights and religion.

Ironically, the totalitarian anti-religion forces are getting unwitting assistance from many passionately religious individuals. These people of faith, many of whom could legitimately be called fanatics, have fallen into the New World Order's divide-and-conquer trap by vociferously advocating their own brand of religion while attacking "rival" faiths. Christian Islamophobes, Jewish chauvinists, Buddhist nationalists in Myanmar, Hindu nationalists in India, and Islamic Takfiri extremists are all unknowingly assisting the New World Order's efforts to eradicate religion. Their actions legitimize the radical secularist discourse that religion is the cause of all the world's division and strife—a claim that Karen Armstrong, among others, has shown to be a Big Lie.[95] The extremists are turning their religions into tribal nationalisms with little genuine spiritual content, sapping their faith tradition of its energy even as they attack and wound the other faith traditions.

Given the New World Order's war on religion, the first priority for all reasonable people of faith should be to promote interfaith solidarity, not inter-religious strife. One program on which virtually all religious people can agree is that religion should play an important role in public life. For religious people, the whole edifice of right and wrong on which the law is based is built on revealed religious tradition; secular logic alone cannot derive the moral postulates that form the basis of social and legal codes. Even the Christian notion of "render unto Caesar what is Caesar's" was never taken to mean that public life and law should be robbed of religiously-based morality—at least not until the radical freemasonic ultra-secularists and their New World Order project emerged in the latter half of the 18th century.[96]

All of the above reflections urge us to mount long-term projects of interfaith activism aimed at preserving and expanding the sphere of religion in social life. We need groups with such names as Reasonable People for the Preservation of Religious Societies to mobilize worldwide, not only in reaction to specific blasphemy incidents, but also to explain to the people of various nations and cultures, in terms they can understand, why some things must be held sacred.

The beginnings of such an interfaith effort may be seen in two recently-formed groups—one founded by Christians to promote Christian solidarity with Islam and Muslims and thereby protect Muslims from Christian attacks; the other founded by Muslims aiming to remind their fellow Muslims that Islam requires that they protect Christians.

The first (Christians protecting Muslims) group is Bridges to Common Ground, founded by the former American Congressman Mark Siljander. Bridges to Common Ground aims to "inspire, educate and mobilize diverse people to a reconciling movement across the divide of cultural and religious differences" and "mediates by demonstration of a courageous, spiritually based model of peacemaking; interceding and effecting change at personal, local and global levels."[97] At a practical level, the group does most of its work disabusing Christians of their false ideas about Islam, and explaining to Christians (and to a lesser extent Muslims) that the two faiths have a tremendous amount of common ground. The many Christians who are hostile toward Islam and/or Muslims, and might therefore be tempted to support blasphemous attacks on Islam, are desperately in need of the good offices of Bridges to Common Ground.

Congressman Siljander was once one of those Islamophobic Christians himself. While Representing Michigan's 42nd Congressional District, Siljander walked out of a Congressional Prayer Breakfast because the prayer was being led by a Muslim. A few years later, Siljander discovered that Muslims venerate Jesus, and that the Qur'an may preserve many meanings of the original, Aramaic-language Gospels better than the over-translated, sometimes mistranslated Bible does. Since discovering the commonalities of Christianity and Islam, Siljander has been an unofficial peace emissary to dozens of nations—and was ironically rewarded for his peacemaking in 2008 with an indictment on terrorism charges trumped up by the neoconservative Islamophobes, who apparently thought that

Christian-Muslim friendship posed a threat to their 9/11-triggered war on Islam.

The second (Muslims protecting Christians) group is the Covenants Initiative, founded by Dr. John Andrew Morrow, a Religious Studies scholar who has also completed the full cycle of traditional Islamic seminary studies. Dr. Morrow's book *The Covenants of the Prophet Muhammad with the Christians of the World* explores documentary evidence that Muslims have been obliged to protect Christians since the earliest days of Islam.[98] Horrified by the growing numbers of attacks on Christians by Takfiri extremists, especially during the war on Syria, Dr. Morrow has become a scholar-activist dedicated to ending these abuses of religion: "And now that we are witness to widespread Islamicist violence against Christians in places like Syria and Egypt—often perpetrated by groups fighting as proxies for the United States and Israel—it is nothing short of providential that *The Covenants of the Prophet Muhammad with the Christians of the World* should see the light of day at this precise historical moment."[99]

Those who participate in such interfaith efforts as Bridges to Common Ground and the Covenants Initiative will necessarily express their defense of religion in terms that can communicate across the boundaries of faith. This communicative effort should also reach out to non-religious people—an even bigger challenge. While radical secularists and committed atheists are unlikely to be convinced that religions need protection, more moderate non-religious individuals could potentially be swayed to recognize that religion and its attendant morality are socially beneficial, and to work together with religious people for peace, justice, and interfaith harmony. Additionally, exposing the many nefarious deeds of the New World Order anti-religion conspiracy could convince many non-religious people to re-think their positions.

The internet communications revolution should make it easier for Christians, Muslims, and other religious people to unite in common defense of their faiths. One thousand years ago, ordinary Western Christians had no access to the truth about Islam. Instead, they were inculcated with Islamophobic myths of Mahound, the Mozarab Martyrs, and so on. Today, accurate information is widely available, and activist groups can easily work to promote it, while calling for interfaith unity in defense of the sacred. Islamic scholar and activist Bediüzzaman Said Nursi was a leading theoretician of "information jihad" which today needs to be directed towards unity of the faiths in mutual self-defense:

> The way of the Risale-i Nur was peaceful jihad or "jihad of the word" (*mânevî jihad*) in the struggle against aggressive atheism or irreligion. By working solely for the spread and strengthening of belief, it was to work

also for the preservation of internal order and peace and stability in society in the face of the moral and spiritual destruction of communism and the forces of irreligion which aimed to destabilize society and create anarchy, and to form "a barrier" against them.[100]

The foregoing reflections suggest that we need to adjust our approach to defending the Prophet Muhammad by fostering more effective civil dialogue between Muslims and non-Muslims. To succeed, Muslims will need to master the linguistic registers and value systems of the cultures they address; and non-Muslims will likewise need to gain a deeper understanding of the beliefs and values of Islam. In the end, we will all have to agree to disagree on certain issues, and to accept the reality that we cannot impose all of our dreams and desires on this very large and very messy world—a world that is at the same time, for monotheists, the perfect creation of a perfect God. But even as we admit the limits of our puny power, we religious people have no choice but to resist the New World Order's absurd attempt to erase the central role of God and His prophets from our hearts, our souls, and our lives.

CHARLIE HEBDO: A CLASSIC EXERCISE IN NATO DISCIPLINE, PLUS SOME COMMENTS IN DEFENSE OF FREE SPEECH

Webster Griffin Tarpley, Ph.D.

Washington DC, March 9, 2015—The terrorist attacks two months ago on the French satirical magazine *Charlie Hebdo* and the Paris Hyper Cacher kosher supermarket have received worldwide attention, but are largely misunderstood. The thesis argued here is that these killings, which must be condemned, do not derive from the polemical-satirical anti-religious cartoons *Charlie* had published for many years. Rather, *Charlie Hebdo* was chosen as a target in order to kill some famous personalities in or close to the French ruling elite in order to prevent and deter France from carrying out policy changes which President Hollande had been preparing. The wife of the slain cartoonist Charb had been a cabinet minister under Sarkozy, and the former head of Charlie had gone on to lead the large radio broadcaster France Inter. Other famous cartoonists were also killed. The accused perpetrators were all "the usual suspects," well known to the Paris police; one wonders how many of them, like the Toulouse shooter Mohamed Merah, were officially listed as informers and assets of the DGSE, France's CIA equivalent.

Hollande's January 5th, 2015 Rebellion Against NATO Policy

In an unusual two-hour interview on France-Inter Radio (the head of which is a former boss of *Charlie Hebdo*) on January 5th, Hollande announced that he was in effect breaking with US, UK, and NATO policy on three key points. First, he demanded an end to the economic sanctions imposed on Ukraine. Second, he rejected the idea that France should militarily occupy Libya, a reckless adventure. Thirdly, he undercut both German Chancellor Merkel and Greek Prime Minister Samaras by assuming a very relaxed posture in regard to the January 25th Greek elections, in sharp contrast to the hysterical scare propaganda being heard around the EU about the apocalyptic dangers of a Syriza victory.

On the Russia sanctions, Hollande stated categorically: "I think the sanctions must stop now. They must be lifted if there is progress. If there is no progress the sanctions will remain…Mr. Putin does not want to annex eastern Ukraine. He has told me that…What he wants is to remain influential. What he wants is for Ukraine not to fall into the NATO camp."

It was pure heresy, one of the biggest breaks with the Anglo-Saxon lockstep since the death of de Gaulle. Hollande trusted Putin! And he wanted to wreck the entire US-UK sanctions regime, which would be finished if France dropped out! At this point Hollande was scheduled to go on January 15th to talks with Merkel, Putin, and Poroshenko in Astana, Kazakhstan. Hollande explained: "I will go to Astana on January 15th on one condition, which is that there should be a possibility of making new progress. If it's just to meet and talk without making any actual advances then there's no point. But I think there will be progress." Hollande obviously wanted to deliver two helicopter carriers to Russia; only Anglo-Saxon pressure had stopped the delivery of the first one.

On Libya, Hollande ruled out French unilateral military intervention: "France will not intervene in Libya because it's up to the international community to take its responsibility," he said. But French forces could still strike Islamist extremists in the country's lawless south.

On Greece, Hollande said that voters there were free to choose. There was no hysteria. As France 24 pointed out, "Hollande's warning not to interfere with the Greek election has been interpreted as a swipe at German Chancellor Angela Merkel, whose government has described a Greek exit from the euro as almost inevitable should Syriza come to power. Hollande simply noted that "there are certain engagements that have been made [by Greek governments] and all those must be of course be respected."

This interview added up to an attempt by the desperately unpopular Hollande to restore some measure of independence to French policy in these key areas, as against the demands of London, Washington, and Berlin. Within forty-eight hours the killing started at the *Charlie Hebdo* offices. On the day of the large Je Suis Charlie march in Paris, Merkel remarked to some press that the Astana conference had been called off—a temporary success for the Nuland faction of the State Department. But the success has not proven permanent. When the four-power conference did occur, it was in Minsk, Byelorus, on February 11th—a conference which has, at least for the moment, quieted down the fighting.

NATO Geopolitical Terrorism Used to Keep US-UK Allies in Line

To anyone with a knowledge of the relevant history, the Charlie attacks continue a long established pattern of NATO intelligence acting to discipline tendencies towards the assertion of national interest by the European countries. France, we must remember, has decades of history frequently punctuated by rebellions against the London-Washington line. The French administration and other institutions are home to a robust French exceptionalism, which is probing how hardy it can be, and which is rooted in achievements of undeniable historical merit. This is a France which can say no and which has said no to the Anglo-Saxon combine.

To identify this phenomenon, it is enough to think of the great French statesman General Charles de Gaulle, who got France out of the colonialism business in Guinea, Algeria, and elsewhere, who insisted on an independent French nuclear deterrent, who kicked the NATO military command out of Versailles, who warned the Johnson administration not to start the war in Vietnam, and who tried to prevent the British infiltration of what is today the European Union. The NATO intelligence answer to these assertions of national interest came in the form of at least thirty assassination attempts against de Gaulle, run through various conduits, and discussed in several studies.

A second case involves the Italian Prime Minister Aldo Moro.[101] In 1977 and 1978, Moro's great political project was to bring the Italian Communist Party into a coalition government with the Italian Christian Democrats, thus providing a stable administration to carry out what Moro saw as Italy's future—carrying out economic development projects in North Africa and the Middle East in general. Italian civil engineers had after all, built the Aswan high dam in Egypt, and were building the city now called Bandar Khomeini in Iran. But, as Henry Kissinger reportedly warned the Italian statesman, allowing a large Communist Party to enter the Italian cabinet was considered by the United States as a violation of the implied Yalta spheres of influence. Moro soon died in spring 1978 at the hands of a Red Brigades organization that had notoriously been penetrated by the CIA, as had the Italian government search committee which tried unsuccessfully to locate and save Moro. Recent statements by Steve Pieczenik remind us of this complex of problems.

A more recent case involves the mass casualty terrorist attack reportedly carried out by one Anders Breivik on the Norwegian government buildings and on a summer camp frequented by the children of that country's Social Democratic Party elite.[102] NATO was at that time engaged in the bombing of Libya, with the goal of overthrowing the government of Colonel Muammar Qaddafi. Norway had participated in the first months of the bombing, but then announced that no Norwegian air assets would be available for operations against Libya after August 1st, 2011. To make matters worse for NATO, the government of the Netherlands soon announced that it intended to join Norway in standing down from the bombing campaign against Qaddafi. Breivik was convicted for the bombs and the shootings, but there were persistent reports of a second shooter in the press.

NATO intelligence has been busy of late because of the powerful centrifugal tendencies gripping the Western camp. Politicians not totally aligned with the dominant austerity, Russophobia, and Arab spring line have been entrapped in sex scandals—see the cases of Berlusconi of Italy (who refused an austerity plan), Dominique Strauss-Kahn (the presumptive French president who, according to two reliable sources, was trying to get Merkel and Qaddafi [sic] to act against the US Fed), and Hollande himself, whose first warning had been when his motor scooter trips to visit his mistress were revealed by the French magazine *Closer*. More recently we have witnessed the assassination of the Russian oligarch Nemtsov, and here the *cui prodest* calculus of who benefits points the finger of guilt towards the enemies of Putin, be they Ukrainian fascists or Chechen terrorists.

Such, we believe, is what actually happened around *Charlie Hebdo*. But we must also attempt to make some sense out of the furor in favor of free speech, and against criticism of Islam, which thoroughly engaged world public opinion in the weeks after the French events.

How Theological Provocations Work

"Sticks and stones can break my bones but names can never hurt me"—so goes the American proverb first recorded in the New England states in the 19th century, probably during the 1860s. In my view, this is excellent strategic and political advice. Stability and serenity are great assets. It is not wise to be thrown into a frenzy by the statements or symbolic actions of some insignificant, obscure provocateur or bigot half a world away. In strategic terms, it is generally not recommended to be overly distracted by the actions of an adversary; one needs to pursue the strategic course that one has already embarked upon. Despite the benefits of modern Internet communications, one prominent disadvantage is that scurrilous comments which might in earlier eras have dissipated into the fog and the night can now be eternalized on the Internet. But the case for ignoring them remains very strong. If one is upset about blasphemers, one can take comfort in the certitude that a divine justice will surely deal with them—so human intervention need not occur.

Western culture has recently been much obsessed with notions of political correctness. This obsession, which is antithetical to free speech, imagines that the free expression of ideas needs to be regulated and constrained so as to avoid offending the feelings of some participants in the debate. This is unquestionably a symptom of the ideological decadence of the Western world at the present moment. The motto of the politically correct quackademic is "your rights end where my feelings begin," and this mentality is doing severe damage to the educational institutions of the Western world. The essence of political correctness is that reality itself must be denied and excluded from discussion. A society which is systematically incapable of coming to grips with large parts of reality is a sick society, and quite possibly a doomed one.

Healthy intellectual life requires the clash of opposing ideas and points of view on important subjects. The civility of the process means very little compared to the need for ruthless comparisons and critiques as a means of getting at the truth. The Socratic dialogue continues to stand as a universally valid model for human intellectual activity. Such a dialogue can get very rough, but it represents the most reliable approach to intellectual progress which humanity has yet devised. It is a grave mistake to hobble the search for truth by limiting or chilling free speech. It is far better to rebut, discredit, and ridicule than to ban. What is forbidden becomes more attractive. US publishers used to try to get their books banned in Boston, since that often meant a runaway best-seller.

The First Amendment of the United States Constitution, representing as it does the most robust protection of free speech available anywhere in the world, is a key to such success as the United States has enjoyed as a country. Of course, the First Amendment is a two-way street: it can be used to attack, and it can be used to counterattack. It is designed to channel political conflicts into propaganda wars so as to prevent civil wars and shooting wars. It offers extreme polemics, but ideally nobody gets killed. Other countries would be well advised to imitate it, but the tendency unfortunately seems to be going in the other direction.

Je Suis Charlie ou Je Suis Hypocrite?

By contrast, the hypocrisy of many who paraded through the streets of Paris sporting the slogan of "Je Suis Charlie" was evident, since many of them do not support any recognizable form of free speech. France in particular still has laws which establish particular interpretations of the history of Europe during the fascist era, and of the Armenians of the Ottoman Empire, as the compulsory doctrine of the French state. Quite apart from the specifics, it is a bad method and likely to backfire, since it makes crackpots into martyrs. President Hollande has talked of the need to ban hate speech, and a representative of the CRIF, the umbrella organization of French Jews, referred to the American First Amendment during a recent France 24 debate as a "problem" which had to be neutralized by working around it. We intend to keep this problem. To be sure, certain forms of free speech must be regulated and have been regulated: there is no right to shout "Fire!" in a crowded theater, nor to directly incite imminent violence. But the examples cited by Hollande appear to fall far short of those clear and present danger situations, and thus to be inadmissible violations of the fundamental human right of free speech.

The issue of free speech has proven extraordinarily difficult for world leaders to master. This issue led to the first major and very lamentable gaffe in the pontificate of Pope Francis, a leader whom we otherwise cordially support. In the aftermath of the *Charlie Hebdo* events, the Pope suggested that criticism of religion was off limits. While on his way to the Philippines in mid-January, Pope Francis remarked to a group of reporters:

> If my good friend Dr. Gasparri says a curse word against my mother, he can expect a punch. It's normal. You cannot provoke. You cannot insult the faith of others. You cannot make fun of the faith of others.

Whatever this may be, it is closer to Botero's *ragion di stato* of than it is to Christianity, although many Christian churches and denominations have indeed responded historically to criticism with violence. Nothing and nobody can escape satire, especially on twitter, where modern Juvenals and Martials abound. Jesus Christ was on a different line, and recommended that we turn the other cheek even if we were actually slapped. The Pope is obviously concerned about Christian minorities in various countries around the world who might be targeted if he were to declare open season on certain religions. The authoritarianism of the Council of Trent may also be at work in the background. This approach is understandable as a tactic, but the fundamental truth remains that the progress of humanity requires speech that is a really and truly free.

Cookbooks for Theological Provocation

Those who wish to harm the Moslem nations are always busily at work, conducting psychological and political profiling with a view to provoking self-destructive reactions. Here are some comments from an Islamophobic columnist and pedant who is heavily invested in parading theological knowledge. Nevertheless, the general line of his attack is clearly delineated:

> It appears that pinpricks can produce chain reactions in the Islamic world. The threat may be termed asymmetrical because Islam is more vulnerable to theological war than Christianity (or for that matter Judaism) . . . As the youngest of the major religions (apart from Sikhism), Islam must defend its historical narrative more fiercely than the older religions. Islam never

withstood the withering criticism of Enlightenment scholars from Spinoza to the Jesus Project determined to discredit sacred texts . . . The fact that Islam has established neither a Magisterium in the Catholic sense, nor an authoritative tradition like that of Orthodox Judaism, leaves it decentralized, divided and fractious. If Turkish intelligence decided to employ its university theology departments to manufacture designer heresies for use in Iran, for example, the capability is in place . . . With a dozen scholars, a score of operatives on the ground, and a budget of a few million dollars, a competent intelligence service could have a handful of Muslim heresies merrily contending for the mantle of the prophet. In another location I suggested that Petraeus' temporary success in the 2008 surge might lay the groundwork for a Thirty Years' War in the region. Weapons are there to be used, and theological weapons may turn out to be some of the nastiest means of war-fighting at hand.[103]

It should be clear from this foray into the imperialist mind that the theological warfare or theological provocation approach to destabilizing the Moslem states—and by extension the world—which is described here has already been in action for quite a few years, perhaps finding its clearest form so far in the illegitimate and abusive declaration of the caliphate by the likes of the CIA asset al-Baghdadi, the friend of Senator John McCain. The Moslem world must recognize that blasphemy, apostasy, heresy, the slander of any religion, and the like are not and will not be considered crimes under the public laws of most Western states, and that any bans on these practices will tend to be untenable in the modern world, if only because of the universality of modern Internet communications. Indeed, the attitude that the publication of a cartoon or the burning of a paperback book halfway across the world might usefully become the suitable object of a violent demonstration—tying a whole country up in knots—constitutes a tremendous ideological weakness, and a strategic vulnerability for any society.

A pilot project for the recent campaign of Islamophobic insults and obscenities designed to provoke an otherwise nonexistent Clash of Civilizations came in the Netherlands during 2004. Two individuals who can only have been operating as conscious provocateurs—Theo van Gogh, of the same family as the famous painter, and Ayaan Hirsi Ali, a feminist from Somalia, launched a vigorous campaign of Islamophobia designed to weaken the traditions which had made the Dutch one of the most tolerant peoples in the world. Van Gogh's distant forebear was the artist, but his father was a member of the Netherlands intelligence service. When Van Gogh was murdered by a self-styled Moslem fanatic in

November 2004, xenophobic demagogues like Geert Wilders became the beneficiaries. In retrospect, the Van Gogh affair appears as the opening move in a campaign to whip up Islam phobia in the smaller NATO states.

Bilderberg Group Behind First Wave of Mohammed Cartoons, 2005-2006

At a time when the US and UK were focused on maintaining the international coalition fighting in Iraq, and were looking for a vassal states to hurl into the Iran campaign that was being planned by neocons in Washington, the scene shifted to Denmark and the Mohammed cartoons of 2006. In contrast to van Gogh, whose impact had remained more circumscribed, this time the NATO provocateurs were able to generate a backlash in about forty countries, with about 140 people being killed in riots or assassinations. At that time, I argued that the best way to defeat provocations of this type was simply to ignore them and leave them lost in deserved obscurity:

> The NATO intelligence provocation appearing in the guise of the scurrilous Mohammed cartoons published by the reactionary newspaper *Jyllands Posten* of Denmark, and then by a series of other European publications, has already done much to mobilize the armies, bases, and treasuries of Europe in support of the lunatic plan to the Bush-neocon clique for a nuclear sneak attack and punitive expedition against Iran over the coming weeks or months....The evidence strongly suggests that the cartoon provocation was presented to Atlanticist oligarchs at the meeting of the Bilderberg group held from May 5th to May 8th, 2005 at the Dorint Sofitel Seehotel Überfahrt in Rottach-Egern, on the shores of the Tegernsee lake in the south German federal state of Bavaria. The first publication of the cartoons in Denmark followed in September 2005 . . . The editor of *Jyllands Posten* who ordered the publication of the cartoons is Flemming Rose, who has extensive connections to Daniel Pipes, another neocon fascist madman who runs Campus Watch, a neo-McCarthyite witch-hunting organization which vilifies American professors who criticize Israel or show sympathy for the Palestinians . . . Our advice to the Moslem world: DO NOT FALL FOR PROVOCATIONS. From Count Thurn's 1618 defenestration of Prague to Bismarck's Ems telegram in 1870, big wars have often grown out of staged provocations.[104]

Still more recently, we have the intelligence operation built around the crude and vulgar 2012 movie variously entitled "Desert Warrior" or "The Innocence of Muslims," produced by the Israeli Sam Bacile. Bacile was closely associated with the notorious Islamophobia Network of the pro-war activist Pamela Geller. Another member of the Islamophobia network was John Bolton, considered by some to have been a candidate for the post of Secretary of State in the Mitt Romney administration. Among the goals of this operation, we may count the defeat of Obama in the 2012 US presidential election, and his replacement by the greater warmonger Romney. This film triggered demonstrations in scores of countries, with a death toll of about 50, plus 700 injured.

The Lessons Learned by the Sixteenth Century Politiques of France

All of this reminds us of some very basic truths about religion and politics, some of which were developed in France. A terrible time in France was that of the wars of religion between Roman Catholics and Calvinist Huguenots, c. 1562–98. Intelligent observers saw that armed bands used religion as a cloak for recruiting dupes, and that apocalyptic-demagogic clergymen delighted in advancing the most sweeping absolute claims for their own faith, while consigning the other side into hellfire. Those who saw through this game were the *politiques*, who asserted that, whatever the clerics might assert, it was up to the civil magistrate—the government, the modern state—to make the final decisions, not in the name of anybody's holy book, but in the name of law and order as the elementary prerequisites for civilized life. Such a solution would allow every faith to develop freely, without the burden of governing.[105] To this was added a little later the horrors of Cromwell's theocratic dictatorship over England, with major-generals in every key city enforcing a very radical Protestantism. These were the ingredients that went into the famous US separation of church and state. Four years ago, the Roman Catholic bishop of Tripoli, Libya told the present writer that Libyans, including Christians, enjoyed far-reaching religious freedom under Qaddafi. Now Libya is in chaos, and the separation of mosque and state, church and state, has been abrogated. These issues are connected.

Time to Wise Up—Don't Fall for Provocations

Intelligence agencies, counterinsurgency, foundations, and greedy opportunists have been scheming on both sides of the divide between Islam and the West. Imagine the utter intellectual sterility of a debate between the philodoxers Bernard-Henri Levy and Tariq Ramadan! Only the imperialists will come home the winners.

Agitators coming forward with extreme demands and extreme rhetoric should be carefully examined hidden agendas and for links to foundations or the intelligence community. The demand for sharia law to be established as binding in the United States, for example, is utterly unrealistic and will only feed an Islamophobic backlash. When Ataturk established the separation of mosque and state, he adopted the Swiss civil law, the Italian criminal law, and the German commercial law. And that was in Turkey almost a century ago. On the other hand, everyone is free under freedom of association to accept mediation and arbitration from any clergy, as long as no laws are violated

At the same time, it is clear that virulent anti-Semitism exists and must be fought. In Europe especially, there are utterly cynical intellectuals who have lost any belief in God, in progress, in their nations, in the working class, or in anything else who affect a pose of anti-semitism because this gives them a comforting feeling of moral superiority over the likes of a Netanyahu. This position leads nowhere.

The French comedian Dieudonné is guilty of a cardinal sin for anyone in his profession—he's just not funny. He thinks death camps and extermination are grist for his jokebook. He goes around gesticulating with a hand signal he obviously regards as a version of the fascist salute, but which on closer examination looks very much like an understated classic Beppe Grillo *vaffa*—and Grillo is not funny either. The result is simply appalling. Dieudonné is reported to be rich, and a close friend of the racist-xenophobic Vichy veteran Jean-Marie LePen of the National Front. Indeed, Dieudonné is reported to be creating a reactionary party called National Reconciliation with a right-wing dropout from the National Front, Alain Soral. This approach also leads to nothing good.

Bill Maher's Islamophobia Rant Refuted

During recent months, an attack on the Moslem religion has been carried forward by the ignorant comedian Bill Maher, who has built his career on the astonishing willingness of Americans to laugh at absurdities. (Maher is also not funny.) Building his superficial arguments on the crimes of Isis and then on the *Charlie Hebdo* events, Maher has characterized Islam as a "mother lode of bad ideas." There would be many ways to refute this denigration, but I believe the most effective one is as follows. The ability of Islam to promote a luminous flowering of science, culture, and civilization is proved beyond doubt by the Baghdad Renaissance under Haroun al-Rashid, the Caliph of Baghdad around 800 AD, and thus the contemporary and even an ally of Charlemagne, King of the Franks. At this point, the Islamic caliphate was probably the most advanced form of human civilization existing anywhere in the world.

At other times, Islamic civilization does not enjoy this same superiority. The waning centuries of the Ottoman Empire are an example, and these of course impacted most of the Arab world. We need to be aware of the way in which imperial powers have attempted to create a synthetic and fictitious Moslem identity, and then impose it on subject populations as a means of imposing weakness, backwardness, and fragmentation on them. British scholars in particular are past masters of the art of identifying the most backward tendencies in any civilization, and elevating precisely those to the status of its immutable essence. Bernard Lewis, once of the British Arab Bureau, and later of the Princeton Institute for Advanced Study, is infamous for his outrageous argument that the Ismailist Cult of the Assassins (active around 1100) somehow embodies the essential features of Islam. In particular, Lewis' view of the Assassin leader called the "Old Man of the Mountain" is widely considered to be the basis of the construction of the public image of Osama bin Laden, and of the self-styled Caliph Baghdadi more recently. Here is a synthetic identity being manufactured and imposed.

In my personal list of the greatest statesmen of the 20th century, Mustafa Kemal Ataturk of Turkey and President Nasser of Egypt figure prominently, alongside Franklin D Roosevelt, Charles de Gaulle, and Sun Yat-sen of China. I would submit that it is the Ataturk-Nasser tradition of anti-imperialism, populist economic development, the scientific-technological modernization, and cultural and social progress in which has generally been the main target of imperialist policy in the Middle East. When Ataturk destroyed the reactionary Ottoman brotherhoods during the 1920s, the British responded by creating the Muslim Brotherhood, specifically as a way to combat the growing anti-colonial nationalism of many Egyptians. The Muslim Brotherhood presents itself as a religious organization, but its leaders are essentially plutocrats—bankers, factory owners, top officials, latifundists, doctors, lawyers, and editors. As so often in history, religion is used as a cloak for the worldly interests of exploiters. Needless to say, the Moslem Brotherhood has been in a close alliance with the CIA for many decades. But Ataturk had established the separation of mosque and state, and Nasserism incorporated this idea in the form of a modern, secular republic, with freedom of religion for all.

The US strategy against the Soviets in Afghanistan during the 1980s is also a case in point. Here we saw the CIA choose the benighted fundamentalist Gulbuddin Hekmatyar, arguably the most barbaric of all the Afghan warlords, as the favored US candidate.

When Arabs Could Choose, They Chose Progress

If we want to know what the Arabs in particular would choose for themselves if they were free from foreign interference and manipulation, we can go back to the 1960s and perhaps the early 1970s. These were years of the Cold War, during which the power of the United States was significantly checked and balanced by that of the Soviet Union and the Warsaw Pact. When the US refused to help build the Aswan High Dam,

President Nasser went to Moscow and was able to get the assistance he needed for this great work of civilization. So what were the choices made by the Arab countries during this time when the imperialists were far less able to dictate political outcomes in Middle East capitals than they are today?

In Egypt, power passed during the 1950s from the decadent British puppet King Farouk to President Nasser and his fellow army colonels. The Nasser model was imitated by many nations. In Iraq, Nasserism took the form of the regime of General Kassem, against whom the CIA deployed the young Saddam Hussein. In Libya, Colonel Gaddafi constructed a government along the Nasser model. The same pattern was observable in Syria under Hafez Assad, in Algeria under Boumedienne, in Sudan, and among the Palestinians under Arafat. In Tunisia under Bourguiba it was a kind of Nasserism run by teachers and professors.

All of these progressive Arab regimes were mercilessly targeted by the NATO imperialists using subversion, assassination, and military attacks by Britain, France, Israel, and the United States. In the case of Libya, the authoritarianism of Qaddafi has been proven retrospectively something of an historical necessity, as seen by the tragic chaos reigning in that country today.

The deep roots of Nasserism in the modern Middle East have now been graphically demonstrated yet again by recent events in Egypt. Here the CIA operation known as the Arab Spring—in reality a preplanned military coup using posturing, computer-loving golden youth in Tahrir Square as a smokescreen—led to the fall of President Mubarak, admittedly a flawed and distorted version of the original Nasser method. President Morsi of the Muslim Brotherhood was in power for about a year with US backing, during which time he was unable to deliver on his promises of an improved economy, but sought rather to acquire a Pharaonic power more absolute than any exercised by Mubarak. His regime was toppled when the Army perceived that Morsi was seeking to embroil Egypt in a war in Syria, and at the same time with Ethiopia. Political power then reverted to the refurbished Nasser tradition in the person of General Sisi.

The lesson to be derived from this short experience is that, as the exorbitant power of the United States in the Middle East declines, it becomes less feasible for Washington to impose obscurantist Moslem Brotherhood regimes on a country like Egypt, where the organic tradition of politics, institutions, and theology go back to President Nasser. As the US presence ebbs, we may witness a rebirth of Nasserism on a large scale, with the Arab world reverting to the normal pattern of following the Egyptian model. The Arab states can thus plausibly argue that significant parts of the barbaric rebellions which afflict them today are not of indigenous manufacture, but rather represent toxic imports, which the NATO states have forced down the Arabs' throat.

Since my speech at the Second Interreligious Conference in Khartoum, Sudan in October 1994, I have been arguing that while it may not be possible to agree about faith, it is certainly possible to agree about hope and charity. Charity here means the good works of advancing the material and cultural welfare of humanity by means of economic development—the *bona opera* of Leibniz. Here Christian charity joins hands with Confucian benevolence and its imperative to make the people prosperous and educated; with the social solidarity of Islam; and with the sedaka (tzedakah) of Judaism. World economic development and the resulting pacification are exactly what the clash of civilizations is designed to suppress. If there are millions of jobless millennials in the Arab world with no education, no job, no wife, no kids, no home, no prospects and no hope who are vulnerable to extremist calls, then the idea that jobs and opportunity should be created is not as strange as some reactionaries think. A new world Development Decade is very much to the point.

CHARLIE? NON MERCI!
FRENCH ISLAMOPHOBIA AND ISLAMOPHILIA IN HISTORICAL PERSPECTIVE

John Andrew Morrow

Introduction

"If you insult my mother," said Pope Francis, "I am going to punch you in the face." Perhaps the Pope went too far but his point was poignant. According to the law of reciprocity, if someone insults your father, you insult their mother. This is "an eye for an eye." You fight freedom of expression with freedom of expression. You fight words with words and images with images. As Gandhi noted, however, the problem with this philosophy is patently clear: "an eye for an eye will only make the whole world blind." Judging by the cinematic circus surrounding the *Charlie Hebdo* affair, it seems that the entire world is indeed blind or, more precisely, blinded. The question, of course, is blinded by whom and blinded why?

Historical Flashes

In order to understand the present, we need to understand the past; in this case, the French and their attitude towards Islam. As difficult as it may be for many Muslims to comprehend, the French were not always foes. Yes, they defended themselves from Muslim invaders in the 8th century convinced that they were idol-worshipping infidels and evil-doers. Had they known, like the Jews and Christians of Spain, that Muslims represented a liberating force spearheading a cultural and scientific revolution, they might very well have responded differently. The propaganda, however, continued unabated, for centuries. They knew only what they were told: horror stories about Islamic rule; scurrilous and scandalous stories about the False Prophet and Anti-Christ and his fanatical followers. For those who are familiar with medieval French literature, it comes as no surprise that the French, the wretched *ifranj* of Arabic literature, played a prominent role in the Crusades until the early 16th century.

The historical hatred of the French towards Islam and Muslims experienced a sudden shift in the mid 16th century when King Francis I of France (r. 1515-1547), and the Turkish Sultan, Sulayman the Magnificent (r. 1520-1566), entered into the Franco-Ottoman Alliance in 1536. Not only was the alliance strategic and tactical, it was also commercial and cultural. What is more, Francis I was eager to ensure the protection of Christians living in the Ottoman Empire in the same fashion that Sulayman the Magnificent was concerned about the welfare of Muslims living in France.

Labeled by its adversaries as "the impious alliance" and the "sacrilegious union of the Lily and the Crescent," this diplomatic alliance between Catholics and Muslims and between Europeans, Turks, and Arabs scandalized the Western world which reeled with anti-Islamic sentiment. Nonetheless, the alliance lasted from the early 16th century until the 19th century, namely, until the Egyptian campaign when Napoleonic troops invaded Ottoman territory, a treacherous breach of the treaty that took placed in 1798-1801. If the alliance lasted so long, it was because it was to the benefit of both parties, proving that Western Christian and Eastern Muslims can co-exist peacefully when the proper policies are in place.

The Sultan who prepared the way for peace between French Catholics and Ottoman Muslims was Selim I (r. 1512-1520) who succeeded in uniting the Middle East from 1516 to 1517 by means of the conquest of the Mamluk Sultanate which encompassed Syria, Arabia, and Egypt. After his successor, Sulayman the Magnificent entered into an alliance with Francis I, the Ottomans and the French exchanged ambassadors. They signed religious, military and financial agreements. They even led joint military campaigns. The Ottomans and the French attacked Genoa and the Milanese in 1534-35. They fought together in the Eight Italian War in 1537-1538; the Ninth Italian War (1542-1546); the Hungarian Campaign in 1543; the Tenth and Eleventh Italian Wars (1551-1559). In 1547, the French even supported the Ottomans in their war against the Safavids. Imagine: French and Muslims in peace; friends, for three centuries, under Francis I, Charles IX, Henry III, and Louis XIV. What is important, so far as Islam is concerned, is that the alliance Sulayman made with the Catholic French was never viewed as grounds to question his sincerity as a Muslim. Tolerance and coexistence between members of other faiths was not abnormal in Islam: it was normative.

The Capitulations of the Ottomans were not one-sided. The French returned the favors of the Ottomans. If the Turks provided churches for Christians, the French provided mosques for Muslims. In fact, when Barbarossa spent the winter in Toulon, France, in 1543-1544, King Francis II (r. 1515-1547) converted the cathedral of the city into a mosque. If French influence was all the rage in Istanbul, Turkish influence was equally fashionable in Paris where the consumption of coffee, Ottoman clothing, including the turban and the caftan, along with reclining on Persian cushions and rugs were all in style.

It is therefore ironic that the French government currently insists on banning the headscarf when high-class French Catholics used to wear the turban and French women used to wear the kaftan and the hijab. Louise de Savoie, the mother of Francis I, used to dress in Muslim fashion, just like a traditional Muslim woman. Even Madame de Pompadour wore the headscarf! French ambassador Charles Gravier de Vergennes sported Ottoman outfits. The French officer, Claude Alexandre de Bonneval, who helped modernize the Ottoman army, used to wear a turban. He looked like a shaykh! As can be appreciated, the situation has certainly changed. I would love to see a French President wear a turban, a French first-lady wear the hijab, and French politicians dress like ayatullahs.

During the early days of the Franco-Ottoman Alliance, an event of major historic importance took place; namely, the publication of the *Testamentum et pactiones initae inter Mohammedem et Christianae fidei cultores* in 1630. Known in Arabic as *al-ʿAhd wa al-shurut allati sharataha Muhammad rasul Allah li ahl al-millah al-nasraniyyah* or *The Covenant of the Prophet Muhammad with the Christians of the World*, the document was discovered in the Levant by Father Pacifique Scaliger de Provins, a Capuchin monk. The content of the Covenant of the Prophet was completely in line with the Ottoman Capitulations. In it, the Messenger of Allah called upon Muslims to defend their Christian allies; granted them freedom of religious belief and practice; protected their lives and property; and excluded priests and monks from taxation. Christians, in return, were to be loyal to their Muslim allies even when it came to conflict with their co-religionists. In short, the Messenger of Allah commanded that Muslims and Christians respect and defend one another.

The discovery of this document elicited a great deal of scholarly debate for centuries. Certain scholars called it into question. Such was the case with Grotius, Voëtius, Hoornbeek, Hottinger, Bespier, Prideaux, Bayle, Mosheim, Döllinger; Jacques, Gieseler; and Guillaume. Father Pacifique, however, was convinced that it was authentic. This was also the opinion of Sionita, Hotman, Salmasius, Saumaise, Nagy de Harsany, Ricaut, Hinckelmann, Marana, Renaudot, Basnage de Beauval, Twiss, Madrazo, La Societé d'Amis de la Religion et de la Patrie, Grassi (Alfio), Miltitz, Addison and Van Dyke, among many others.

This favorable attitude toward the Covenant of the Prophet lasted only briefly after the establishment of the French Republic. In 1795, the Committee for Public Education decided that the government would print the *Covenant of the Prophet with the Christians of the World* in Arabic and French and distribute it to the consuls of the Republic in the Levant in order to circulate it throughout the Otttoman Empire. During the course of the meeting it was decided that copies of the Covenant of the Prophet would be sent to every library in the Republic and to all the schools in the Levant. Furthermore, copies would be sent to leading scholars across Europe.

Suddenly, however, everything changed. The translation and publication project was cancelled. The attitude of the French government suddenly, and unexpectedly, became hostile towards Islam and Muslims. If the French government treated the Covenant of the Prophet as authentic it now mocked it and denigrated it. What happened? The French Revolution. The execution of Louis XVI. The Universal Declaration of Human Rights. The start of secularism. The invasion of Egypt by Napoleon in 1798. The beginning of French imperialism in the Muslim world. The invasion of Algeria in 1830; that of Tunisia in 1831. The division of Africa among European countries at the Berlin Conference in 1884. The conquest of the Western Sahara in 1890. The French occupation of Morocco in 1904.

After the French Revolution, complete silence prevailed. The translation of the Covenant of the Prophet, which was supposed to be published internationally, was cancelled, and had to be published, independently, and in a tiny run, by the translator himself. Only a single copy has survived. The copies of the Covenant of the Prophet edited by Sionita, Fabricius, Nissel, Harsany, and Hinckelmann disappeared. It is a miracle that a few copies have reached us. The Covenants of the Prophet, which were found in many places throughout the Middle East, started to disappear. They were hidden. They were seized. They were destroyed. Neither Christians nor Muslims wanted to hear about the Covenants of the Prophet. Why? It was because neither side wished to respect them. Eventually, they were completely forgotten until they were rediscovered in the first decade of the second millennium.

Within half a century, the French Empire would collapse. Although French colonialism was short-lived, the damage it did to Muslim countries was devastating. Rather than being humbled by their defeat, the French remained angered, redirecting their animosity toward North African Muslim immigrants who were forced to immigrate to France due to the destruction of their countries of origin. Although the French no longer had an Empire, they maintained their imperialistic mentality; namely, their sense of superiority over others. Rather than attempt to integrate immigrants, they marginalized them both geographically and culturally. Regardless of how much they would assimilate, losing their language, culture, and even religion, they continued to be treated as second-class citizens. As absurd as it may sound, French children, born in France to French parents, and who have French grandparents, continue to suffer discrimination on the basis of the origin of their ancestors. It would seem that unless one traces back one's roots to the Franks, one cannot be truly French. People with origins in North Africa, for example, are therefore excluded from social integration and participation. The situation of

Muslims in France is therefore comparable to the historical treatment that African Americans have received in the United States.

If 99.9% of French people are oblivious to the fact that the Catholic French Kingdom was a friend and ally of the Ottoman Caliphate, an equal number of Muslims ignore the fact that they once co-existed in peace and prosperity with Western Christians and even waged wars together against common enemies. If the French maintain an imperialist mindset, Muslims maintain a victim mentality. This master-slave dichotomy can only lead to clashes. The master seeks to keep the slave in his or her place. The slave takes every opportunity to lash out against the master. Few, if any, remember the time when French Christians and Turkish and Arab Muslims were not adversaries but rather friends, allies, and partners. Unless we have a general understanding of French and North African history, the mass media can take full advantage of such myopia to manipulate public opinion, as we can see with the case of *Charlie Hebdo.*

Charlie Hebdo and French Hypocrisy

Despite concerted efforts to present *Charlie Hebdo* as the emblem of freedom of expression against religious fanaticism and obscurantism, people who are not puppets responding to the movements of their manipulative masters see it as the symbol of hypocrisy and salient double standards. The satirical publication is no stranger to controversy. Previously known as *Hara-Kiri*, it was banned briefly in 1961 and again, in 1966, for a span of six months. After mocking the death of Charles de Gaulle in 1970, the paper was banned definitely forcing the editors to regroup and rename it *Charlie Hebdo.* The paper ceased publication between 1981 only to reappear with a vengeance in 1991. Although it claims to uphold freedom of expression, *Charlie Hebdo* fired Mona Chollet in 2000 after she objected to an article by Philippe Val that described Palestinians as "uncivilized." In 2008, the paper terminated veteran political cartoonist Maurice Sinet, known as Siné, for suggesting that Jean Sarkozy planned to convert to Judaism. The paper only believes in freedom of expression when it suits secularist, atheist interests.

In an attempt to make Muslims appear irrational imbeciles, the mass media has insisted that they were outraged that the Prophet Muhammad was represented as an image—something which is supposedly outlawed by the *shari'ah.* The fact that the Prophet has long been represented in images is never part of the equation. The media makes it appear that Muslims are merely mad because somebody dared to draw Muhammad. At times, an image of the "Prophet" with a bomb on his turban is shown as an example. Although I read papers from around the world, and am media savvy, I have never come across an article that honestly addressed the real nature of the scandalous cartoons: namely, images of the "Prophet" naked, his balls hanging, and his anus in the air saying "a star is born;" cartoons of the "Prophet" having his posterior filmed while asking: "Do you love my ass?" Poor taste? Yes, indeed, just like the images of Jesus sodomizing God the Father while Christ has the Holy Spirit inserted in his rectum. Oh, did you Christians miss that one? How about the Pope holding up a condom and using it as the Eucharist? What about blasphemous mockery of Christ and the Virgin Mary portrayed in *Charlie Hebdo*'s *The Real History of Little Jesus*? Did that escape Christians as well? Certainly some Christians took notice and protested, but by and large contemporary Christians have become jaded to blasphemous portrayals of Christ and the Virgin in the mass media—party due to the fact that the media usually fail to report Christian protests. And the anti-Muslim satires of Charlie Hebdo have definitely been much better reported than their anti-Christian ones.

What is free speech? Free speech is the right to express one's religious and political views without fear of political or legal retaliation. The intent of liberty of expression is to prevent coercion. It is not a license to slander, libel, and defame. With every right comes responsibility. As the *Declaration on Religious Liberty* explains: "In availing of any freedom people must respect the moral principle of personal and social responsibility: in exercising their rights individuals and social groups are bound by the moral law to have regard for the rights of others, their own duties to others and the common good of all. Everybody must be treated with justice and humanity" (no. 7). Every nation that defends freedom of expression places limits upon it. Countries that permit pornography outlaw child pornography. Nations that permit freedom of expression prohibit hate propaganda and incitement to violence.

Stéphane Charbonnier did not die for free speech. He died because of his own sheer stupidity. If a man enters a lion cage, he is bound to be devoured. The lion is not to blame. There is a legal distinction between assault and aggravated assault. The law distinguishes between first and second degree murder. *Charlie Hebdo* was not innocent. The paper deliberately set out to offend the sensibilities of Christian and Muslim believers. Tellingly, however, the paper never provoked Jews. In France, for example, is it against the law to stir up hatred against a nation, a race or a religion if it encourages discrimination, hostility or violence toward a specific group. The French State shows zero tolerance toward anyone who denies the Jewish or Armenian Holocaust. It acts swiftly and decidedly against anything it perceives as an expression of anti-Semitism.

When it comes to Islam and Muslims, however, the hypocrisy of the French is hideous. The French are prepared to ban *Hari-Kiri* for mocking Charles de Gaulle; however, they support the publication when it humiliates the Prophet Muhammad. They charge French authors and comedians with hate speech when they criticize Israel; however, hate-mongers who defame Islam are given free reign. Despite repeated legal actions against *Charlie Hebdo*, the paper consciously chose to continue its campaign of anti-Islamic propaganda, deliberately insulting what Muslims hold most sacred. The paper alleged that it was not mocking the Prophet; rather, it was making fun of Islamists. The overwhelming majority of Muslims would not object to poking fun at pseudo-Muslim psychopaths and terrorists. They do it all the time on radio, on television, and in printed media. *Charlie Hebdo* did not decide to portray Osama ben Laden or Khalid Shaykh Mohammed in provocative poses. On the contrary, they targeted the Prophet Muhammad, the beloved leader of 1.5 billion Muslims. In so doing, they took aim at an entire community.

Do I side with Salafi serial killers? Absolutely not! Do I sympathize with *Charlie Hebdo*? Never. As a Muslim, I am certainly not Charlie for unlike Charlie I respect God; I respect His Prophets and Messengers; I respect religion; and I respect the feelings of my fellow human beings. *Charlie Hebdo* is not composed of free speech advocates: they are pornographers and *agents provocateurs* at the service of atheist secularist fundamentalism. The mass march that took place after the unfortunate but almost inevitable shootings was a parody. There, side by side, marched some of the greatest violators of human rights in the world all identifying themselves with *Charlie*. The stance of the French State vis-à-vis Muslim sentiment was clearly conveyed when it granted nearly 1 million Euros to support the magazine. The Digital Innovation Press Fund, funded in part by Google, donated 250,000 Euros to support the weekly which was matched by the French Press and Pluralism Fund. The Guardian Media Group also came forth with a pledge of 100,000 pounds. While it is commendable to defend freedom of speech, it must always be met with moderation.

France, like most of the Western world, has clearly positioned itself as *dar al-kufr* or the Abode of Disbelief and *kuffar al-harbi*, infidels at war with Islam. For several centuries, however, the French actually belonged to *dar al-'ahd*, the Abode of the Covenant and, rather than *kuffar al-harbi*, they were categorized as *ahl al-kitab* and *ahl al-dhimmah*, the People of the Book, and the People of Protection. Such co-existence between Christians and Muslims was made possible by the Covenants of the Prophet Muhammad which represents the foundation of rights in Islam. The principles proclaimed in the Covenants protected all citizens, regardless of their religion. They differ from the modern conception of "human rights" and "secularism" in the sense that the sovereignty of God reigns supreme. It is God who is giving these rights; not Man. This Covenant-based system provided the same social benefits of secularism by means of a religiously-rooted divinely-decreed system. The Covenants of the Prophet raises human rights to the level of Divine Rights.

If Muslims and Christians were friends and allies in the past, it was because they both believed in monotheism and respected one another's religious traditions and sensibilities. As offensive as this may seem for many, the French Revolution was a fiasco that eroded and eventually eradicated Christian values and ethics. To be frank, the French were better human beings when they were Catholics. Having essentially succeeded in exterminating Christianity, to the detriment and moral decay of France, French atheists seek to secularize all in their midst. While Islam is a shadow of what it once was, and the Muslim Tradition is in a coma and on life-support, it is the only socio-political and spiritual force that continues to resist secularism, materialism, and hedonism, to its dying breath. Resultantly, Islam must be made out to be public enemy number one and an existential threat to Western civilization. For people who profess to follow the Enlightenment faith, this is not progress. Far from evolution, it is devolution. It is a return to ignorance, hostility, and animosity; to the time when the Franks were at war against the Saracens as opposed to the time that Catholics and Muslims co-existed under the Covenants of the Prophet. If the people are blinded it is to prevent them from seeing this reality.

Conclusion

In closing, it is compellingly clear that killing someone for slander, defamation, and libel is not a just and equitable act. The case of *Charlie Hebdo* called for the *jihad* of the pen and not the *jihad* of the sword. Consequently, I condemn, in no uncertain terms, those who abuse the Prophet in the same fashion that I condemn those who kill his abusers. Although both parties are blameworthy—namely, those who abuse freedom of expression to offend and provoke Muslims, and those psychopath reactionaries who commit crimes in the name of Islam, printing blasphemous cartoons pales in comparison to premeditated mass murder. Likewise, if Jews had assassinated some German neo-Nazis involved with disseminating anti-Jewish caricatures, this would have been neither morally defensible nor wise. But it would certainly have been understandable.

In the current legal system prevailing in France, people may have the right to insult the Virgin Mary, Jesus, and Muhammad; however, this does not mean that they have the moral right to do so. One also has the right to sleep with intravenous drug-using transsexual prostitutes with STDs; this does not mean that it is the ethical thing to do. Law establishes the limits of allowable behavior. In other words, they set the lowest standard. Morals and ethics, however, show us how we should strive to behave. The cartoons published by *Charlie Hebdo* may have been legal; however, this does not change the fact that they were blasphemous, immoral, and unethical.

As for the terrorists involved in the Paris attacks, they are far from being the product of Islam. In reality, they are the product of Western society; to be precise: they are the product of French ghettoes. In Orwellian fashion, the French, like the British, the Americans, and the Israelis, simultaneous support and oppose what they describe as "radical Islam." The French secret services, for example, have been linked to the G.I.A. or the Armed Islamic Group, the death cult that was used to discredit the Muslim movement in Algeria. The French government has also been one of the staunchest supporters of the Syrian opposition. They support Takfiri terrorists abroad and then complain when Takfiri terrorists turn against them domestically. Since the Islamic, or shall we say, Satanic State, was created by Western powers, many political and military analysts find it highly suspicious when such groups attack targets in the Western world. No Muslim in his right mind would ever intentionally kill non-combatants or engage in acts of terrorism. Slaughter of the sort soils the image of Islam in the world and results in a brutal backlash against Muslims living in the West.

Islamist terrorists are not fighting for Islam. They are a proxy army, a fifth column, at the service of the secular New World Order. Secularist fundamentalists use religious extremists to destroy religion and discredit the Islamic option. Takfiri terrorists are used as a pretext for military intervention, war, and occupation. The end-game is not regime change, democracy, human rights, and freedom of expression. The strategic objective is the acquisition and control of natural resources. The war is not moral: it is material. Who, then, is this "Prophet" that these pseudo-Islamic forces claim to have avenged? If it is the Prophet Muhammad, they have done nothing but insult his name and his legacy of mercy and compassion. As Dalil Boubakeur, the Paris Imam, put it plainly, Takfiri/Wahhabi terrorists cannot possibly be talking about the historical Muhammad for the only "Prophet" they follow is Satan. As for the *Charlie Hebdo* affair, I can only describe it as an orchestrated blasphemy against Islam, similar to the actions of ISIS, serving to provoke Muslims; incite animosity against them; provide a pretext for creating a security and surveillance state; and justify imperialistic actions abroad.

A TALE OF TWO CITIES:
DISTURBING PARALLELS BETWEEN THE NEW YORK AND PARIS 9/11s

Barbara Honegger

In the wake of the January 7ᵗʰ Paris shootings, commentators in the U.S. and Europe have asked: "Could these attacks be 'France's 9/11'?" On the surface, this refers to the official claim and widespread belief that extremist Muslims perpetrated both events. But the question is also surprising, as the raid on the Charlie Hebdo offices and follow-on shootings at a kosher market killed only seventeen individuals compared to the mass murder of nearly 3,000 and the spectacular destruction of the World Trade Center on September 11ᵗʰ. Just beneath the surface, it is also darkly jarring because it hints at a disturbing constellation of facts that point to a very different and parallel reality behind the attacks on Paris and New York City.

To expose this parallel reality, we will begin with the historical context and key facts surrounding 9/11 and New York City.

The founders of the state of Israel knew it could not exist in the middle of the Muslim world without the backing of a major foreign power. Theodore Herzl, Israel's ideological founding father, had originally hoped this would be Germany; but during World War I the Zionists decided on the UK, and when Britain later had second thoughts, used terrorism to get their way.[106] After Israel's founding in 1947, the United States became the main state sponsor, and the U.S. Israel lobby grew enormously in influence with the objective of making America the enabler of Tel Aviv's foreign and security policies.

To this end, in the years leading up to September 11ᵗʰ, Israel's chief foreign policy goal was to engineer a major U.S. military presence in the Middle East, a goal finally fulfilled by the U.S. response to the 9/11 attacks. The very night of the attacks, when Benjamin Netahyahu—who in 1979 had organized the Jerusalem Conference on International Terrorism whose proceedings[107] became the blueprint for the War on Terror declared in the immediate aftermath of the 9/11 attacks—was asked what they meant for U.S.-Israeli relations, he responded "It's very good."[108] Also on 9/11 itself, former Israeli prime minister Ehud Barak told the BBC that Osama bin Laden was the likely perpetrator,[109] instantly assigning the blame that catalyzed the U.S. military into the greater Middle East before any serious investigation could have even begun.

In 1996, a group of U.S. Zionists known as neoconservatives or "neocons" had written a white paper entitled *A Clean Break*[110] for then newly-elected Israeli prime minister Benjamin Netanyahu calling for "regime change" in Iraq, the second target of U.S. military attack and occupation after Afghanistan justified by the false official narrative of 9/11. The next year, 1997, these same neocons founded the Project for a New American Century (PNAC), which in September 2000—a full year before 9/11—published a manifesto entitled *Rebuilding America's Defenses* calling for a "catastrophic and catalyzing event, like a new Pearl Harbor."[111] That New Pearl Harbor, we now know, was the attacks of September 11th, 2001.[112] The PNAC manifesto's signatories and participants soon took over all the major levers of power in the new Bush-Cheney Administration needed to carry out the inside attacks of 9/11, including Vice President Cheney himself, Cheney's top aide I. Lewis Libby, Secretary of Defense Donald Rumsfeld, Deputy Secretary of Defense Paul Wolfowitz, Rumsfeld's Assistant Secretary of Defense for Policy Douglas Feith, head of Rumsfeld's Defense Policy Advisory Board Richard Perle, Elliott Abrams, and soon-to-be Ambassador to the newly-occupied Afghanistan Zalmay Khalizad. Dov Zakheim, Rumsfeld's Pentagon Comptroller, had written an even earlier paper advocating a staged catastrophic event to force the U.S. into war to reconfigure the Middle East in Israel's interest which he had presented to PNAC, and is credited with the actual "New Pearl Harbor" quote in its manifesto. And Philip Zelikow, the executive director of the 9/11 Commission who headed its cover up and wrote a detailed outline of the "results" of the "investigation" before it even began, in 1998 co-authored an article laying out the changes the U.S. government would need to make in the wake of "catastrophic terrorism," beginning with the chilling subtitle "Imagining The Transforming Event."[113] That "Transforming Event" was "imagined" as an attack on the World Trade Center in New York City.

Then on September 11th, a group of Israelis were arrested after being observed dancing and celebrating after the *first* World Trade Center plane hit, which their cameras were ready to record.

This historical context and fact nexus points clearly at U.S. and Israeli Zionists as the real masterminds and high-level perpetrators of the 9/11 attacks, the corollary of which is that the official story—that 19 Muslim hijackers armed only with box cutters, run by a man in a cave in Afghanistan in urgent need of dialysis overcame the entire multi-trillion-dollar U.S. defense establishment on 9/11—is a Lie of State. That it is a lie has been proven many times over by the scientists, scholars and investigators of the worldwide 9/11 Truth Movement. Just some of the facts that constitute this proof, any one of which alone refutes the official story, are:

1) The precursor of the 9/11 attacks, the World Trade Center 1 bombing in 1993, was orchestrated by the FBI which provided the bomb material and explicitly let the attack go forward; in fact, every high-profile U.S. terrorism plot of the last decade, with only four exceptions, were FBI sting operations.[114]

2) Up to ten of the alleged "hijackers" turned up alive after 9/11[115] including alleged lead hijacker Mohammed Atta, whose father said he called him the next day, and when asked how to get in touch with him, said "Ask the [Israeli intelligence service] Mossad, he works for them";

3) None of the pilots and co-pilots on any of the four planes on 9/11 squawked the easy-to-send hijack code;

4) Cell phone calls couldn't be connected over 1,800 feet on 9/11, yet the official story claims that dozens of calls, which formed the core of the "hijacker" story, were made from planes flying at 35,000 feet;

5) The alleged Pentagon plane pilot, who is supposed to have flown a high-speed corkscrew descent in a large airliner that top gun Navy pilots have said *they* could not perform, was a terrible pilot who couldn't even pass training muster on a small Cessna;

6) There was fire and destruction in the two innermost rings of the west side of the Pentagon, one and two rings *beyond* the alleged C Ring "exit" hole—the furthest that any part of the alleged plane penetrated according to the official story;

7) The plane that hit WTC 2 in New York City was without markings and gray, and so could not have been any United Airlines commercial airliner;

8) Pieces of Flight 93 began falling from the sky eight miles before the alleged crash site near Shanksville, Pennsylvania; and

9) In the lead up to 9/11, known Al Qaeda operatives were provided with U.S. visas by the CIA and allowed to enter the country, train and carry out the attacks.

Now that we have established that the evidence overwhelmingly supports that U.S. and Israeli Zionists masterminded and orchestrated the 9/11 attacks, framing Muslims to justify the invasion and occupation of Muslim lands in the greater Middle East in fulfillment of Israel's foreign and security policy goals, we will now turn to the historical context and facts surrounding the Paris shootings of January 2015. We will see that they follow a recurring pattern in the "war on terror," that virtually all of those involved in or linked to major terrorist attacks—from 9/11 to the London subway, Madrid train station and Boston Marathon bombings—have suspicious relations with one or more Western "security" service.

In the years leading up to the Paris shootings, Israel faced a growing demographic crisis—the need for more Jewish citizens to counter its ever-growing Arab population; and in the weeks leading up to the attacks, France had taken two major geopolitical steps that infuriated Israel. In the wake of similar moves by Britain, Ireland, Sweden and Spain, the lower house of the French Parliament voted to recommend the recognition of Palestine as a state[116], to which Israeli prime minister Netanyahu warned that France was making a grave mistake; and France had voted in favor of International Criminal Court (ICC) membership for Palestine at the United Nations. France was also spearheading an effort at the U.N. to pass a Security Council resolution to restart *and* conclude the Israeli-Palestinian peace talks, and the French foreign minister had stated publicly that if it failed, France would officially recognize Palestine as a state. With France taking multiple official measures openly sympathetic to Muslim Palestinians, real Islamic zealots would never have chosen such a time to murder innocent French civilians. President Hollande had also called for the lifting of sanctions against Russia and was preparing to sign a compromise agreement on Ukraine in Astana on January 15th.

On January 7th, just eight days before this potential détente with Russia at Astana, two highly-militarily-trained commandos in black face masks, making it impossible to prove their identities during the act, and speaking perfect French attacked the Paris offices of cartoon satirists *Charlie Hebdo* killing individuals from a target list called out by name despite two police officers already being inside the company offices. The shooters had been tracked, monitored and tapped by French, British and U.S. authorities for more than a decade—one having been convicted on a prior terrorism offense, and the kosher market shooter having even met at the French presidential palace with then president Nicolas Sarkozy in 2009.[117] The deputy editor of Israel's IBA Channel 1 just happened to be on the scene and began posting photos of the shooting. The shooters claimed that the attacks were inspired by U.S. Muslim imam Anwar al-Awlaki[118] who according to 9/11 Commission executive director Philip Zelikow was a key contact for some of the September 11th Pentagon plane hijackers; attended a special post-9/11 Pentagon luncheon for allegedly "moderate" Muslims and was invited to give a sermon at the U.S. Capitol;[119] and had been exposed as an undercover FBI asset and Al Qaeda recruiter by some 900 documents obtained by Judicial Watch under the Freedom of

Information Act revealing that he left voicemails and emails with FBI agents for years after 9/11, at one point being released from custody at JFK airport on FBI orders despite there being a warrant out for his immediate arrest. It's therefore not surprising that al-Awlaki was targeted and killed by a U.S. drone attack in Yemen in 2011.

The French and EU governments, and even Charlie Hebdo—which had been purchased by the Rothschilds only weeks before the attacks[120] that massively increased its print run and sales—had been prepared for an attack for months. The shooters escaped the building, abandoning a get-away car outside a café closely linked to the Israeli Defense Force (IDF), conveniently leaving an ID in the car—like 9/11 "lead hijacker" Mohammed Atta conveniently leaving documents in his rental car at the airport and the "hijacker ID" that miraculously survived the World Trade Center inferno in New York City. No real terrorist would leave identification behind, especially having gone out of their way to hide their identities by using face masks, which makes it likely that the masked shooters were not the same men the ID sent the police chasing after. The shooters then robbed a gas station in full battle gear on the way to a hideout.

French President Hollande arrived at the Charlie Hebdo offices to make announcements within just half an hour. Like President Bush continuing to sit in the Florida classroom after the second WTC tower had been attacked on 9/11, how could he or his security detail know he would be safe unless the attacks were not what they seemed?

The videos and photos of the shooters on the street show all the signs of a staged Hollywood-style event or counterterrorism drill—like the hijack-scenario "exercises" being run by NORAD and the National Reconnaissance Office on 9/11—including the clearly simulated point-blank AK-47 sidewalk shooting of a police officer in the head with no recoil and no blood[121] as brilliantly detailed by Swedish investigator Ole Dammegard.[122]

Like the wrong kind of Islamic head scarf—Shiite instead of Al Qaeda-Sunni/Salafi—miraculously "found" unburned at the 9/11 Pennsylvania "crash" site, the Paris shooters were filmed thrusting the wrong finger—from the left rather than the right hand, which no Muslim would do—in the air while yelling "Allahu Akbar" ("God is great").

Five hundred police and special forces personnel, including tanks, were sent to the location where the shooters were holed up, while the police commissioner from the area where the shooters had lived, who was clearly one of the French authorities who had been following them for years, was found shot in the head the night of the attacks in the middle of writing a report on the shootings[123] after refusing an order from a superior to stop his investigation and his family was denied access to the results of the autopsy as provided by French law.[124]

The shooters made certain they were quickly portrayed as Muslim members of Al Qaeda linked to al-Awlaki, and in the case of the kosher market shooter of ISIS, by calling a French television station and going on the record saying so. All three shooters were finally surrounded and killed, so there was no risk of their being able to testify to having been part of a years-long covert military-intelligence operation.

French President Hollande asked Israeli Prime Minister Netanyahu not to take part in the Sunday, January 11th mass demonstration and march attended by more than forty world leaders[125], posted 4,700 police to guard 700 Jewish schools, and deployed 10,000 troops to guard "sensitive sites."[126] (Is it just a coincidence that this is the same number—10,000—of police and National Guard forces that were deployed, also with tanks, in the U.S. in the wake of the Boston Marathon bombings?) Netanyahu exploited the heightened fear from the attack on the kosher market to call on all French Jews—Europe's largest Jewish population—to mass emigrate to Israel as the one place where they can feel safe from terrorism, and repeated the "invitation" at the burial *in Israel* of the four French victims of the Paris kosher market attack.[127] At the funeral, Israel's president told the Jews of France that "we yearn to see you settle in Zion [Israel]." In mid-February, Netanyahu said "We are preparing to absorb a mass immigration from Europe. Jews of Europe, Jews of the world, I say Israel is waiting for you with open arms"[128] and his cabinet approved a $46 million dollar plan to "encourage" still more Jewish immigration from France, Belgium and Ukraine. Chillingly, President Hollande responded to French Jews, "If terrorism succeeds in driving you from the land of France, from the French language, from French culture, from the French republic which emancipated Jews, then terrorism would have achieved its goal."[129] Though the official interpretation is that he was saying Muslim terrorists would have achieved the goal of terrorizing French Jewish citizens, there is another possibility: that Israel was a secret hand behind the attacks designed to fan the fear of violent anti-Semitism toward the goal of mitigating its growing demographic crisis by increasing Jewish emigration to Israel.

What is not in question is that the Paris attacks, which were immediately used by French authorities to crack down even further on free speech, especially on the Internet, will be exploited by both Israeli and European Zionists to further conflate anti-semitism with legitimate criticism of Israel's illegal occupation and violence against the Palestinians. This is why it is so important not to officially recognize Israel as a "Jewish state," as were this to happen, the pressure would increase exponentially to criminalize and use the state apparatus to punish all criticism of Israeli policy and actions—even those that violently violate the human rights of Palestinians—as being "anti-Jewish."

Like Anwar al-Awlaki, the U.S. imam who despite inspiring some of the 9/11 alleged hijackers was invited to a special Pentagon luncheon for "moderate" Muslims after the Pentagon attack, the Charlie Hebdo shooters had returned from Syria where they had fought with the so-called "moderate" terrorists[130] supported and trained by the U.S., Israel and NATO countries, including the French government. These Islamist forces are a continuation of the Sunni jihadist terror cells that have been supported and trained by the U.S. and its allies since 1979, and since 1996 are the Gladio B successors of the secret NATO Gladio A forces which perpetrated attacks on European civilians during the Cold War to falsely blame communists.[131] The whole purpose of the CIA-NATO-Mossad Operation Gladio was, and is, to frighten European civilians—and in the "American Gladio" attacks of September 11th, U.S. civilians as well. In particular, according to NSA documents revealed by whistleblower Edward Snowden, American, British and Israeli intelligence worked together to *create* the brutal Sunni jihadist organization Islamic State of Iraq and Syria (ISIS; also known as IS or ISIL), whose leader is reported to be Mossad-trained agent Simon Elliot[132] and which President Obama is seeking a new Authorization for the Use of Military Force from Congress and billions of U.S. taxpayer dollars to fight. Stinger and TOW missiles used by ISIS are reported to be from Israeli stockpiles,[133] and in 2014 Netanyahu confirmed that the Israeli Defense Force is supporting Al Qaeda terrorists in Syria through a logistics base in the Golan Heights. And Netanyahu had the unmitigated gall to address a joint session of Congress in early March 2015, only weeks after the Paris shootings, in an attempt to rally the American public in the fight *against* "radical Islam."

Since the day of its founding, Israel has refused to officially define its borders, and the radical Zionist enterprise, led by Netanyahu, still holds to the goal of achieving a Greater Israel—not as commonly believed extending from the Jordan River to the Mediterranean, but from the Euphrates in *Iraq* to the Nile in *Egypt*. So it should come as no surprise that Israeli-guided ISIS just happens to be taking large swaths of territory inside Iraq, and that ISIS is also now reported to be gaining strength in the Sinai Peninsula where they are fighting the Egyptian government, the ideal base from which to launch a proxy assault on Egypt.

In light of these facts, it is time for France to add a fourth battle cry to its eternal "Liberty! Equality! Fraternity!": ***Reality!***

PRE- AND POST-9/11 FALSE FLAGS:
HOW WEAPONS OF MASS DECEPTION ARE INTERDEPENDENT

Kevin Barrett

We interpret new information by comparing it to past experience—more precisely, to stories we tell ourselves about past experience. If we have perceived an apparent pattern, such as angry Muslims reacting violently when their Prophet is insulted, we assume that each new incident, such as the Charlie Hebdo attack, must fit the same template. It is these "pubic myths," as they are called by self-styled public mythmaker Philip Zelikow, that structure the social reality we inhabit. And as Zelikow notes, it doesn't matter whether or not they are true; the important thing is that they are widely believed to be true.

One of the public myths that grounds Americans' and Europeans' understanding of their political systems is the myth of the lone nut. Assassinations of powerful and influential individuals, like other spectacular outbursts of violence with political consequences, are generally attributed to marginalized people or groups, rather than to the powerful individuals and institutions that stand to benefit from the crimes. Each new incident, each new lone nut, each new terrorist attack, is written off in advance as another example of senseless violence, of the lashing-out of the marginalized.

But what if there are other patterns at play? What if such violence is more often instrumentalized than random? What if much of the spectacular mayhem fed to us by the media has been fabricated by those who gain from it?

Lance deHaven-Smith writes in his groundbreaking *Conspiracy Theory in America*:

> The tendency to consider suspicious political events individually and in isolation rather than collectively and comparatively is not limited to the conspiracy-theory literature; it is built into the conspiracy-theory label and has become a pervasive predisposition in U.S. civic culture. For Americans, each assassination, each election breakdown, each defense failure, each war justified by "mistaken" claims is perceived as a unique event arising from its own special circumstances. While Americans in the present generation have personally witnessed many political crimes and tragedies, we see them as if through a fly's eye, situating each event in a separate compartment of memories and context.[134]

Smith asserts that the bias toward considering each suspicious political event as a separate case prevails even when those events are closely connected. For example, he suggests, despite obvious circumstantial evidence that John and Robert Kennedy were killed by the same people (right-wing US military and intelligence personnel backed by conservative oligarchs) for the same reasons (to maintain the Cold War in general and the Vietnam war in particular) the two assassinations are generally "seen as entirely unrelated" even by those who recognize them as inside jobs.[135]

Another series of apparent State Crimes Against Democracy (SCADS) that should be viewed as a coherent group, but often is not, is the subject of this chapter: The continuing progression of suspected false flag events serving as a public relations campaign for the so-called Global War on Terror (GWOT). From the questionable World Trade Center bombing of 1993, the "al-Qaeda" attacks on the US embassies in Dar es Salaam and Nairobi in 1998, the attack on the USS Cole in October 2000, to the subsequent false flag atrocities of 9/11-anthrax, Bali, Madrid, London, and Mumbai, to the Fort Hood shooter, the underwear bomber, the Boston Marathon bombing, the Times Square bomb attempt, the chemical weapons attack at al-Ghouta, Syria, and Islamic State atrocities and beheading videos, to the late 2014 through early 2015 attacks in Canada, Australia, France, and Denmark, the ongoing phenomenon of extremist, apparently strategically counterproductive terror attributed to radical Islamists but actually performed or enabled by Western intelligence agencies and their privatized spin-offs, demands to be considered as a unified phenomenon, not a series of isolated events.

Those who question any one of these alleged Islamic terror incidents in isolation are at a disadvantage in relation to the purveyors of the official story, who can draw on a larger narrative that synthesizes the whole series of events as examples of an alleged Islamist threat. For example, 9/11 truth-seekers are routinely challenged about other alleged Islamic extremist attacks, especially those that preceded 9/11, by defenders of the received notion equating terrorism with radical Islam. The larger notion of a radical Islamist terror threat, for mainstream thinkers, has become a myth that conditions the interpretation of any specific event purporting to involve Islam and terrorism. Because they have accepted the Islamic terror myth as a mode of interpreting reality that is ontologically superior to mere facts, defenders of the status quo are impervious to challenges questioning the empirical evidence supporting a conventional interpretation of any specific terror incident.

9/11-Anthrax: Lynchpin of a Terror Myth

The mythic interpretive template directing Americans to blame Muslims for terrorist incidents was hammered deep into public consciousness on September 11th, 2001. Almost from the moment the Twin Towers were destroyed in spectacular controlled demolitions,[136] TV news anchors, expert guests and political leaders began chanting the magic words "al-Qaeda" and "Bin Laden" despite the lack of evidence supporting such an interpretation. The very next day, as if by magic, a list with 19 names of alleged radical Muslim hijackers materialized, supposedly discovered in Mohamed Atta's suitcase, which (we were told) had somehow failed to make the transfer between the commuter plane Atta took from Portland, Maine to Boston and the doomed Flight 11.[137] Though the list of 19 names included two who died before 9/11 and ten who were alive after 9/11[138], and though Atta's suitcase included incompetently forged documents such as his supposed will beginning with a botched bismillah reading "In the name of God, myself and my family"[139]—and though the idea of Atta putting his will and a list of hijackers in a suitcase headed for oblivion makes even less sense than the story of his driving from Boston to Portland on September 10th so he would have to catch a commuter flight with a tight connection to Flight 11—the absurdly improbable account was uncritically accepted by mainstream institutions including the media, the courts, Congress, and most of the academy. Even when a former high-level intelligence official admitted to the *New Yorker* that the so-called evidence implicating the alleged hijackers was obviously planted, saying "Whatever trail was left was left deliberately—for the FBI to chase," mainstream investigative journalists were unwilling to dig deeper to discover who had planted the evidence and left the false trail.[140]

9/11-anthrax appears to have been designed to etch in stone the mythic template equating Islam and terrorism.[141] One year earlier, in September 2000, the neoconservative Zionists at Project for a New American Century had called for a "catastrophic and catalyzing event—like a New Pearl Harbor."[142] As 9/11 Commission scriptwriter Philip Zelikow had written in a 1998 *Foreign Affairs* article envisioning a terrorist attack destroying the World Trade Center: "Like Pearl Harbor, this event would divide our past and future into a before and after."[143] Zelikow, that self-described expert in the "creation and maintenance of public myths,"[144] knew that 9/11 or its equivalent would be remembered in the collective imagination as the kind of primordial event similar to the creation of the world in creation myths. Such events are remembered as transformative catalysts that divide time into a nebulous long-ago-and-far-away "before" and an "after" that is the world as we know it. Zelikow and his fellow Zionist neocons also knew that the new world "after" 9/11 would be dominated by a mythic interpretive framework demonizing Muslims as terrorist enemies. After the creation of the public myth of Islamic terror via the "catastrophic and catalyzing event" of 9/11-anthrax, maintenance of that public myth could be performed by intermittently creating or publicizing smaller terror events.

Thus 9/11-anthrax played a central role in the creation of the Islamic terror myth. Prior to the autumn of 2001, such high profile but far-from-catalyzing events as the 1993 World Trade Center bombing, the African embassy bombings, and the USS Cole attack paved the road to 9/11-anthrax by creating a plausible enemy image on whom the coming "New Pearl Harbor" could be blamed. While space does not permit a detailed analysis of these three events, I will briefly summarize key points cited by those who argue for the false flag interpretation of the three major pre-9/11 alleged Islamic extremist attacks.

Pre-9/11 False Flags: Creating a Plausible Enemy

Compelling evidence indicates that the 1993 World Trade Center bombing, like 9/11, was an inside job. Such evidence includes testimony by an outraged Emad Salem, the FBI informant and agent provocateur who hatched the plot and directed its logistics, that the FBI had promised him that it would build a phony non-explosive bomb but "we didn't do that."[145] As the *New York Times* reported: "'Do you deny,' Mr. Salem says he told the other agent, 'your supervisor is the main reason of bombing the World Trade Center?' Mr. Salem said Mr. Anticev did not deny it."[146] Additionally, the official story that the FBI cracked the case when Mohammed A. Salameh, who had rented the truck used in the bombing, was arrested when he returned to the rental company to ask for his deposit back makes no sense.[147]

Like the 1993 World Trade Center bombing, the bombings of two US embassies in Tanzania and Kenya in 1998 appear to have been inside jobs facilitated by an American agent provocateur. The undercover American agent who arranged the African embassy bombings was US Army Sgt. Ali Mohamed. Though the official cover story holds that Sgt. Mohamed infiltrated the US military on behalf of al-Qaeda rather than the other way around, the preponderance of evidence suggests the contrary. Mainstream investigative journalist Peter Lance, pretending to support the cover story while publishing evidence against it, reports:

> Ali Mohamed ... was something of an al Qaeda super-spy who managed to work with terrorists, the Green Berets, the CIA and become an FBI informant, even while ensuring Osama bin Laden's safe passage around the Middle East. For years, *Triple Cross* alleges, the FBI and specifically

[prosecutor Patrick] Fitzgerald, knew about him but allowed Mohamed's activities to continue unchecked.[148]

University of California professor Peter Dale Scott confirms that Sgt. Mohamed "worked for the FBI, the CIA, and U.S. Special Forces."[149] Scott reports that Sgt. Mohamed's FBI handler John Zent facilitated the African embassy bombings by telling the Royal Canadian Mounted Police to release Mohamed, who had been held as a terrorist suspect.[150] Scott cites numerous similar examples showing that Mohamed enjoyed official US government protection while carrying out his terrorist activities.

Like the 1993 and 1998 bombings, the October 2000 attack on the USS Cole in Yemen, which killed 17 sailors and wounded 49, appears to have been facilitated or orchestrated by corrupt US government officials. Handicapped teenager Tawfiq Bin Attash, publicly billed as a mastermind of the attack, was in no position to succeed with his harebrained scheme of filling a dinghy with explosives and attacking the next American ship that passed by. Attash and his friends must have had professional inside help finding out when the USS Cole would be passing within range; their booby-trapped dinghy provided cover for a pre-planted explosion from within the ship that did most of the damage. (The modus operandi echoed the false flag sinking of the USS Maine by a bomb planted inside the ship, blamed on a nonexistent Spanish attack from without.)[151] In July, 2001, the Yemeni government's investigation concluded that the American government had bombed its own ship as a pretext for military action of some kind, possibly including a planned invasion and occupation of the port of Aden.[152] But in retrospect it seems that the overriding strategic purpose of the USS Cole bombing was to pave the road to 9/11-anthrax by hoisting the false flag of al-Qaeda to the level of plausible patsy.

Post-9/11 False Flags: Maintaining a Public Myth

Just as an intermittent series of relatively small false-flag attacks set the stage for 9/11-anthrax and its enshrinement of the Islamic terror myth, another series of relatively minor attacks since 2001 has kept the terror pot boiling. The first major 9/11-anthrax follow up was the Bali bombing, which Australian journalist Joe Vialls argued was accomplished by an Israeli miniature nuclear weapon.[153] While this may come as news to consumers of the Western mainstream media, most Indonesians recognized the false flag from day one. As Sidney Jones reported in *The Observer* two weeks after the crime: "Absurd, as it may seem, if talk shows and media commentaries are any indication, the most likely candidates in most Indonesians' minds are the U.S. government and the Indonesian army."[154] The Indonesians were likely right. Eyewitness Dmitri Khalezov has testified that former Israeli Mossad chief Mike Harari was arrested in

Thailand for orchestrating the Bali bombing, then released under pressure from foreign governments. Khalezov has provided documents supporting his assertion.[155] An American-supported Israeli mini-nuke attack has emerged as the most plausible scenario for the Bali bombing.

The next spectacular international attack attributed to al-Qaeda was the Madrid train bombing of March 11th, 2004—which, coincidentally or not, occurred exactly 911 days after 9/11. French journalist Mathieu Miquel, relying exclusively on official court documents and from Spanish mainstream media sources, reports: "As incredible as it may seem, the evidence that supposedly confirms the theory (that Islamists carried out the attacks) cannot stand up to rigorous analysis. And the suspicious behavior of certain elements of the police forces clearly indicates the existence of an intent to sabotage the investigation."[156] If the police framed innocent Muslims and sabotaged the investigation, the attack must have been yet another false flag designed to maintain the Islamic terror myth.

Then came the London mass transit bombings of July 7th, 2005. Once again, the official attempt to convict Islamist terrorists falls apart upon close inspection. Scholar and author Nafeez Ahmed has written a book raising questions about the official story,[157] while another British academician, Nick Kollerstrom, has written an even longer book demonstrating at length and in detail that the event was clearly a government-sponsored false flag attack and that the Muslim patsies were innocent.[158]

In November 2008 another spectacular, supposedly Muslim extremist attack occurred in Mumbai, India. Pakistani TV host and defense analyst Zaid Hamid has cited evidence that this attack, known in India as 26/11, was the product of Hindu extremists in Indian intelligence in collaboration with the Israeli Mossad.[159] It later emerged that CIA agent David Headley had orchestrated the attack.[160] Headley apparently masterminded the attack on behalf of Zionist elements in US and Indian intelligence, with Mossad behind them, in order to falsely blame the attack on Pakistan: "Although American and Indian investigators have used David Headley in order to link him with Pakistan, yet his real connections are concerned with Indian secret agency RAW [India's most powerful intelligence agency] and American CIA."[161]

For simplicity's sake, I will focus for the remainder of this overview of post-9/11 synthetic terror on the USA, the would-be unipolar world hegemon whose acceptance of the Islamic terror myth is most crucial to the neoconservative-Zionist program.

After a hiatus lasting most of the decade, the false flag of Islamic terror was re-hoisted in the USA following the Fort Hood shootings of November 2009. (Technically this event cannot be classified under the terrorism rubric since the victims were soldiers, not civilians.) American historian and terror analyst Webster Tarpley writes that the Fort Hood massacre attributed to Major Nidal Hasan unleashed "an articulated campaign of media hysteria and mass manipulation."[162] Tarpley went on to question the official story of the shootings by citing reports of multiple shooters, adding: "There remains the question of whether Major Hasan's psychosis has been artificially produced through a program of brainwashing and heavy-duty 'Clockwork Orange' psychological manipulation." That question would re-emerge in 2014 in connection to another likely Manchurian Candidate terrorist, the leader of Islamic State and self-proclaimed Caliph Abu Bakr al-Baghdadi.

If the Fort Hood shooting was tragic, the follow-up incident involving a so-called underwear bomber was pure farce. While the American people were told that a terrorist named Umar Farouk Abdulmutallab had packed his underwear full of plastic explosives in hope of blowing up a jetliner, they were not told that Abdulmutallab did not have a detonator—and that plastic explosives cannot explode without a detonator. Worse, eyewitnesses saw Abdulmutallab boarding the Detroit-bound plane in Amsterdam without a passport, escorted by a "sharply-dressed man" who appeared to be some sort of security agent. A cameraman on board the plane was clearly complicit in the attack, beginning to film shortly before the attack began, and panning seamlessly to capture the entire episode as if on cue. Passenger and eyewitness Kurt Haskell, a Detroit attorney, has published convincing evidence that the whole affair was a poorly-disguised false flag operation.[163] ABC News reported Haskell's courtroom testimony: "I am convinced that Umar was given an intentionally defective bomb by a U.S. agent to stage a false terrorist attack."[164]

A subsequent headline-garnering reminder of the alleged Islamic terror threat was the Times Square bombing attempt of May 1st, 2010. Like the underwear bombing incident, the Times Square scare involved an utterly incompetent terrorist patsy and a so-called bomb that was highly unlikely to explode. According to former US intelligence insider Gordon Duff, editor of Veterans Today, the fake attack was "part of a CIA false flag against Pakistan."[165]

The next major American myth-maintenance operation was the Boston Marathon bombing of April 2013. If anything, this alleged Islamic terror incident was an even more crushingly obvious false flag than its predecessors. Photographs taken at the scene show that the exploded backpack the FBI claims held a bomb was not worn by either Tsarnaev brother, but instead by an unknown man wearing a cap with insignia of Craft International, a Blackwater-style outfit owned by "American Sniper" Chris Kyle specializing in mercenary mayhem whose motto is "Sometimes violence *does* solve problems." Craft and the officials who hired them hid from the media and refused to either deny or explain the mercenaries' presence at the Marathon.[166] Video taken at the scene reveals apparently staged carnage complete with theatrical pseudo-amputations of artificial limbs and poorly-distributed amounts of cinematic fake blood..[167] The FBI murdered a key witness, Ibrahim Todashev, execution style while he was in custody.[168] The Tsarnaevs' uncle Ruslan Tsarnaev was married to Samantha Fuller, daughter of controversial CIA agent Graham Fuller, until 2004.[169] Graham Fuller has allegedly been implicated in a number of scandals including the Iran-Contra affair and the creation of al-Qaeda.[170] He provided support to Chechens fighting against Russia.[171] Fuller has advocated "guiding the evolution of Islam" and has been called the CIA controller for the ethnic Turkish USA-based Fethullah Gulen organization which controls over $20 billion in assets and has been accused of trying to overthrow the government of Turkey.[172] While in Turkey in May 2011 I met with Turkish journalists who said Fuller, who headed the CIA station in that country in September 2001, threatened them shortly after the attacks, telling them not to question the official story of 9/11 in print.

In a February 20th 2015 email to this author, Fuller derided the allegations, saying "My voluminous writings over the years make abundantly clear what my position is on a wealth of issues and my consistent criticisms of US policies; these ridiculous allegations are simply utterly inconsistent with what I say, do or write." Given his manifest opposition to neoconservative-driven Islamophobia, it is conceivable that Fuller has been slandered by neocon operatives, and that the accusations against him are baseless or exaggerated.

With or without Graham Fuller, think tanks and covert operations professionals have certainly "guided the evolution of Islam" not only by propping up such "moderate Muslim" Zionist apologists as Fethullah Gulen, but also by promoting the appalling and repulsive sectarian cruelty of so-called Islamic State, formerly known as ISIS or ISIL. This extremist group, which primarily attacks Muslims and to a lesser extent Christians as it destabilizes Israel's potential enemies, was armed and trained at CIA bases in Jordan and unleashed against the Syrian government of President Bashar al-Assad and later Iraq.[173] According to an American mainstream media report that has been scrubbed from the internet, as well as numerous Iraqi reports, self-styled caliph Abu Bakr al-Baghdadi was held by US forces at Camp Bucca at least four years despite official denials.[174] The official attempt to cover up al-Baghdadi's four year stay at Camp Bucca suggests that the self-styled caliph may have been enlisted or even mind-controlled while in US custody.[175] The preponderance of evidence suggests that Zionist elements of US-NATO manufactured ISIS not only to destabilize Israel's potential enemies, but also to maintain the public myth of Islamic terror and the clash of civilizations it spawned.

The Emerging Counter-Narrative

By considering the above series of high-profile false flag attacks attributed to Muslims as a coherent phenomenon, rather than a series of isolated events, we are preparing the ground for an emerging counter-narrative challenging the myth of Islamic terror. This counter-narrative begins with the observation that no rational American should fear terrorism of any kind, since it poses a threat to human life and limb far below the level of lightning strikes and bathtub drownings.[176] It continues with the observation that according to the American FBI, only 6% of terrorist attacks on American soil are even attributed (whether correctly or incorrectly) to radical Muslims, who statistically pose less of a terror threat than radical Jews, leftists, or hispanics—despite hysterical media coverage suggesting the contrary.[177] Finally, it asks who created and promoted the false notion of an Islamic terrorist threat, and for what ends . . . and answers the question by pointing to neoconservative Zionists, whose political philosophy is based on the need for an enemy, whether actual or mythical.[178]

In the absence of a coherent counter-narrative, those questioning the official story of any alleged terror attack are at a serious disadvantage. A high-level aide to George W. Bush, reputed to be Karl Rove, famously suggested to journalist Ron Suskind that artificially-created public myths have superseded empirical reality:

> The aide said that guys like me were "in what we call the reality-based community," which he defined as people who "believe that solutions emerge from your judicious study of discernible reality." I nodded and murmured something about enlightenment principles and empiricism. He cut me off. "That's not the way the world really works anymore." He continued "We're an empire now, and when we act, we create our own reality. And while you're studying that reality—judiciously, as you will—we'll act again, creating other new realities, which you can study too, and that's how things will sort out. We're history's actors . . . and you, all of you, will be left to just study what we do."[179]

While narratives can certainly take leave from reality, especially when fabricated by liars, they can also serve as honest efforts to communicate reality. The reality-based community should recognize the power of narrative and fight back against the empire of lies by telling truthful stories that outstrip the false ones promulgated by political hacks. And perhaps the most important truthful counter-narrative available today is the above-sketched revisionist account of the so-called War on Terror.

WITCH HUNT ON TERRORISM

Anthony Hall

Scores of skeptical observers are noticing the abundant signs of crisis engineering displayed in the supposed Islamic terror episodes that took place in Ottawa Canada last October, in Sydney Australia in December and in Paris France in January of 2015.

The probable nature of this series of Mossad-style operations can best be understood as the Shock Doctrine in action.[180] The triumvirate of deception in Ottawa, Sydney and Paris seems to have been carried out through real, yet covertly manipulated, acts of lethal violence finessed by operatives tasked to advance the rebranding of the 9/11 Wars.

In an article in *Veterans Today* entitled "Paris Terror, The Smell of False Flag," Senior Editor Gordon Duff reflects on the apparently staged theatrics accompanying the ruthless murders carried out at the offices of the Charlie Hebdo satirical magazine. He writes:

> Killing twelve French citizens to manipulate public opinion in a nation increasingly unfriendly to Israel simply fits a pattern. That pattern has recently included synagogue attacks as well. The first thing [that should be] asked when there is a terror attack is "who benefits." No, the mainstream media doesn't ask. Intelligence agencies don't ask either. They already know. 80% of the time one of them did it, either directly or through a terror group they either created and operate, like ISIS/ISIL or one they took over, perhaps like Boko Harum or Al Shabab. No one ever asks where those satellite phones and new Toyota pickup trucks come from, as though they magically arrive from outer space.[181]

Veterans Today, Israel, and Global Security

Like many members of the close knit circle that operate in and around *Veterans Today*, Gordon Duff is a veteran of US special forces involving several branches of the US intelligence services including the CIA. What this group of VT insiders have most in common is a shared sense of betrayal that the instruments of US foreign policy, but especially its most covert branches, have been subordinated to Israeli control.

What I have come to see as a Canadian outsider without any military background myself is the shared acknowledgement by VT insiders that they took part in some very dark operations on behalf of the US deep state. The view seems to be that in earlier times these operations did serve in one way or another some genuine US interests, even if only those of certain branches of the US corporate sector.

The evidence, assert VT insiders, no longer support these conclusions. The subjugation of US foreign policy under the dominant prerogatives of the Jewish lobby, including The American Israel Public Affairs Committee, is but one facet of a more general takeover by a broad coalition of criminal co-conspirators whose operatives are in the process of effectively plunging all humanity, indeed all life on earth, into a hellish abyss.

While the writers at *Veterans Today*, myself included, cover all manner of subjects a common understanding shared by most VT writers and its many avid readers is that the events of 9/11 were engineered from within US agencies at Israel's behest. A primary aim was to transform Israel's regional enemies into the global enemies of the so-called "West." In the process the otherwise obsolete agencies that had emerged from the capitalist side of the Cold War were delivered a new transnational foe to seek out, combat and vanquish.

Increased military budgets, widened police powers and enhanced political prestige for those who successfully made the transition from anti-communism to anti-terrorism were thereby secured. The neo-liberal transition from the social welfare state to the stock market state was transacted providing governments with new justifications for intrusive intervention in everybody's personal and commercial business.

9/11, therefore, was partly about maintaining the industrial viability of the permanent war economy that had grown up in the United States since the attack on Pearl Harbor in 1941. While this false flag operation maintained some elements of continuity in the US political economy, the 9/11 Black Op also provided the new overlords of Western geopolitical strategy with the keys to the castle of the world's dominant national security apparatus.

The installation of the new directors began in earnest with the expertly engineered media misrepresentations of the events of 9/11 in ways that brought the creation, amplification, manipulation and exploitation of Islamophobia to new heights of diabolical cunning.

This subversion of mass media was the essential component of the global coup d'état, one that hastened the transfer of imperial power from US institutions to Israel and to the many worldwide networks of Zionist banking, media, military and security interests that have come to be identified with the power, prestige and Machiavellian duplicity of the Jewish state.

Thanks in significant measure to the work of VT insiders it is becoming more broadly understood that the upper echelons of all major military and intelligence forces in the world are well aware that Israeli-American neocons were the directing masterminds who pulled off 9/11, albeit in a flawed way that fell far short of the full extent of the destruction planned for that day.

The indicators are strong that in recent months Gordon Duff and other VT insiders have received a major cache of new material exposing many heretofore unknown operational facets in and around the September 11 event. The origins of the new information are said to involve Edward Snowden and material passed through ex-KGB figures who are also among the VT circles of special forces operatives, weapons experts, and geopolitical analysts.[182]

Part of the new revelations concern the application of new generations of secret nuclear technology to produce the tremendous surges of energy that transformed three of the world's premier steel frame skyscrapers into vapour and talcum-power-like dust in three unprecedented displays of controlled demolition.

The use of mini-nukes and related nuclear technology is tied to more far ranging accounts of how nuclear weapons have been stolen and passed along, including to Israel, to provide material that has already been detonated in a variety of military and false flag theatres. These thefts together with military responses to the sabotage from within speak of ongoing divisions within the martial and intelligence apparatus of the ailing superpower. These divisions have become deeply intertwined with the myriad of complexities in the covert operations of the privatized terror economy.

As I have come to understand over the years, source materials garnered from insider interactions among operatives in state intelligence agencies and their corporate spinoffs often fail to provide the certainty of fixed points of published references that can be cited, checked, checked against other sources, and listed in bibliographies as academicians are accustomed to doing.

Intelligence operatives are prone to play one another, to trade info, to finesse various agendas and even to sprinkle bits of disinfo into rich stews of new revelations. In some instances the difference between life and death hangs in the balance of deviation from the unwritten rules of transaction among spies, counterintelligence operatives and the like. Written accounts recording their transactions among themselves are therefore sometimes subtle and tricky narratives to interpret.

Notwithstanding such interpretive problems, provisos, and cautions, however, the stark outlines of a newly exposed landscape of contemporary history is being revealed at VT clarifying the nature of the origins and ongoing machinations in the still unfolding 9/11 Wars. A primary attribute of the 9/11 Wars is the audaciousness of the psychological operations entailed in the aggressions. A previously undercover world is emerging into the light of skeptical examination in the Age of the Internet.

As a platform of resistance to tyranny for personnel who have worked, or do now work, at the heart of the ailing superpower's elaborate Armed Forces, *Veterans Today* renders some protection to those soldiers of conscience who refuse to collaborate in silence with the sabotage from within. As the investigation into 9/11 proceeds it becomes increasingly difficult for those thousands of operatives who played parts in the 9/11 assaults and the enormous deceptions that followed to hide from their more conscientious peers.

On 9/11 itself many personnel at, for instance, NORAD or the Pentagon, might have been unaware of the consequences of their actions because of need-to-know obfuscation, narrow circumscribing of assigned responsibilities, and the fog of confusion created by concurrent drills meant to resemble the real assault on America that did take place on that bright September morning in 2001. Now, however, the hiding places are diminishing.

Veterans Today provides some sanctuary and a base of operations for whistle blowers within the military. The controversial news platform is also turning the tables on those soldiers that chose the route of upward mobility with the makers of the global coup d'état over loyalty to the people and Constitution of the United States as well as to the real safety and security of the global community.

Benjamin Netanyahu's Strange Excursion to Paris, January 2015

The convergence of all these many forces seemed to be on display in Benjamin "Bibi" Netanyahu's strange behaviour during the official ceremonies of mourning following the murder of twelve people at the head offices of the Charlie Hebdo satirical magazine in early January. Within hours of the violent episode the alternative media was thick with observations that the whole operation stank of a Mossad-style intervention aimed a cranking up Islamophobia and with it the current round of anti-terrorist initiatives.

It seemed that Netanyahu was simultaneously seeking to take credit for the operation while joining in the procession of world leaders marking the occasion. Netanyahu had been asked by the French president, Francois Hollande, not to attend at all. He nevertheless showed up but was snubbed by the organizers who did not put the Israeli prime minister and his security police on the first bus to the site of the world photo opportunity.

For a time Bibi was in the second row of the procession. But he then pushed his way to the lead row and proceeded to wave victoriously to onlookers like some sort of conquering Caesar who had taken control of the French City of Lights by force of arms.

It was almost like Bibi is playing to two audiences. The biggest but secondary audience were the masses of ordinary folks that are prey to the deception that all the false flag events are not staged but rather genuine and independent acts of Islamic jihadism motivated by nothing more than raw hatred and contempt for the freedom and liberties of citizens in the Judeo-Christian West.

Netanyahu's less numerous but more important audience is composed of those that are well aware of the Likudnik leader's instrumental role in the invention and oversight of the Global War on Terror in all its various Islamophobic incarnations. Try as some of us might to break the spell of the deception, Bibi is well aware that the elaborate illusion is for the time being protected by networks of co-conspirators in charge of large numbers of media operations seemingly spread across a wide spectrum of political and ideological perspectives.

Bibi's importance in the Paris anti-terrorist rituals is based on his leading role in formulating the general concept of a war on terror with his series of conferences culminating in the publication of his edited book in the early 1980s, *Terrorism: How the West Can Win*. Bibi's paradigm was given fuller academic expression in the 1990s by Samuel Huntington's *Clash of Civilizations* which, in turn, built on Bernard Lewis's earlier work.

Following 9/11 Bibi is on record as having repeated several times the proposition that the events of 9/11 were good for Israel. The most prominent Israeli politician in the world has been unrelenting in playing the lethal semantic game of basically equating the movement for Palestinian survival and self-determination with terrorism at every turn.

Netanyahu is skilled in his cunning condemnation of ISIL, the hugely hyped Islamic terrorist group that tellingly wants only to fight other Muslim groups and strangely never wants to fight Israel. Netanyahu never misses an opportunity to confuse the Islamic State, which is not a state, with the Islamic Republic of Iran which is becoming a global superpower in spite of the cyber attacks, economic warfare, assassination plots and blatant propaganda directed its way by the complex of Western governments that take their lead from Israel.

The shootings at the Charlie Hebdo offices were followed by the shooting of four Parisian Jews in a kosher market. This episode was quickly seized upon by Mr. Netanyahu as an opportunity to promote Jewish immigration to Israel from France and elsewhere in Europe.

At the Great Synagogue in Paris Benjamin Netanyahu's security detail manhandled the French Prime Minister, Manuel Valls, directing him where to sit. Valls audibly protested the insult to France's dignity and jurisdiction. President Hollande subsequently exited the religious venue just as the the Israeli Prime Minister was about to speak. The imperiousness of Netanyahu throughout begs the question of whether or not he conceived of himself as the executive in chief of the entire "Je suis Charlie" operation.

The rebranding of the 9/11 Wars, initially sold to the public in the name of the Global War on Terror, involves the Dark Op rejigging of the imagery of the Islamic terrorism. The largely manufactured imagery of Islamic terrorism involves the creation of media representations combining some elements lifted from reality with the scientific fabrication of Disneyesque archetypes and caricatures of evil meant to leverage the potent political currency of fear.

Since 9/11 the implanting, cultivation, manipulation, and exploitation of public fears of Islamic terrorism have become big business. The generation of Islamophobia through fear of Islamic terrorism has become a core element in the lucrative public perceptions industry. The illusions produced by this business provide grist for the propaganda mill that regularly injects the deadly toxin of industrial-strength hatred into the contaminated mainstream of most media of mass communications these days.

The biggest part of the public relations industry derives its most lucrative profit streams from the promotion of aggressive warfare through the engineering of public opinion hostile to the demonized Other. Since 9/11 this promotion of aggressive warfare leans heavily on the enterprise of whipping up readily exploitable hatred towards Islamic religion, Islamic philosophy, Islamic culture, Islamic people and Islamic countries.

As the core polity at the convergence of all these elements, the Islamic Republic of Iran is subject to an especially concerted campaign of engineered Islamophobia in the West. Where Iran under the Shah's rule was an obedient servant of Western interests, the very strength and viability of Iran's Islamic revolution since 1979 has made the national bedrock of Persian civilization the primary obstacle to the imperial aspirations of Likudnik Israel.

Iran, like Islamic people more generally, has therefore been especially subject to the subversive deployment of fraudulent media coverage to produce the necessary mental environment for foreign wars combined with domestic pacification of dissidence at home. Unfortunately, purposely induced Islamophobia is being integrated into the top-down regimes of governance imposed on most of the so-called Western democracies.

From Red Scares and Anti-Communism to Islamophobia and Anti-Terrorism

The mixture of the spectacle of made-to-order violence in Ottawa, Sydney, and Paris with the orchestration of highly engineered media coverage is reminiscent of the brand of media manipulations developed by Madison Avenue's PR guru, Edward Bernays.[183]

A nephew of Sigmund Fraud, Bernays culminated his career as the pioneer of photo ops and spin doctoring with a series of elaborate media ruses. Designed for the CIA and the US Armed Forces, the aim of these media deceptions was to misrepresent purposely the US-backed coup in Guatemala in the early 1950s.

To protect the monopoly of power amassed by the United Fruit Company the Guatemalan elected leader, social democrat Jacobo Arbenz, was removed from power in favour of a series of imposed military dictatorships. This strategy of US domination through covertly engineered regime change would become a staple of US foreign policy throughout the Cold War.

The Guatemalan psy op became the archetypal psychological operation designed by America's Father of so-called Public Relations to promote the interests of those companies attached to the US-led side of the Cold War. The PR creation of invented narratives as a replacement for the truth extends with even greater force into the present age when the memes of anti-terrorism have been made to replicate many of the Bernaysian memes of anti-communism.

A primary factor governing the relatively smooth transition from one enemy to the next was the the will to maintain the prestige, wealth and political clout of the many elite interests tied to the elaborate and corrupt apparatus of the national security state. There is nothing accidental in the fact that the class who derived much power from dominating and exploiting Cold War anti-communism retained and even strengthened its position of omnipotence in the era of institutionalized anti-terrorism. Dick Cheney is a primary personification of those who maintained their class privilege by shifting gears to exploit first anti-communism and then anti-terrorism.

As the sophistication of Cold War propaganda progressed, Bernays' brand of anti-communist spin was combined with the fabrication of concocted terrorist events in NATO's oversight of Operation Gladio in Europe. Concurrently, the CIA covertly purchased the services of thousands of journalist in Operation Mockingbird to slant, subvert and subordinate news reporting in ways thought to advance US foreign policy.

The early days of Operation Gladio and Mockingbird can be looked back upon as experimental child's play compared to its contemporary extensions involving higher levels of institutionalized professional subversion. From this subversion flows the 24/7 provision in the mass media of false public narratives to cover over the real nature of the crimes against humanity forming the stock in trade of the world's dominant criminal cabal.

The masters and agents of this Organized Criminal Cabal have seized illegitimate forms of control over the very life support systems, both natural and man-made, on which we all depend for survival. We are therefore universally held hostage to the gross malfeasance of the psychopaths and kleptocrats whose comparative advantage in ruthlessness has enabled them to make strong claims to most of the main inheritances of both natural history and of human civilization.

As Naomi Klein and many others have documented, a key device in the manufacturing of consent among domestic populations for foreign wars or for otherwise unpopular alterations of the political economy of home countries has been to create and exploit disorienting disasters. While Klein emphasizes the deployment and exploitation of shock to implement disaster capitalism, her timid analysis does not go nearly far enough.

Especially disappointing was Ms. Klein's characterization of 9/11, the most jolting and iconographic illustration of her main thesis illuminating the Shock Doctrine's effectiveness as an instrument of social control. Klein's deceptive depiction of the events of 9/11 as the outcome of a mere "intelligence failure" is representative of the kind of cowardice or worse in critical analysis that is crippling the political effectiveness of the progressive left. How can the antiwar movement have any significant impact at all if its leadership refuses to address clearly and cogently the deeper nature of the origins and attributes of the 9/11 Wars?

The Anatomy of Fraud, Deception, and Mass Murder Through State Terrorism

The necessary precondition for mounting with popular support aggressive assaults on targeted groups is to dehumanize target populations in the minds of the aggressor populations. Julius Streicher's Der Stürmer once performed this task of propaganda, preparing German public opinion for the mass slaughter of Jews during the culminating years of the Third Reich.[184]

The role once played by Der Stürmer set patterns once again on display in the barrage of anti-Islam messages that have become the specialty of the Zionist run media as epitomized by Rupert Murdoch's communications empire including Fox News.[185]

Ever since the full power of the Shock Doctrine was illustrated on 9/11, the pace of false flag terrorism combined with unrelenting manipulation of the mass media has been accelerating as the need grows to turn aggressor populations more radically and ruthlessly against target groups. While so far the target populations are mostly Muslim, the anti-terrorist propaganda is in no way limited to Muslims. It now extends to purposely vague and ill-defined concepts making potential enemies of those accused by state inquisitors of "radicalization" or "extremism."

To accomplish the task of smearing targeted groups the so-called intelligence agencies tasked with so-called counter-terrorist activities have been very active in identifying unstable individual as assets to be played and exploited. A classic example of such an unstable, drug addicted individual in constant trouble with the law was Michael Zahef-Bibeau, the supposed "recent Muslim convert" and alleged ISIL supporter said to have been the Ottawa shooter.

After committing a lethal "act of war" at the main war cenotaph in Canada's national capital, where he was conveniently photographed by an unnamed tourist at the key moment, Zahef-Bibeau received a police escort to the Canadian Parliament Buildings from which his body disappeared after some sort of loud but unseen shooting exchange.

The supposed killer of Zahef-Bibeau, Parliamentary Sergeant at Arms, Kevin Vickers, then received a medal for his act of bravery from Israeli Prime Minister Benjamin Netanyahu. This strange sequence was all reported dutifully and without even minor skepticism by Canada's Zionist-run press corps on the opening day of Parliament just as Canada's Zionist federal government led by Prime Minister Stephen Harper was bringing in expanded police powers to evade due process of law in the name of anti-terrorism.[186]

The repertoire of deception is extensive extending to the hiring of patsies to be blamed for concocted acts of violence necessary for creating the political and monetary currency of commodified fear. Miraculously discovered passports, counterfeit or real, have become one of the hallmarks of false flag terrorism. Such identification documents are planted and quickly found in the rush to put forward designated culprits for instant trial by media.

Most of the time there is no semblance whatsoever of careful police investigations or objective reporting of these manufactured episodes. Because deceased patsies, crisis actors and accomplices can tell no tales, they are increasingly being made to die in the course of the sensationalized events. In Paris Helric Fredou, the Police Commissioner in Charge of investigating the Charlie Hebdo shootings, supposedly committed suicide in the midst of his endeavours.

When terror shock is made to strike many crucial but vulnerable protections of law are sacrificed to open yet more space for the unbridled machinations of power politics. The achievements derived from generations of gradual progress in the slow evolution of juridical safeguards are overturned in a moment as media-generated hysteria feeds the rapid growth of the privatized terror economy.

The endless imagery of Islamic terror in news media becomes the stuff of caricature in, for instance, the French satirical magazine *Charlie Hebdo* or the some of the cinematic offerings of the Hollywood propaganda machine. The core tactic in promoting genocide and facilitating other crimes against humanity is currently on clear public display in Clint Eastwood's propaganda classic, *American Sniper*.

A movie star who emerged from the classic tradition of American Westerns glorifying the westward expansion of the United States through genocidal wars directed at Native Americans, Eastwood has extended this tradition to the US invasion of Iraq in utter disregard of international law.

As I have made clear in my introduction to *The American Empire and the Fourth World*, US propaganda to justify its assaults in the Middle East draws heavily from the language of the American Indian wars as essential to the imagined ascent of civilization over savagery.

Chris Kyle, the real life sniper on which the Eastwood film is based, made it clear that he saw those who passed in front of his weapon of mass murder as Islamic savages, as equivalents of those American Indians who were the primal enemy that the US Armed Forces were initially created to defeat.

This Hollywood blockbuster demonstrates how far the arts and science of propaganda have come since Adolf Hitler and Leni Riefenstahl got together in 1935 to make *Triumph of the Will*. If Leni Riefenstahl's capacity to escape prosecution in the war crimes proceedings of the Nuremberg Tribunal is a precedent, it is quite likely that film director Clint Eastwood will be able to evade legal accountability for his anti-Muslim production whose intent is to provide false justification for US crimes against humanity in Iraq.

While the post-9/11 role of the Israeli government in promoting the US invasion of Iraq is never explicitly mentioned in *American Sniper*, it is quite clear how the film's neocon director conceived of the movie's larger geopolitical function as justification for the spearheading by the US Armed Forces of the Jewish state's wars.

Where the Jews of Europe were once the target of this kind of sinister media manipulation, today it is Arabs, Persians and the worldwide community of Muslims, the ummah, who are becoming the object of the new Holocaust of systematic murder and persecution.

Increasingly this new Holocaust of state-sponsored mass murder, displacement, and public denigration of Muslims is integrated into the foreign and domestic policies of those Western countries subject to domination by the Zionist media cartels including Crown corporations like the BBC in Great Britain, the CBC in Canada, and ABC in Australia.

The hypocrisy and double standards have become stupendous. They are marked in the disparity between hate speech laws designed to silence criticism of Israel and Zionism on the one hand and officialdom's encouragement and embrace of expressions of Islamophobia on the other.

What can be said of the massive public valorization in Paris of *Charlie Hebdo*'s Muslim-bashing cartoons as the quintessence of free speech, especially after France's banning of Islamic dress and pro-Palestinian demonstrations, and after the sustained efforts to censor and criminalize the humor of Dieudonne M'bala M'bala[187] and the cartoons of Zeon?[188]

Officialdom's expression of support for freedom of speech in the capital of the French Enlightenment and of the French Revolution is especially farcical given the high level of censorship that prevails now in all of the mainstream media, in much of the so-called alternative media, and in the academy as well. This veil of censorship is imposed in increasingly obvious ways in the vain effort to hold together a growing, yet simultaneously collapsing, sand castle of lies and fabrications to maintain the big deceptions on which the dominant criminal cabal depend to maintain the illegitimate rule of their murderous kleptocracy.

PREQUEL TO CHARLIE HEBDO:
THE MARCH 2012 MOHAMED MERAH AFFAIR (A MOSSAD-DCRI CO-PRODUCTION?)

Laurent Guyenot (translated by Kevin Barrett)

"The important thing to understand is that the trauma of Montauban and Toulouse struck deep in our country, a little—I do not want to compare the horrors—a little like the trauma that followed the events in the US and New York in September 2001 . . . September 11th."
  –Nicolas Sarkozy, 23 March 2012, broadcast on Europe 1[189]

The Charlie Hebdo affair comes three years after the Mohamed Merah case. The two incidents have extremely disturbing similarities, as if they employed the same script, the same staging and the same troupe of actors. First, consider the many factual similarities: the suspects' profiles, the two dubiously-connected episodes of each tragedy, the all-night sieges keeping the audience riveted to their television screens, the implausible executions of the suspects, and a whole series of inconsistencies in the official story. Additionally, in both cases, the authorities have produced no convincing evidence that the executed suspects were actually involved in the crimes. Another connection: the four Jewish victims of the grocery store hostage episode "are buried in the same cemetery as the Jewish victims of Mohammed Merah."[190]

But the most striking similarities are in the repercussions of the two cases—especially the virtually-identical government/media response. Two days after the killings in a Jewish school March 19, 2012, Foreign Minister Alain Juppé went to Jerusalem for the funeral of the victims. There he met Shimon Peres in the presidential palace, where Juppé assured Peres of his support in the war on terror and anti-Semitism (both implicitly skillfully combined in this scene). Then the next day, Juppé met Prime Minister Benjamin Netanyahu to pledge his support.[191] In a public tribute to the victims (and implicitly to Zionism) Alain Juppé, wearing the kippa, spoke of "a national tragedy, a catastrophe that has struck France. (. . .) When a Jew is targeted in France, the whole of France is affected. The attack on Jews in France is the business of 65 million French people. Your grief, your pain is ours (. . .) Anti-Semitism is unbearable for us. France will not yield to terrorism." Note the subtle equation that makes "terrorism" and "anti-Semitism" two interchangeable terms.

A similar swiftly-orchestrated response followed the deaths of Jewish hostages in the Hyper-Kosher grocery store in 2015, following the supposedly related shootings at the headquarters of Charlie Hebdo. Israeli Prime Minister Benjamin Netanyahu took charge of France's officially-sanctioned nationwide demonstration, before going to the Great Synagogue of Paris where, before a cheering crowd, he gave a speech about his favorite topic: the fight against terrorism and anti-Semitism.

Each of the two cases took place shortly after brutal Israeli attacks against the Gaza Strip, and each was used to consign those atrocities to the memory hole—or at least to drown out the chorus of disapproval. Each also allowed Israel to remind the Jews of France (the largest Jewish community in Europe) that they live in a hostile land and would do well to emigrate to Israel. Both affairs also gave Israel a pretext to oppress the Palestinians and attack unfriendly Arab and Muslim countries. In March 2012, Israel was seeking to launch a war against Iran, and the Merah affair drummed up French support.[192] Likewise in 2015, Israel was trying to stop a G5+1 nuclear deal with Iran, and the Charlie Hebdo and supermarket shootings once again helped the Zionist cause.

Additionally, each of the two affairs helped terrorize French Jews (the largest Jewish community in Europe) to encourage them to emigrate to Israel. When, on October 31st 2012, Netanyahu made an official visit to France, he said at a press conference with Hollande (who would accompany him the next day to Toulouse for a ceremony honoring the victims): "In my role as Prime Minister of Israel, I always say to Jews everywhere: Come to Israel and make Israel your home."[193]

Finally, in both cases, immediately after the event, a PATRIOT Act type of law censoring free speech and focusing on anti-Semitism—equated with criticism of Israel—was imposed on the French public. In the days following the killings in 2012, President Sarkozy announced his plan to create a new criminal offense and place internet users under surveillance: "Any person who habitually visits websites that justify terrorism or incite hatred or violence shall be prosecuted and penalized."[194] Apparently the concept of "condoning terrorism" is almost limitless.

The new anti-terrorism acts were presented by Sarkozy to his Cabinet on April 11th, 2012, but were eventually rejected by Parliament. So, it seems, we had to start all over again in 2015.

And indeed, a few days after the killing of Charlie Hebdo, taking advantage of public emotion, François Hollande proposed a new law: to censor the Internet. "To fight an enemy, you must first know and name it. Anti-Semitism has changed its face. It has not lost its ancient roots. Some of these springs have not changed since the dawn of time: conspiracy, suspicion, falsification. But today, it also feeds on hatred of Israel. It imports conflict from the Middle East. It claims that Jews are somehow responsible for people's misfortunes. It keeps alive conspiracy theories that spread without limits, even those that have led to the worst of horrors."

Hollande stressed the need to "be aware that conspiracy theories are propagated through the internet and social networks. But we must remember that it is words that prepare the way for mass extermination . . . We need to act at the European and even international levels to define a legal framework, so that the internet platforms running social networks face their responsibilities and are penalized for violations," he emphasized. Holland said his government will support the call of several Jewish organizations "against Holocaust denial on the Internet." It seems that the concept of negation or "denial," usually associated with Holocaust denial, has been curiously extended to include negation of the official account of the Charlie Hebdo case.[195]

To underline the similarities between the two affairs, and gain a better perspective on the Charlie Hebdo incident, here is a reminder of the facts in the Merah case, highlighting anomalies and advancing a plausible hypothesis.

The first act begins with the March 11th, 2012 murder of the soldier Imad Ibn Ziaten in Toulouse, followed by the March 15th shooting that killed two other soldiers of the 17th Parachute Engineer Regiment (RGP), Abel Chennouf and Mohamed Legouad, and seriously injured a third in front of their barracks in Montauban (Tarn-et-Garonne). Several witnesses described the scene. *La Depeche du Midi* published the testimony of Monique, a psychiatric nurse who had been accompanying a patient to the ATM and the tobacco shop: "The three young soldiers came to the ATM. (. . .) When I heard the first blast, I thought they were just playing. Almost immediately, I saw a man with a black helmet firing at them. He shot the first soldier several times, then the second. The third, who was withdrawing money, tried to escape. But he fell too, almost before my eyes. The shooter was only targeting the military. Aiming at their heads. I was right there, he could also have killed me. He went back to his scooter and fled towards the city center. This was someone young, I think, of stocky build. He fired around fifteen shots at the very least."[196] Martine, another woman who testified to police, but preferred to remain anonymous in media interviews broadcast by RTL and TF1, said she was jostled by the killer, whom she described as "quite corpulent": "When he turned around, the movement raised the visor of his helmet a few inches. I saw a tattoo or scar on his left cheek. I also caught a glimpse of his eyes through the visor. He had a cold look, of frightening clarity. A look that I will never forget."[197] She would repeatedly reaffirm these details, saying of the tattoo: "He has a tattoo on his face, of that I'm sure."[198]

The three victims of the March 15th shooting, like the March 11th victim, were from the Maghreb. The crime appeared to be racially rather than religiously motivated, since one of the victims was Catholic. Suspicions quickly focussed on a group of neo-Nazis serving in the 17th Regiment, as was revealed by two newspapers, *La Depeche du Midi* and *Le Canard Enchainé*: Sergeant Jamel Benserhir had lodged a racial discrimination complaint against three soldiers pictured in the newspapers saluting Hitler while holding the flag of the Third Reich. The army tried to cover it up, then penalized the three soldiers with a slap on the wrist. So the first suspects after the Montauban killings were neo-Nazis seeking revenge. The three soldiers were questioned but exonerated. However, the neo-Nazi trail remains the most plausible one, especially since tattoos (above all in cobweb designs) are a distinctive feature of this subculture. But this line of inquiry was suddenly abandoned when the killings occurred in the Jewish school, which was immediately viewed in connection with the attacks on the soldiers.

This was the second act. On Monday, March 19th at 8 am, in front of the Jewish religious school Ozar-Hatorah in the residential area of la Roseraie, shortly before the opening of the school, a man on a motorbike opened fire, killing one adult and three children and injuring five others. The victims were Jonathan Sandler, 30, a professor of Jewish religion, his two son Arieh (5 years) and Gabriel (4 years), and Myriam Monsonego (7 years), daughter of Rabbi Yakoov Monsonego. The whole area was immediately cordoned off and many police officers were deployed there. A young Lyonnais intern at Ozar HaTorah school testified: "I saw the killer, he had green eyes. It could have been anyone. Was he a neo-Nazi or something else?"[199] Aside from this eyewitness account, the public is entirely dependent on police sources, such as the prosecutor speaking before the cameras at the crime scene, saying the killer "shot at everything in front of him, children and adults, and hunted down children within the school."[200] A statement was nevertheless collected by BFMTV: that of Nicole Yardeni, regional president of CRIF. It went unnoticed by viewers who heard her testimony that in reality, she did not witness the crime, but merely claimed to have viewed images filmed by surveillance cameras— images never made public, even partially. But did she really watch any such images? At the trivial question "What color was the bike?" She stumbled: "White, at least that's what they told me."[201]

What is even more troubling is this: Under the pretext that Jewish custom requires burying the dead within 24 hours, it seems that the remains were repatriated to Jerusalem without an autopsy, in violation of the most basic procedures of criminal investigation. The President of CRIF Midi-Pyrenees, Nicole Yardeni, confirms that the authorities were "very attentive" to CRIF's requests to forego "unnecessary" autopsies.[202]

It seems, in fact, that no autopsies were performed—a fact which has raised eyebrows and fueled suspicions. The four victims were Israeli citizens whose families belonged to the Ozar Hatorah network, an ultra-Zionist organization founded in 1945 that is now close to the Likud Party.

Could it have been an operation orchestrated by the Israeli secret services? Could they have exploited an unsolved crime, transforming an anti-Arab racist hate crime into an anti-Semitic incident? The Mossad, after all, is the most active secret service in the world. It can count on its worldwide network of tens of thousands of trained agents, "black" informants (that is to say, infiltrators of Arab communities), and especially sayanim, devoted helpers in the Diaspora willing to lend a hand in committing illegal acts in their country of residence. (Jacob Cohen, author of *Springtime of the Sayanim*, believes there are about 3000 in France.) Israel has a long history and rich expertise in the field of false flag attacks, fomenting civil war in hostile countries, and terrorizing Jewish populations into emigrating to Israel. This tradition began in the 1950s with Operation Susannah in Egypt, consisting of bombings falsely attributed to Muslim extremists, and in Iraq with the false flag attacks documented by Naeim Giladi in *Ben-Gurion's Scandals: How the Haganah and the Mossad Eliminated Jews*. Mossad's PsyOp division also knows how to take advantage of situations it may not have caused. For example, when TWA Flight 800 crashed off Long Island on July 17th, 1996, killing 230 people, Mossad launched a vigorous disinformation campaign suggesting that it was an assassination hatched by Iran or Iraq. More than one hundred articles echoed this lie.[203]

The Toulouse killings could therefore be the umpteenth false anti-Semitic act brought to us by those who, for Israel's sake, assign themselves the mission of maintaining the victimization of Jews in a country where real anti-Semitic acts are too rare for their liking. Let us remember the false anti-Semitic attack on the RER D train on July 9th, 2004.[204] Or the fire at a Jewish social center in Paris on August 21st 2004 that turned out to have been set by a Jewish center employee, Raphael Benmoha.[205] Then there are the cases of Rabbi Gabriel Farhi who, in January 2003, mutilated himself and reported a fake anti-Semitic assault; and Alex Moses, a Likud member and general secretary of the Zionist Federation in France, who in January 2004 sent himself anti-Semitic emails.[206] The scenario is always the same: The media wolfpack howls about anti-Semitism, and politicians scramble to outdo each other emitting screams of indignation; and then when the investigation reveals the hoax, the whole affair is hushed up, with the culprit written off as a lone nut.

However, the national context of the presidential elections also casts suspicion on the French secret services, at least in the eyes of those who remember the doubts surrounding the case of the hostage-taking of

Neuilly in 1993 where Sarkozy risked his life to save the children before the cameras.[207] But hidden from cameras, the suspect, called the Human Bomb, was rendered unconscious and then, when all the children were released, he was shot three times at close range, on the pretext that had moved his arm in his sleep. Super Sarko surged in the polls. Then in March 2012, President Sarkozy was in trouble in his reelection campaign: "The only chance for Sarkozy to win the election is if an event outside of his campaign occurs. An international, exceptional or traumatizing event," said the director of L'Express shortly before the Toulouse killings.[208]

And Sarkozy did indeed rise in the polls and win re-election. Since we know that the secret services are run by very close associates of Sarkozy—namely Bernard Squarcini, nicknamed "Shark" (read *The President's Spy*[209]) at Interior Intelligence (DCRI) and Erard Corbin de Mangoux at External Security (DGSE) (whose appointment departed from standard procedure and raised concerns), we can easily imagine them giving a boost to their boss. In 2008, Sarkozy purged the French secret service, under the pretext of regrouping General Intelligence (RG) and the Department of Territorial Surveillance (DST) to form the General Directorate of Internal Security (DCRI). Squarcini intensified surveillance of Muslims in France and strengthened cooperation with the Israeli secret services, according to journalist Wayne Madsen.[210]

The suspicion of a Mossad-DCRI joint venture was reinforced after Mohamed Merah was identified as the suspect, his "Salafi" profile disseminated, his apartment beseiged, and his summary execution completed during the late night and early morning of March 21st. After dreaming about it all Tuesday night, the French public awakened Wednesday morning to learn that Merah had been shot dead with thirty bullets in his body, two in the back and one in the head after an assault in which 300 rounds were fired.[211] Soon leaks allowed the public to see some of the puppet strings attached to the corpse. On the one hand, they learned that Merah had been under long-term surveillance by the DCRI. Bernard Squarcini told *Le Monde* that during the siege of Merah's apartment, "he wanted to speak with the officer of the Regional Directorate of Internal Intelligence (DRRI) in Toulouse whom he had met in 2011," and declared to him in a tone that betrayed familiarity: "Anyway, I had to call you to tell you that I had the tips to give you, but actually I was going to smoke you."[212] Yves Bonnet, former head of the DST, concludes that Merah was an informer for the DCRI.[213] On the other hand it was learned Tuesday, March 27th, 2012, by the Italian newspaper *Il Folio*, that Mohamed Merah had traveled undercover for the French secret services under the direct command of Erard Corbin de Mangoux of the DGSE (which the latter denies). In return, the young man was to supply information to French counterintelligence officials. Additionally, according to Israeli security sources (and the information is confirmed by Squarcini) Merah had traveled to Israel on a three-month tourist visa in September 2010, prior to his travels to Arab countries by way of a checkpoint on the Jordanian border. This should have been impossible for a young Muslim Algerian. It also should have denied him access to Syria and Lebanon unless he held multiple passports.[214] Once again, the trails of the Mossad and the French secret services cross.

So the hypothesis that took shape gradually, through the collective work of many on-line researchers, is that of a joint venture between the French secret service and Mossad. A plot of this nature is doubly effective: if one of the two countries falls under suspicion, the other will come to its aid (at least in one of two possible cases). To preserve "plausible deniability"—the golden rule in covert operations of this type —the responsibilities of the two services are kept separate and operate in two distinct phases.

Here is the sequence of events, according to the most plausible recapitulation. In the context of its preparations for launching a war against Iran, the Israeli government was trying to secure the support of NATO. For the United States, Israel could count on the neoconservatives (read: crypto-Likudniks) and the powerful pro-Israel lobby, which according to John Mearsheimer and Stephen Walt had already led the Americans into the Iraq war. But Israel was also looking for a way to ensure the support of the French government, and perhaps in the context of the French presidential elections, to cash in on its aid to Nicolas Sarkozy, the most Atlanticist and pro-Israel president France has ever known—a president who, betraying fifty years of independence, returned France to NATO.

With the Montauban killings, the Mossad seized the opportunity to conduct a psychological operation, manipulating French and world public opinion to portray Israel as a victim and make us forget its massacres in Gaza. In all likelihood, the operation was the work of Lohamma Psichologit, the psychological warfare department of the Mossad. The idea was to create a second false crime, clearly anti-Semitic, linked to the real crime of Montauban. The link conditioned the public to suspend any doubts: Since the first crime was real, nobody would question the reality of the second, provided that it was attributed to the same killer. The bet was risky, because the Montauban crime had nothing anti-Semitic about it. But it had the advantage of sending an implicit message to the public: Those who protest the war in Afghanistan, and the coming war in Iran, are killers of Jewish children. Thus the Mossad activated its agents, and a small network of sayanim, to stage the false killings in the Jewish school. Meanwhile, the Mossad had made a deal with a faction of the French secret service, probably at the highest level. But in this world, everyone tries to outsmart everyone else; it is not impossible that the Mossad blackmailed France with evidence of the involvement of the DCRI in the first killing at Montauban, which had been perfectly timed to blame the National Front party, take the wind out of its sails, and re-elect Sarkozy.[215]

This is only a hypothesis. Many gray areas remain that only a thorough investigation could clear up. What, for example, do we make of the young intern at the Ozar HaTorah school, Aaron "Bryan" Bijaoui, aged 15 and a half, who was taken to the hospital after being shot on March 19th? What about the various emails received by the same Jewish school (one of which said that the killings were not over) signed in the less-than-Islamist style, "the French vigilantes and true Frenchmen"?

One thing is certain: Whether or not there were any killings in the Toulouse school, Mohamed Merah had nothing to do with it. He was selected by the secret services to take the blame, probably because he was known to both the Mossad and the DCRI. In other words, Mohamed Merah was the patsy, if one defines the term as a suggestible person sent at the right time to the right place to be captured, convicted and executed, in order to cover the tracks of those who orchestrated the operation. The patsy serves to divert attention from the real culprits to the enemy (real or imaginary) that the operators wish to stigmatize. The choice fell on a young offender recruited while in prison. Not very religious, loving money and adventure, Mohamed Merah had been persuaded to take part in an undercover operation infiltrating Islamist networks. He was sent to Afghanistan, Pakistan, Turkey, Syria, Lebanon, Jordan, and Iraq. Most of these trips, in fact, were probably fictitious. They are the "legend" of Merah, that is to say, his fictional biography as an ostensible Salafi. For the purposes of the DCRI, it is sufficient to find Immigration stamps on one passport in his name.

The choice of Merah as patsy proved rather unfortunate, but probably the secret services had nothing better at hand. The problem is not only that the puppet strings of manipulation, that is to say, Merah's links to the DGST, the DCRI and the Mossad, are easily visible. It is also that his physical appearance does not match the description given by "Martine," nor to that given by the child at the Jewish school who saw the green eyes of the killer. These testimonies exonerate Merah. Furthermore, the Salafist legend contradicts the description of Merah provided by his associates. As soon as the press, fascinated by the invented character, rushed to interview anyone who knew Merah, it became obvious that he did not match the profile of a fundamentalist. Though his family was silenced (except his father), none of his colleagues, whether coach, lawyer, or jailer, can imagine him as an Islamist. He loved cars, football, video games, movies and nightclubs.[216] The people in his neighborhood described him as "nice, quiet, respectful and generous."[217] The lawyer who followed him since his earliest days of juvenile delinquency says "I have never known Merah to be religious."[218] Although we are told that he must have been indoctrinated in prison, his 2008 prison guard does not remember having seen him show any interest in religion. Finally, as noted by Jean Cohadon in an article published on the website of the *La Depeche du Midi* on April 9th, the alleged itinerary of the supposed killer defies comprehension: "What can one make of a boy of 23 years capable of killing three soldiers Thursday, March 15th, and then treating himself to a pair of fashionable basketball shoes to hit the nightclubs with his friends on Saturday night? Or of executing three children with shots to the head on Monday morning, then spending the afternoon laughing and playing football with the kids ... of a 'female friend' at Izards?"[219] On top of all this evidence, the story told by "a woman" to a reporter from the Brest *Telegramme* can not be taken seriously: According to her, Merah supposedy kidnapped her son to show him unbearable al-Qaeda videos full of throat-cuttings: "There was a HUGE Quran in his living room and GIGANTIC swords hanging on the wall . . ."[220] Finally, Merah's internet records show that "he did not visit Islamist websites." Curiously, it was the DCRI that in 2011 requested that the telephone and internet surveillance of Merah be suspended.[221]

But never mind the facts! The key to the success of a false flag attack is the speed with which the official version, that is to say, the guilt of patsy, is imposed. The most important task is to cut short any alternative theory, which can then be denied as baseless rumor. Official pronouncements must drown out the public's efforts to discover its own meaning in the event, express doubts, or debate. If, during and after the initial shock, the government speaks with confidence, authority and unanimity, it will convince the naive and intimidate skeptics. Studies show that information received in a time of emotional stress, during which rationality is suspended, are integrated into the memory of the trauma, so the distinction between facts and their explanations is abolished. Less than 24 hours after the second killing at Toulouse, the Secret Service had the full biography of Mohamed Merah, complete with photos and videos displaying his supposed religiosity and his career as a "Salafist." Live from the "siege" of Merah's apartment on the evening of Tuesday, March 20th, Interior Minister Claude Gueant took it upon himself to summarize this beautiful "legend," just as Merah had supposedly confirmed it to the "negotiator" with whom he had established a "relationship of trust": "He talked a lot. He went over his whole itinerary. He explained how he had received instructions from al-Qaeda during his stay in Pakistan. He trained there. He was even offered the chance to lead a suicide attack, which he refused. But he accepted a general mission to commit an attack in France."[222]

The second rule of a good false flag attack is to quickly eliminate the patsy. Once he understands the role in which he has been cast, the patsy also realizes that he has nothing to lose by proclaiming what he knows. Therefore, a good patsy is a dead patsy. On the evening of March 20th, after his "contact" was satisfied that he was at home, Merah was besieged in his house by RAID (Research Assistance Intervention Deterrence). According to one resident of the unnamed building, Merah was shot down quickly, but RAID kept gesticulating for thirty hours to prolong the suspense before the cameras and under the watchful eye of Claude Gueant.

It was also necessary to silence Merah's family, who knew too much and could not be fooled. So they arrested his mother, his sister, and his brother Abdelkader as quickly as possible, and found words to convince them—at least the mother and sister who were soon released; while the brother was put under investigation for "complicity" and placed in solitary confinement in the prison of Fresnes (Val-de-Marne). "He cannot speak with any other inmate in the prison and is constantly accompanied by two guards to go to the exercise yard," a prison source affirmed.[223]

The siege of Merah's apartment was a gargantuan media spectacle and a triumph of mass hypnosis. TV news recited lyrically before a pumped-up viewership the terrible assault, the real "eruption of violence"[224] when Merah "sprang from his bathtub like a devil." Interior Minister Gueant personally undertook the task of storytelling with the emotion for which he is so well known: "The killer came out of the bathroom, firing with extreme violence. (. . .) RAID officials tried, of course, to protect themselves, and fought back. And in the end, Mohamed Merah jumped out the window with a gun in his hand, continuing to shoot. He was found dead on the ground." More lyrical still is the testimony of the commander of RAID, Armaury Hautecloque, who delivered an exclusive featuring killer's last words: "I am a mujahideen, I want to die with weapons in hand, you're going to kill me and I am very proud, very honored to do battle with RAID, I will try to kill as many of you as possible."[225]

These epic tales have mystified many. One ends up wondering aloud, as did the founder of the GIGN, Christian Prouteau: "Why didn't we use gas to capture Merah alive?"[226] Such doubts have been amplified by poorly controlled elements of the media. Thus, a radio reporter for the British network Sky News, deployed to the scene, allowed himself to express his disbelief at the sight, and his discomfort in finding that, during the decisive phases, it was the Interior Minister who seemed to be giving orders. When it was announced that Merah had wounded three RAID agents, the reporter saw only two, one evacuated limping, the other "in a state of shock," without any trace of blood. (The video since been suppressed.)[227]

Therefore it was necessary to alleviate the doubts of the French people, who have trouble taking M. Gueant at his word and are annoyed by the servile discipline of the French media. Such a contingency was anticipated, which is why "evidence" linking Merah to the crime was fabricated. Ebba Kalondo, editor of France 24, received about 1 a.m. Wednesday a phone call from a young man claiming to be Mohamed Merah. There then followed a 10-minute conversation during which Merah confessed to his crime and his affiliation with Al-Qaeda. And that's not all: Merah had filmed his killings with a mini-camera strapped to his person. Besieged in his apartment, he supposedly confirmed the existence of this camera and "told the police how to find it. Investigators then got hold of 'the bag he had entrusted to someone containing a Go Pro camera which he had strapped to himself, allowing him to film the entirety of the three killings of which he was guilty' confirmed the Paris prosecutor Francois Molins Thursday."[228] Mohamed would have sent her the video file on a USB to the Paris bureau of Al-Jazeera. The police claim to have watched the video, which they describe as "a very, very clean job. This is not a low-quality, blurry film. The montage is professional with songs intercut between the scenes."[229]

Unfortunately, once again, someone did not do his job properly, leaving evidence that the claims are bogus. The phone call could not have been made by Merah. It was placed from a phone booth over a mile from the home where Merah was under strict surveillance, two hours before the first assault of RAID. To place this call, Merah would have had to surreptitiously leave his apartment right under the noses of the officials who were watching him, walk one kilometer, and then return home quietly, still without being noticed. This assumption, we are told, is "seriously envisaged by the police."[230] As for the USB, the first audits conducted by investigators from the Police Judiciaire show that neither Mohamed Merah nor his brother could have sent it to Al-Jazeera, since the postal cancellation stamp is dated Wednesday, when Merah was surrounded by RAID and his brother was in custody. Caught in their contradictions, the police services suddenly warned that there was perhaps "a third man."[231] In any case, of course, the public will never see the video, even if the authorities pretended for a week to worry about its possible circulation on the Internet.

And in any case, doubts will remain doubts. President Sarkozy, along with the Ministers of Interior and Defense, Claude Gueant and Gérard Longuet, refused to hold Senate hearings investigating the directors of the intelligence services in connection with the shootings in Montauban and Toulouse that killed seven people.

PLANTED ID CARD EXPOSES PARIS FALSE FLAG

Kevin Barrett

"It was their only mistake."

French Interior Minister Bernard Cazeneuve says the terrorists who attacked Charlie Hebdo would never have been caught had they not made one fatal mistake: They conveniently left an ID card in their abandoned getaway car.[232]

Since when did criminals leave their identification cards in abandoned getaway cars?

An ordinary citizen, taking no precautions, might accidentally leave a wallet or purse in their parked car. I have driven automobiles approximately 50,000 times in my life, and I think my wallet might have slipped out of my pocket and fallen into the crack between the driver's seat and the door . . . once.

What are the odds that skilled terrorists who have just carried out a highly professional special-forces style attack, taking precautions to avoid being identified, will accidentally leave their ID card in the abandoned getaway car? Effectively zero.

So why did police report an event that cannot have happened?

Assuming that French police really did find terror suspect Said Kouachi's ID card in an abandoned getaway car, that card must have been planted by someone wishing to incriminate Kouachi. Even the legendary French idiot detective, Inspector Clouseau, could not fail to make this thunderingly obvious inference.

The discovery of Kouachi's ID does not implicate him; it exonerates him. It shows that he was an innocent patsy framed by the real perpetrators.

Police and intelligence agencies routinely plant evidence to support false narratives, convict innocent people, and exonerate themselves. American police who kill unarmed citizens often plant a gun on the corpses to support their claims of having killed in self-defense. Such throw-down guns, which the police call "ham sandwiches," are kept in police locker rooms and carried in police cars in case they are needed.[233]

Likewise, throw-down ID cards and other "incriminating" documents are routinely used by the military, intelligence, and special forces professionals who orchestrate false flag operations. Consider the ludicrously-obvious planted evidence used in the mother of all false-flag operations: the September 11th, 2001 inside job.

Intelligence agents planted not just one, but two "magic suitcases" designed to incriminate Mohamed Atta, the innocent Egyptian man framed as alleged ringleader of the crimes of September 11th. According to Der Spiegel's book *Inside 9/11: What Really Happened*, the first Atta suitcase was handed to German police by a self-described "good samaritan burglar." The so-called burglar claimed to have stolen Atta's suitcase during the course of a burglary and discovered terrorism-related information in it. As an honorable citizen, this kind-hearted burglar felt compelled by his conscience to deliver the suitcase to the authorities.

According to Der Spiegel, the German police, not being fools, knew that the self-styled burglar was not really a burglar at all, but an intelligence agent planting fake evidence against Atta. Der Spiegel quotes German police as saying: "The only question is, which intelligence agency was he working for?" ("CIA and Mossad," answered former German Intelligence Minister Andreas Von Bülow in his book *The CIA and September 11th*; former Italian Prime Minister Francesco Cossiga agreed, saying "all democratic circles in America and of Europe, especially those of the Italian centre-left, now know that the disastrous attack was planned and realized by the American CIA and Mossad with the help of the Zionist world, to place the blame on Arab countries and to persuade the Western powers to intervene in Iraq and Afghanistan."[234])

Despite its absurd origins, this suitcase full of fabricated documents provides virtually the only purported evidence supporting the official story of Atta's supposed terrorism-related activities in Germany. Aside from the good samaritan burglar's suitcase, it seems that the original Egyptian Atta —the one in Germany—was a gentle, shy, sensitive, soft-spoken architecture student with no connections to terrorism of any kind. Yet the "Atta" who made a spectacle of himself in Florida before 9/11, staging memorable public scenes while all but wearing an "I am an al-Qaeda terrorist" sign around his neck, was a coarse, obscene, violent loudmouthed braggart who dated strippers, disemboweled kittens, and spoke fluent Hebrew.[235]

The Hebrew-speaking Atta's second and better-known "magic suitcase" was the one he allegedly checked in on his early morning flight from Portland, Maine to Boston on September 11th, 2001. According to the 9/11 Commission Report, the suitcase was miraculously preserved and delivered to the authorities when it somehow failed to make the transfer from Atta's Portland-to-Boston commuter flight onto Flight 11, which Atta supposedly piloted into the North Tower of the World Trade Center. Had the suitcase been transferred as it should have been, we are told, it would have been destroyed in the crash.

This magic suitcase provided the only evidence allowing authorities to identify the alleged 19 hijackers within 24 hours of the event. (None of the 9/11 passenger lists contained any Arab names; no airline employees remember having ticketed or boarded any of the alleged hijackers; and none of the hundreds of security cameras at Boston's Logan Airport, Washington D.C.'s Dulles Airport, or Newark Airport took a single authenticated frame of any of the 19 Arabs blamed for 9/11.)[236]

This suitcase not only contained a list of the 19 patsies, but also Atta's supposed last will and testament. (Why would a suicide hijacker check his will onto a doomed plane?) Britain's dean of Middle East journalism Robert Fisk has ridiculed Atta's alleged will, pointing out that it begins with a botched bismillah: "In the name of God, myself, and my family..." No Muslim would ever write such a thing. As Fisk suggests, the document purporting to be Atta's will must have been forged by an incompetent intelligence agent. The suitcase was obviously planted.[237]

And that is not just Robert Fisk's opinion. Seymour Hersh, the dean of American investigative journalism, quotes a senior US intelligence source as saying, with regard to Atta's magic suitcase: "Whatever trail was left was left deliberately—for the F.B.I. to chase."[238]

Atta's two magic suitcases are not the only examples of clumsily-planted 9/11 evidence. Another is the "magic passport" of alleged 9/11 hijacker Satam al-Suqami. That passport, looking as pristine as the "magic bullet" of the JFK assassination, was allegedly discovered by an anonymous individual, with no chain of custody, near the two flat spots of smoking ground where two 110-story towers somehow exploded into very fine dust.[239]

Two other "magic passports" were discovered in Shanksville, Pennsylvania, next to the 10-by-15-foot hole in the ground where Flight 93 supposedly disappeared, leaving no discernible wreckage. These were the passports of Ziad Jarrah, a Lebanese agent of the Israeli Mossad, and Saeed al-Ghamdi, a Saudi CIA asset.

But the magic suitcases, and the equally magic passports, pale beside the most pathetically-planted 9/11 item of all: The "Fatty Bin Laden confession video" supposedly discovered in December 2001 by an anonymous US soldier in Jalalabad, and delivered with no chain of possession to be brandished by the Bush Administration as supposed proof of Bin Laden's guilt. Professor Bruce Lawrence, a respected expert on Bin Laden, has categorically stated of this video: "It's bogus!" Lawrence adds that his many acquaintances in the US intelligence community's Bin Laden units know that the video is bogus—but are afraid to say so in public, because they are afraid of the implications of Bin Laden's innocence.[240]

9/11 isn't the only State Crime Against Democracy (SCAD) in which planted evidence has been used to implicate patsies.[241] In an article entitled "The Lost and Found ID Oddity in Terror Cases—Stupid or Sinister?"

journalist Russ Baker points out that the alleged assassins of President John F. Kennedy and Martin Luther King, Jr. also conveniently dropped identification allowing the authorities to quickly "solve" those cases.

Lee Harvey Oswald, the accused assassin of JFK, supposedly dropped his wallet at the scene of the murder of Officer J.D. Tippet—the crime that somehow connected Oswald to the assassination of the president. Initial police reports describe finding Oswald's wallet next to Tippit's body. But when the discovery was met with a wave of skepticism, the police re-wrote their reports to remove references to the magic wallet.

Another famous patsy, James Earl Ray, was similarly framed. Near the site where the Memphis Police Department's best sharpshooter, a mafia asset named Earl Clark, shot Dr. King, a bundle of items linked to Ray was dropped. It contained Ray's rifle, binoculars, clothing, and radio, along with a newspaper clipping referencing King's lodgings. A 1999 civil jury verdict proved Ray was framed by the real killers: A domestic assassinations unit consisting of CIA officials and high ranking US military officers commanding the 111th Military Intelligence Group and the 20th Special Forces Group.[242]

These and other examples show that the intelligence agents who orchestrate false-flag events often do not even bother to disguise the blatantly-fabricated nature of the planted evidence used to implicate patsies. So we should not be terribly surprised when the French police tell us—with a straight face—that a highly professional fleeing terrorist would leave his ID card in an abandoned getaway car.

PART 2:
SHATTERING THE MYTHIC CONSENSUS

WILL CHARLIE HEBDO RELEASE EUROPE FROM WASHINGTON'S HEGEMONY?

Paul Craig Roberts

The Charlie Hebdo attack has many characteristics of a false flag attack. If Western intelligence services are responsible, the attack has had the unintended consequences of empowering the nationalist anti-immigration parties in Europe and the UK. Indeed, whether the attack is real or not, the consequences are the same.

The Charlie Hebdo attack consists of two essentially unrelated attacks in Paris on the same day. In the main attack, allegedly two Muslim brothers enraged by the cartoon assaults on Islam by the French cartoonists attacked the office of the magazine with military rifles, killing eleven people and wounding ten, five critically. In a separate attack, Amedy Coulibaly allegedly killed Jewish patrons of a Jewish deli. Allegedly, the two separate attacks were part of one plot.

The question is: "Who benefits?"

Clearly, not Muslims.

Just prior to the attacks the French government had voted in favor of the Palestinians, a vote that was against the position of the US and Israel, and France's President Hollande had stated publicly that the sanctions against Russia should end.

Washington and Israel saw this as France taking a foreign policy position independent of Washington's and Israel's. Charles de Gaulle had rolled over in his grave and told Hollande to get out there and represent France instead of Washington.

The alleged terror attacks served to bring the French government back in line with Washington and Israel.

A number of commentators including myself, although none from the presstitute media, have raised questions whether the attacks were orchestrated for the purpose of forcing France back in line.

Among the curious aspects of the attacks are the misidentification of the getaway car driver. Authorities identified the driver as Hamyd Mourad, who at the time was in class 145 miles distant. When this accused terrorist heard his name on social media as part of the attack, he realized his danger and quickly turned himself into the French police before he could be murdered by police as a terrorist.

The obvious question: As French intelligence is completely wrong about Mourad, why believe that French intelligence is right about Cherif and Said Kouachi?

The official answer is that the highly professional kill team that decimated the Charlie Hebdo office conveniently, and unprofessionally, left their ID in the get-away car.

We have heard this far-fetched story before. Remember, US intelligence, allegedly caught off-guard by the 9/11 attacks, identified the culprits in a matter of hours from an undamaged passport found as the *only intact item* in the ruins of the Twin Towers.

The improbability of this story was so extreme that US authorities changed the story. In the amended version, the passport was in luggage that had not made the flights into the World Trade Center Towers.

Another curious aspect of the Charlie Hebdo story is the alleged suicide of a French police official whose responsibility was to investigate important parts of the case. In the middle of the night while writing his report, he allegedly decided to commit suicide. Moreover, the French government refused to release the autopsy report to his family, and there is no word about his report, what it said finished or unfinished or what has become of his report. No one knows, because the presstitute media is unconcerned.

Deep-sixed is the most likely explanation.

Yet another curious aspect is that the Kouachi brothers and Amedy Coulibaly were shot dead despite the fact that capturing them was a piece of cake. Videos of Coulibaly in the deli show that he was pushed or for some reason ran into the line of fire with no weapon in his hands, which appeared to be tied at the wrists, and stumbled or was shot down and easily could have been captured. Instead, the police poured rounds into the fallen figure at their feet.[243]

The brothers who allegedly carried out the highly professional attack on the Charlie Hebdo office were transformed a couple of days later into bumbling incompetents who easily could have been captured but were executed instead.

Dead men tell no tales and cannot contradict official stories. The public doesn't need facts when they are fed stories by the presstitute media about how the Kouachi brothers' mother committed suicide and, thereby, turned the brothers into Islamist murderers.[244]

There are many other suspicious parts of the official story, such as the empty escape street and the ease of escape. Others have or will take up these parts of what appears to be a pre-packaged story. I have mentioned enough to make readers alert, and now I turn to the unintended consequence of Charlie Hebdo.

Charlie Hebdo served Israel's destruction of Palestinians and stifled rising European opposition to Israel's theft of the West Bank and military assaults on Gaza. In this sense, if Charlie Hebdo was a false flag attack, it was a successful one. However, the greatest beneficiaries of the official

Charlie Hebdo story are the nationalist parties in France, UK, and Germany.

Charlie Hebdo established Muslims as a threat to Europe, and this has boosted the nationalist political parties that oppose immigration. Marine Le Pen's party in France is now much stronger and more broadly supported. Nigel Farage's Independent Party (UKIP) has been elevated several notches. Germany's PEGIDA anti-immigration party has gained leverage from the Charlie Hebdo attack.

In the presstitute media the message of the strengthening of the European nationalist parties is their stance against immigration. However, the real message is that officially these nationalist parties are opposed to the EU, to the submergence of their sovereignty into the euro, and their vassalage to Washington via NATO.

Charlie Hebdo boosted the nationalists parties and has set in motion a possible unwinding of the EU and, therefore, NATO.

By deciding to curtail France's independent foreign policy, has a false flag attack set in motion the dissolution of Washington's Empire?

THE EMPIRE STRIKES FRANCE

Alain Soral (translated by Kevin Barrett)

Transcript of a lecture filmed January 11ᵗʰ 2015, four days after the Charlie Hebdo attacks, and the same day as the "Je suis Charlie" demonstrations in which four million people marched in cities throughout France.

In the face of this mass-mediated political terror operation targeting people's emotions, whose purpose is to prevent reflection, we are obliged to return to rational, chronological, historical analysis. Today I am simultaneously seized by anguish and by satisfaction (of a sort): The satisfaction of seeing that everything I have been predicting for years is coming true, which validates my analyses. But at the same time it is terrifying to be so right.

The unanimous facade of compassion we see in the media under the "I am Charlie" slogan is there to hide a program of political terrorism. Take for example the journalist who declared on France 2 today: "It is precisely those who 'are not Charlie' who need to be tracked down—those who, in certain schools, refused to participate in the moment of silence (for the victims); those who dissent in social media; those who don't see why this is their battle. These are the ones we need to locate, treat, and integrate or re-integrate into the national community. Educators, police, and politicians have a grave responsibility."

This kind of talk is terrorism aimed at forcing submission. Today's demonstration (which included almost four million people marching in various French cities) is a show of force by the power centers allied with NATO——the forces I call The Empire.

The demonstrations are also a counter-strike against recent French tendencies toward independence, notably the recent (purely symbolic) recognition of Palestine by the French National Assembly, and the legitimate French effort to avoid full collaboration in the economic war against Putin's Russia. We are witnessing a real rollback program. And we need to remember the threats of Benjamin Netanyahu, who announced in no uncertain terms that if France recognized the existence of Palestine we would have terrorist attacks in France. He declared to the French people on August 7ᵗʰ, 2014, in an interview with i-Télé: "This is not Israel's battle. It is your battle, it is France's battle. It they succeed here, if Israel is criticized instead of the terrorists, if we do not stand in solidarity, this plague of terrorism will come to your country."

If we do not understand Netanyahu's statement as a disguised threat, it is absurd, since there is obviously no reason why recognizing Palestine and standing in solidarity with Gaza would provoke Islamist attacks in France. But there is every reason why it would provoke reprisals from Israel. It is at the very least bizarre that this "prediction" or "threat" from Netanyahu—who is leading today's march—should come true.

What we have just witnessed is the complete destabilization of the French state by three individuals who belong to a social substratum I have always characterized as "Islamo-scum." How is it possible that these three individuals could have, in less than 24 hours, completely paralyzed the French state, triggering a State of Emergency (the Vigipirate Plan) and an emergency ministerial meeting? The TV news even speaks of a "total mobilization of the highest levels of the State."

There are hundreds or thousands of such manipulable and manipulated young people in France. Imagine what would happen tomorrow if these three individuals were thirty, and if the double-operation (the magazine and supermarket episodes) were multiplied by ten? We would arrive at what I have been predicting for years: civil war, and the complete blockage of the French state. This is the implicit threat which, by way of this operation, has been aimed at the heart of France.

So we must view this operation as a French 9/11.

But it also reminds us of the desecration of Jewish cemetery in Carpentras (on the night of May 8th to 9th 1995) and its political exploitation. We now know that it was deceptively used by the secret services to undermine the National Front, since they knew from the beginning that the perpetrators were skinheads who had nothing to do with the National Front. It also reminds me of the 2002 "mobilization against the National Front" demonstrations that drew 1.3 million people when National Front leader Jean-Marie Le Pen made the second round of the 2002 presidential elections. We are seeing here the same kind operation, with the same perfect alignment of the state apparatus and the mainstream media (which would normally be a an independent "fourth estate"). And it also demonstrates the ease with which the kindness of the French people can be exploited to subjugate them to a totalitarian system. The speed with which the slogan *je suis Charlie* ("I am Charlie") was propagated globally, on millions of posters and giant banners, is so dramatic that we cannot imagine it being a spontaneous initiative. For all this to be put in place so quickly and intensely, it had to be arranged by political and media networks of both right and left (the neo-conservatives on one side and the neo-Trotskyites on the other, who have been operating together for years).

The slogan imposed on the demonstration today by Prime Minister Manuel Valls, in honor of the victims, is *je suis Charlie, je suis flic, je suis juif*

— "I am Charlie, I am a cop, I am Jewish." It's the triumvirate of the police state, media propaganda, and Zionism. With this threesome, one approaches a dictatorship of great modernity and subtlety. Valérie Pécresse, former minister and government spokeswoman, issued a Tweet demanding a "French Patriot Act," that is to say, a state of emergency in the name of a "terrorist threat." This much-vaunted "terrorism" is an abstraction that is never defined, in order to impose an anti-historical, anti-political and anti-rational approach that uses emotion to prevent thinking. This is extremely disturbing, especially since the forces resisting such manipulation are minuscule.

Charlie Hebdo perfectly embodies the right-left merger that has occurred. This consolidation is illustrated by the couple consisting of the murdered cartoonist Charb and his girlfriend Jeannette Bougrabe, who insisted that her companion should be interred in the Pantheon. Charb, who was originally a journalist from the pro-Palestinian left-wing, somehow formed a domestic partnership with a former Secretary of State serving Nicolas Sarkozy—a radical anti-Islamist who once said "I do not know of any moderate Islam." Charlie Hebdo was originally a libertarian newspaper, in the positive Gallic sense, before being turned 180 degrees and made a neoconservative Zionist mouthpiece by Philippe Val. Its function then became to insult Muslims and Catholics—while firing one of its leading cartoonists, Siné, for a single jibe directed at the power of the Jewish community.

Presumably Philippe Val, former member of comedy duo Font and Val, was controlled through his proximity to Patrick Font, who was sentenced in 2008 to four years in prison for raping eleven girls and one boy aged 9 to 12. The scheme is well-known: A person involved in a sexual scandal is blackmailed in order to transform an anti-imperial publication into a pro-imperial one. My friend Jacob Cohen has reminded me that this was also the fate of the journal *Les Temps Modernes*, a left-leaning magazine founded by Jean-Paul Sartre that subsequently fell under the control of Claude Lanzmann, the father of the ideology of the *Shoah*, the French name for the Holocaust.

By the same kind of process, *Charlie Hebdo*, since its publication of caricatures of Muhammad, taken from a Danish far-right newspaper, became an openly neoconservative organ in the service of the "Clash of Civilizations," the dominant post-Cold-War ideology invented by Bernard Lewis and propagated by Samuel Huntington. This "clash of civilizations" consists of a declaration of war against a fabricated fantasy enemy, "radical Islam." The matrix of this artificial Islam is the Gulf sheikhdoms working hand in hand militarily with the United States—not Muslim nations that have resisted the US, such as Iran, Syria, Libya, and Iraq,

Muslim-majority countries where religions have peacefully coexisted. (Iraq under Saddam Hussein had a Christian foreign minister, Tariq Aziz.)

This ideology of "the clash of civilizations" was set up in the late 90s by the new right-wing globalists, the neoconservatives. The neocons are from a Jewish intellectual circle emanating from *Commentary* magazine, the official organ of the American Jewish Committee. Strangely, they came mainly from the Trotskyist left, but became hard-core American imperialists and militarists when American hegemony and the Clash of Civilizations became necessary for the survival and expansion of Israel. Understanding all this requires considerable historical knowledge, acquired by serious effort. That is why, unfortunately, the battle for the masses seems already lost. We cannot measure up to an emotional wave manipulated by big media and the corrupting power of money.

By its constant provocations against Islam, Charlie Hebdo targeted vulnerable populations, and helped push clueless ghetto youths towards radical Islam. It has now been twelve years since I began engaging with disadvantaged young people, urging them not to fall into the trap of becoming Islamo-scum, that is to say, accepting a dumbed-down takfiri version of Islam which actually leads to Islamo-Zionism, meaning that it validates imperial and Zionist domination. This deviant "Islam" is promoted by the Saudi and Qatari regimes who are allies of the US-Zionist empire. Both the Shiite Sayed Hassan Nasrallah and the Sunni Sheikh Imran Hosein have warned for years against this trap. We must continue to denounce it: Muslim extremism is the necessary complement of American-Zionist imperial domination. Together, they form a Janus mask with two faces.

We should also remember the process that led such disinherited young people as the Kouachi brothers or Coulibaly to be more or less manipulated into falling for radical Islam. Initially, we had in the early 70s the "family reunification" in which a great mass of immigrant proletarians from a Muslim background were brought to France when we were already in a period of high unemployment. Secondly, in the 1980s under President Mitterrand, we made sure that these immigrants could not be assimilated into the French nation: Instead of pursuing a social policy to help raise their economic and educational level, we made them socially decommissioned sub-proletarians. And to make matters worse, we created an official anti-racist ideology, which provides a convenient excuse for crime and bad behavior. Thirdly, since September 11th, 2001 we have seen the systematic manipulation of radical Islam by Western intelligence services. For we know that these jihadists are not directed by their own ideas; rather, they are piloted by remote control to serve the interests against which they believe they are fighting. Using the official anti-racist ideology, they incited the Muslims against traditionalist French people accused of racism; and now, by the synthetic terrorism we have just seen in action, they incite the French against the Muslims. This is the second act of the strategy of chaos, which establishes a climate of tension, mistrust and ultimately civil war. And this is the hidden side of the "Clash of Civilizations" which is preparing the French to participate in a new war in the Middle East. It is to fight against this Clash of Civilizations project that, alongside Dieudonné, I recently created the party Réconciliation Nationale.

Recall that *Charlie Hebdo* consistently lost money for years. It was on the verge of bankruptcy in November 2014. It no longer had any talent, intelligence, or wit. Its journalists had all betrayed their original ideals— those of the founders, Professor Choron and Jean-Marc Reiser. Charb was the apotheosis of this lack of talent and betrayal. It almost seems that the newspaper was financed at a loss for years to produce this result, as if it had been stuffed like a goose for foie gras. Yesterday its sponsors finally turned a profit, even considering the costs of security and the years spent losing money.

Today we learned on the news: "On the verge of bankruptcy before the attacks, *Charlie Hebdo* has received nearly a million euros in 72 hours, thanks to donations from 15,000 people. Google also paid 250,000 euros to the magazine. The Minister of Culture promised that she would release, if necessary, another million euros in addition to structural aid."

They are up to their eyeballs in support from the State—which is to say, from the Empire. It is obvious that the completely bankrupt *Charlie Hebdo* will be saved by the Empire's money, that is to say by the people against whom they are ostensibly fighting. Their sponsors are international Zionism and neo-imperial American domination. From the perspective of the manipulators, what happened there a few days ago completely validates Charb's provocations. Charb validated by his death what he was paid to demonstrate: that Muslims are dangerous people, incapable of dialogue; if their prophet is insulted they take violent revenge. All this is very strange: Either there is a divine purpose by which all this has been accomplished; or there are a lot of perverse manipulators and dupes at work.

Nonetheless, although Charb was an enemy to me, a bad guy for whom I had no respect, I obviously regret his death. Even more do I regret the deaths of Wolinsky and Cabu, because they represented the old guard. Even if they had become slightly senile and a little bit lame, they had a long trajectory and real talent. Yet I must point out that had they been honest—had they been truthful enough to admit that the *Charlie Hebdo* for which they worked had betrayed the *Charlie Hebdo* for which they engaged in their youth—they would not have been present at the fateful meeting. Their biggest mistake was to sanction by their talent, and their long history, the garbage purveyed by Charb and Philippe Val. Sadly, they paid with their lives.

We can draw a parallel between what we are living through today in France and the years when Aldo Moro's Italy was trying to free itself from American domination. What happened to the patriotic Italians, whether citizens of the right or the left, in the 1960s and 1970s, is what we are experiencing in France today. General de Gaulle permitted us to defer for thirty years this process of forced submission by terror. In Italy, the forces resisting submission to the US Empire were, on the one hand, Italian neo-fascist youth, and on the other hand, Communist forces. Operation Gladio and the "strategy of tension" aimed to neutralize these forces of resistance by preventing them from coming together in an alliance of "moral values of the right, labor power of the left" and ensuring that they would fight to the death against each other. That was the purpose of the assassination of Aldo Moro on May 9th, 1978. Today we have the hindsight to know that the red Brigades were manipulated by the US empire to kill Aldo Moro. Even though he was a Catholic bourgeois of the right, he was trying to forge a somewhat independent policy—on Libya in particular. Today we see nearly the same situation in France, except that the Italian neo-fascists and Communists have been replaced, on one side, by the radical Islamists manipulating angry immigrant young people, who have plenty of virility and energy yet are stuck in sub-proletarian impotence, and on the other side the partisans of French Identity, who are also fighting a legitimate battle over legitimate concerns, but are also manipulated. And when you look at who is behind the French Identity movement, who funds and sponsors them, it is the same force that sponsors the manipulation of legitimately angry ghetto youths by "radical Islamic" takfiri networks. Today we had the attack by the Coulibaly and Kaouchi brothers; but you can be sure that tomorrow we will have the counter-attack by the partisans of French Identity.

Despite the hypocritical calls by politicians and intellectuals "not to mix people together" (i.e. not to blame all Muslims)—an attempt at social engineering by the media—the mixture of peoples, and the blaming of Muslims as a group, is inevitable. For the past thirty or forty years, mass immigration from North and Sub-Saharan Africa has been imposed on the people of France, who do not want it, and who do not see any positive result, except for increased crime and opposition to French traditions and identity. Today (in the wake of this massacre) to the people we humiliated by calling them racists, despite their legitimate concern and anger, we say: "You can express your anger." Today Alain Finkielkraut dares to declare on television: "We must not stigmatize Muslims, but the least that we owe the cartoonists of *Charlie Hebdo* is to question the concept of Islamophobia" (meaning to legitimate hatred of Islam). We must therefore expect increased tensions and clashes in the street between angry French traditionalists and angry French people of immigrant origin. And we must expect it especially among adolescents, since adolescence is a time of testosterone, desire for commitment, and lack of cultural, historical and political perspective. This is the weak link in the population, the easiest category to manipulate. We have seen it before, with May 1968 in France. May 1968 was an imperial manipulation of angry, violent youth; its purpose was to get rid of De Gaulle when he tried to resist the same American-Zionist empire. We are exactly in the same situation today, except that Gaullism is dead.

Who benefits from the double killing of *Charlie Hebdo* and Hyper Kosher? *Cui bono?* There is no doubt about it: while traditional France rebelled against Islam, at the exact same moment, François Hollande and Manuel Valls accompanied Benjamin Netanyahu to the Great Synagogue of Paris, where they were greeted with cries of "Long live Israel, Israel will conquer!"

This is not, of course, the only reason to suspect that the events were meticulously manipulated. The most disturbing question is how suburban thugs could know the exact day when all the *Charlie Hebdo* journalists would be present. How did the two brothers gain access to this information? Someone must have given it to them. Who gave it to them, and who knew? Those who knew are those who were responsible for security at *Charlie Hebdo*'s offices (where much of the magazine's protection was withdrawn shortly before the attacks).

Second question: How did the current Minister of the Interior, who will never be anything more than Manuel Valls' stand-in, know, simply from watching the images we all saw, that there were three terrorists, not two? (He made it clear in his initial statements that he already knew there was a third terrorist, Coulibaly.)

Even more troubling, we now discover that the individual who is supposed to have recruited these young men, Farid Benyettou, is a nursing intern at the Salpetriere Hospital in Paris—an example of how dangerous jihadists are entirely under control of people recycled through the public sector. Similarly, with Kouachi and the Coulibaly brothers, we have people who are said to be out-of-control terrorists, yet we discover they are very much on the radar screens of the security services and the media, or have even physically encountered Sarkozy. All have a past that was publicized in the media at some point, which means they have all been puppets in the hand of the deep state.

A third suspicious element concerns the police commissioner Helric Fredou, who was responsible for drafting a report on the family environment of *Charlie Hebdo*, including Charb's alleged girlfriend Jeannette Bougrabe. On the very day of the attack, he supposedly committed suicide with his service weapon. His surviving family members do not believe it was a suicide.

The script is amazingly effective. Consider the characters' profiles: two Algerian-born French radical Islamists attack freedom of expression, sparking the ire of the French against the immigrant underclass; while a black Frenchman of sub-Saharan origin mounts a radical Islamist attack against Jews, triggering a wave of protests against anti-Semitism. The only thing missing is a blue-eyed Gallic French convert to Islam. (They may be saving that one for next time.)

The most striking thing is that the two killings form a very strange diptych: First a symbolic attack against "freedom of expression" by the Kouachi brothers, and the next an anti-Semitic murder in the Kosher grocery store. Thus, in the popular mind, anti-Semitism—and by extension any criticism of Israel—is associated with an attack against our sacrosanct freedom of expression. We thus have an intersection of Voltaire's France and a kosher grocery store, attacked simultaneously. The goal, obviously, is an alliance between France-under-attack and the State of Israel. This is the import of Netanyahu's message to the synagogue in Paris: "Extremist Islam does not hate the West because it hates Israel; it hates Israel because Israel is an integral part of the West and its values of freedom." Netanyahu had unleashed exactly the same logic after 9/11/2001, stating that the Islamists hate Israel because Israel is an ally of the United States; while the reality is, of course, precisely the opposite. Let us not forget what Netanyahu embodies: Israel's far right and its militarist, racist theocratic state, given to extremes of war-mongering violence. Netanyahu is a war criminal and he will one day be condemned as such if international justice does its job. What happened two days ago—seventeen people killed by three thugs—is nothing compared to what Israel has done to the Palestinian civilian population, even just this past summer.

To those who accuse me of not shedding enough tears for these seventeen people, I reply that my eyes are dry from crying over the hundreds of thousands of deaths resulting from the destruction of the Libyan state. My tears have been exhausted by the annihilation of hundreds of thousands of Syrians. And my eyes have dried up for having seen how, for more than a decade, we have turned the daily lives of Iraqis into pure hell.

DOES IT MAKE SENSE TO IDENTIFY WITH CHARLIE?

John Cobb

My short answer is an emphatic NO! For my part, I will say "*Je ne suis pas Charlie.*"

Does that mean I sympathize with the murderers? No, it certainly does not, whoever they may have been. But why would one ask? There are victims of crimes with whom one can strongly identify. I could strongly identify with the murdered Dr. King. Some seem to think that Charlie suffered an attack because it was a model of heroism supporting the weak against their oppressors and exposing pretense and evil wherever they occurred. If I agreed, then of course, I would be glad to join those who say: "Je suis Charlie." But the facts are far otherwise. Islam and Muslims are not the oppressive power in France. They are an unpopular minority that one can ridicule with impunity.

Even sensitive and beautiful pictures of Mohammed are offensive to many Muslims. They believe that pictures as a whole are to be avoided. They read Moses' prohibition of graven images to be of images generally. And whereas Christians have even painted pictures of God, most Muslims have observed the prohibition of images.

Most Christians think that we should be sensitive to the feelings of those who practice other forms of faith. Further, we should be especially sensitive to the feelings of minorities who are not able to defend themselves. We may defend the right of abusers to abuse, but that should not lead us to identify with them.

Some seem to consider the use of humor to be a great virtue regardless of who is ridiculed and whether there is any justification for the humor. Using this enthusiasm for humor as a basis of identifying with Charlie assumes that the cartoons of Mohammed are humorous. Perhaps some of the Charlie cartoons are funny. I have certainly not examined them all. But many are not.

What of the cartoon showing Mohammed kissing another man? What is funny about that? What point can be made by such a depiction that is so important that one is driven to cause great offense to many? A picture of David embracing Jonathan might serve some purpose, although any possible gain would be undercut by treating it as the butt of a joke. So far as I know there is no basis for supposing that Mohammed was gay. So what is the humor in depicting him that way? Even if he was gay, where is the humor?

Do I think that people should be killed because they offend and ridicule minority groups? No. Do I want stricter laws controlling such matters? No. But do I identify with this cruel vulgarity and abuse of the weak? No. And I am appalled to see millions of people doing so.

The irony goes further. In the wake of this event, the French are restricting freedom of speech. They are arresting all sorts of people, mostly Muslims, on suspicion, just as we do here. No evidence of wrongdoing is needed any longer. Guilt by association suffices. The mass identification with Charlie seems to support Charlie's anti-Muslim efforts but not personal freedom or the rule of law.

Since that glorious "free speech" march, France has reportedly opened fifty-four criminal cases for "condoning terrorism." The Associated Press reported that "France ordered prosecutors around the country to crack down on hate speech, anti-Semitism and glorifying terrorism." Incidentally, a comedian was arrested for his comments on Facebook. Apparently the celebration of humor has its limits in France.

Now many readers who will at least acknowledge that I have a point thus far will not want to read farther. They may recognize that their enthusiasm for supporting free speech has been used for ends of which they do not approve. They may not be in full agreement with my telling of the story, but they are likely to recognize that I have valid concerns.

However, many who might otherwise be supportive will consider it unreasonable to question the truth of the story that has had these consequences. If it is important to you to believe that our newspapers and governments are basically truthful, I would leave you to your truths. Read no further. The rest of this piece is likely to be offensive. It is written for those who are open to the possibility that "common knowledge" is subject to manipulation even if questioning its accuracy is called "conspiracy theory."

When an event occurs that is quickly escalated into the justification of new policies or removes obstacles to courses of action that are quickly taken, my first question is *"cui bono?"* or "who gains?" Clearly not the advocates of free speech who are supposedly being celebrated. Clearly not the Islamic community. Apparently it is instead those who favor tighter controls over citizens and more militant foreign policies, justified by a not so vague association of Islam and terrorism.

If this were my only reason for suspicion, I would keep my doubts to myself. But I find the official story intrinsically implausible. I am disturbed that those critics who are in position to influence public opinion raise so few questions.

Consider the course of events as they have been reported. Three men whose identity was thoroughly concealed by their clothing killed several employees of Charlie. They are regarded as having professional skills. However, they left behind incontrovertible testimony to their identity, so that no investigation was needed. The police immediately went after them and killed them on the spot. The police know that no one else was involved; so no investigation is needed. The one official who was engaged in investigation committed suicide.

This sequence of events is very different from what I would expect if, indeed, three Muslims attacked Charlie and killed several people there. If they were skilled killers, they would make it difficult to be traced. Identifying suspects would take time. The suspects would be arrested and interrogated. A matter of great concern would be to discover the larger network of conspirators to which the perpetrators belonged. Investigation would not be ended by a single "suicide."

Of course, the difference between what happened and what I think would have been likely to happen if three Muslims committed these murders does not prove anything. Any oddities of these kinds are outweighed in the minds of many people by the authority of the French government, the police, and the media. Calling attention to oddities expresses a disposition toward "conspiracy theory," and this disposition is known to be sick if not worse. People like me should not disturb the peace.

So why am I spouting off? I am tired of seeing the fires of Islamophobia stoked in order to justify the erosion of human liberties and vicious imperial policies. I am tired of seeing sincere and well-meaning people hoodwinked again and again and of watching their healthy responses exploited for unhealthy ends.

It happens that in this case there is one bit of evidence undermining the official story that even the most credulous might take seriously. Very soon after the event, a film was shown in which the killers are displayed attacking Charlie. A little later one scene was removed from the film. It was a scene in which an attacker supposedly killed a policeman. We see the shooting at point blank range and the policeman falling to the sidewalk. "Seeing is believing." No more evidence is needed!

However, on careful examination of the deleted segment, it is obvious that the bullet (or more likely blank round) harmlessly hits the sidewalk and the policeman is not shot at all. Since copies were made before it was deleted from the official showings, those who are interested can examine this film clip for themselves. I consider that its deletion from the film for official purposes supports my description of what it shows.

Suppose I persuaded people not to take all they hear from government and media at face value. What good would that do? Very little,

I suppose. But if we could generate a desire for serious investigation of supposed terrorist actions, and if it turned out that elements of national governments in non-Islamic countries have been involved in many of them, people might acquiesce less readily in surrendering their freedom and supporting global imperialism. That would be a significant gain.

AN ISLAMIC RESPONSE
TO CHARLIE (9/11) HEBDO

Imran N. Hosein

May peace and blessings be upon Prophet Muhammad—despite the filth that a corrupt and decadent civilization of Gog and Magog has been consistently throwing at him all through its barbaric and blood-stained history. He is indeed a true Prophet of the God of Abraham, and Islamic eschatology allows us to anticipate that it will not be long before the historical process delivers a spectacular validation of Islam's claim to "truth." It is the same "truth" in Islam that came with Moses and with Jesus (peace be upon them both), and that one "truth" rejects, among so many other things, the marriage of a man with another man that the corrupt and decadent civilization of Gog and Magog now validates.

Prophet Muhammad prophesied an End-time in which "there would be great liars—so beware!"

Muslims are not the only people who have recognized the fulfillment of the above ominous prophecy in CIA/Mossad false-flag terrorism all the way up to Charlie 9/11 Hebdo. We know for certain there is more to come—since that is their *modus operandi*. The CIA/Mossad are assisted by a not-so-concealed network of hidden hands within the British, French, Australian, Saudi, Pakistani and other Intelligence Agencies. The acts of false-flag terrorism, and the mountain of orchestrated lies that support them, are all designed to advance Israel's long-term agenda of replacing *Pax Britanica* and *Pax Americana* with a *Pax Judaica* (see my books entitled *Jerusalem in the Qur'ân* and *An Islamic View of Gog and Magog in the Modern World*).

Response to 9/11 and response to Charlie Hebdo

I was present in New York, as the Director of Islamic Studies for the Joint Committee of Muslim Organizations of Greater New York, when the 9/11 terrorist attack on America took place. I responded four days later, on Saturday September 15th 2001, with a public lecture before a large gathering of Muslims at an Islamic Center in Queens, New York. At the end of my lecture, I invited all those present to join with me in praying to the God of Abraham to curse with an eternal curse, and to punish with a punishment that would be eternally inflicted, all those who were responsible for planning and executing that 9/11 act of terrorism. I was proud and happy when all those present in the Islamic Center joined with me in that prayer, with no one abstaining. Having made that prayer, I then invited the Zionist Jews and their Rabbis who were mysteriously away from the WTC buildings on that fateful day, to do likewise. It is almost 14 years since I so invited them, and it should be obvious to readers why they can never make the prayer that we Muslims made.

I now invite the Jewish supporters of the State of Israel, as well as their Christian allies, to publicly pray to the God of Abraham to curse with an eternal curse, and to punish with eternal punishment, all those who were in any way responsible for planning and executing this Charlie Hebdo terrorism in France. Let us warn those who charge innocent Muslims for Charlie 9/11 Hebdo that they will face the consequences of their false accusation in their graves. They must know that Charlie 9/11 Hebdo is part of an unjust war on Islam and innocent Muslims that is supported by a mountain of lies that are more dangerous than a standing army. However, the universe is a moral order—and truth must always eventually prevail over their bogus ISIS, their lies, deception and oppression; it is only a matter of time.

It is important for our gentle readers to know that Prophet Muhammad (peace be upon him) prophesied a great End-time war called the *Malhama*. It is known in Christian and Jewish eschatology as *Armageddon*. The Prophet prophesied that the city of Constantinople would be conquered after the *Malhama,* and this prophecy allows us to recognize that Russia will survive that war with sufficient military capacity intact with which to wage naval warfare. The world can now understand why the Zionist-installed Young Turk government of a secular Republic of Turkey, chose to not only change the most commonly-used name of that city, but to also mysteriously prohibit (a legal prohibition in Turkey) any use of the name "Constantinople."

When I spoke on Islamic eschatology at the State University of Moscow in 2013, I found my Russian audience delighted to learn that our two eschatologies, Christian and Islamic, had similar beliefs on the subjects of the Great War and the Conquest of Constantinople. They were delighted to hear from an Islamic scholar, that when the city of Constantinople is conquered, not only would the name of the city be restored to Constantinople (which is the name used by the Prophet), but that the Cathedral of *Hagia Sophia* which, from the date of its construction in 537 until 1453, served as an Eastern Orthodox cathedral and as the seat of the Patriarchate of Constantinople, would be returned to the Orthodox Christians with a sincere Muslim apology for the monstrously wicked and sinful Ottoman conversion of an orthodox Christian cathedral to a *Masjid*.

It is now absolutely certain that Russia's recent success in recovering its territory of Crimea will lead to an intensification of false-flag Charlie 9/11 Hebdo terrorism designed to justify, as well as facilitate, the launch of a global nuclear war against Russia, China and Pakistan in particular, as well as Arabs and Muslims in general. I expect that nuclear war to take place within the next year or two, but I hope that I am wrong. Europeans and North Americans are likely to suffer most directly from such a nuclear war which would not only be the first, but also the last of its kind in history. The Qur'ân is clear that many others will also perish:

"And [bear in mind:] there is no town/city which We will not destroy before the Last Day, or punish with terrible punishment: all this is laid down in Our decree." (Qur'ân, al-Isra, 17:58)

One of the Signs of the Last Day in Islamic prophecy is *Dukhan* (i.e., 'smoke') which will be plainly visible in the sky:

"Wait, then, for that Day when the skies shall bring forth a pall of smoke which will be clearly visible." (Qur'ân, al-Dukhān, 44:10)

Europeans and North Americans are likely to have a first view of the mushroom clouds from nuclear explosions which would fulfill that End-time prophecy of "smoke." Those who choose to ignore the warning, and to continue to reside in Paris and other big cities of the modern world, would either perish instantly in the war, or perish less instantly in the anarchy that would follow the war as the frantic search for food and water turns violent. The rest of us should flee to the remote countryside and not only stock-up on food, water and other vital supplies, but also acquire survival skills.

Why must history end this terrible way? Why are the Zionists so obsessed with attacking nuclear Russia? Many may not know the answers to these questions, but they should at least know that orthodox Christian Russia—where men cannot marry men—will never bend its knee in submission to those who pursue their decadent messianic agenda with wickedness, lies, injustice and oppression.

MOURNING THE PARISIAN "HUMORISTS" YET CHALLENGING THE HYPOCRISY OF WESTERN MEDIA

Rabbi Michael Lerner

As the editor of a progressive Jewish and interfaith magazine that has often articulated views that have prompted condemnation from both Right and Left, I had good reason to be scared by the murders of fellow journalists in Paris. Having won the 2014 "Magazine of the Year" Award from the Religion Newswriters Association, and having been critical of Hamas' attempts to bomb Israeli cities this past summer (even while being equally critical of Israel's rampage against civilians in Gaza), I have good reason to worry if this prominence raises the chances of being a target for Islamic extremists.

But then again, I had to wonder about the way the massacre in Paris is being depicted and framed by the Western media as a horrendous threat to Western civilization, freedom of speech and freedom of the press; I wondered about the over-heated nature of this description. It didn't take me long to understand how problematic that framing really is.

When right-wing "pro-Israel" fanatics frequently sent me death threats, physically attacked my house and painted on the gates statements about me being "a Nazi" or "a self-hating Jew," and called in bomb threats to *Tikkun*, the magazine I edit, there was no attention given to this by the media, no cries of "our civilization depends on freedom of the press" or demands to hunt down those involved (the FBI and police received our complaints, but never reported back to us about what they were doing to protect us or find the assailants).

Nor was the mainstream or Jewish media particularly concerned about Western civilization being destroyed or freedom of thought and association undermined when various universities denied tenure to professors who had made statements critical of Israel, or when the Hillel association, which operates a chain of student-oriented "Hillel Houses" on college campuses, decided to ban from their premises any Jews who were part of Jewish Voices for Peace. Nor was the media much interested in a bomb that went off outside the NAACP's Colorado Springs headquarters the same day as they were highlighting the attack in Paris. Colorado Springs is home to some of the most extreme right-wing activists. It was a balding white man who was seen setting the bomb, some reports claim, and so the media described it as an act of a troubled "lone individual," rather than as a white right wing Christian fundamentalist terrorist. Few Americans have even heard of this incident.

And when the horrific assassinations of twelve media people and the wounding of another twelve media workers resulted in justifiable outrage around the world, did you ever wonder why there wasn't an equal outrage at the tens of thousands of innocent civilians killed by the American intervention in Iraq or the over a million civilians killed by the U.S. in Vietnam, or why President Obama refused to bring to justice the CIA torturers of mostly Muslim prisoners, thereby de facto giving future torturers the message that they need not even be sorry for their deeds (indeed, former Vice President Cheney boldly asserted he would order that kind of torture again without thinking twice)?

So don't be surprised if people around the world, while condemning the despicable acts of the murderers in Paris and grieving for their families and friends, remain a bit cynical about the media-circus surrounding this particular outrage while the Western media quickly forgets the equally despicable acts of systematic murder and torture that Western countries have been involved in. Or perhaps a bit less convinced that Western societies are really the best hope for civilization when they condone this kind of hypocrisy, rather than responding equally forcefully to all such actions repressing free speech or freedom of assembly. I could easily imagine (and regret) how some Islamist fundamentalists will already be making these points about the ethical inconsistencies of Western societies with their pomposity about human rights that never seem to constrain the self-described "enlightened democracies" from violating those rights when it is they who perceive themselves as under attack.

Yet there is a deeper level in which the discourse seems so misguided. As *Tikkun* editor-at-large Peter Gabel has pointed out, there is no recognition in the media of the dehumanizing way that so much of the media deals with whoever is the perceived threatening "other" of the day. That media was outraged at the attempt by some North Korean allied group to scare people away from watching a movie ridiculing and then planning to assassinate the current (immoral) ruler of Korea, never wondering how we'd respond if a similar movie had been made ridiculing and planning the assassination of an American president. Similarly, the media has refused to even consider what it would mean to a French Muslim, living among Muslims who are economically marginalized and portrayed as nothing but terrorists, their religious garb banned in public, their religion demeaned, to encounter a humor magazine that ridiculed the one thing that gives them some sense of community and higher purpose, namely Mohammed and the religion he founded.

To even raise this kind of question is to open oneself up to charges of not caring about the murdered or making excuses for the murderers. But neither charge is accurate. I fear those fundamentalist extremists just as much as I fear the Jewish extremists who have threatened my life and the Christian extremists who are now exercising power over the U.S. Congress. Every form of violence outrages and sickens me.

Yet the violence is an inevitable consequence of a world which systematically dehumanizes so many people who are made to feel powerless and despairing and deeply depressed about the possibility of finding the milk of human kindness anywhere. The representation of evil dominates the media, and becomes the justification for our own evil acts. And that evil is made possible because so many among us avert our eyes and shut our ears to the cries of the oppressed.

The U.N. estimates that some 10,000 children will die of starvation or diseases related to malnutrition today and every other day in 2015. 2.5 million live on less than $2 a day, 1.5 million on less that $1 a day. Every day thousands of young women are sold into prostitution or "voluntarily" join it in order to raise enough money to help feed their families. Tens of millions of others work in horrendous "sweat shop" conditions. When some of them and some who know about them and feel outraged turn to various forms of nationalist or religious fundamentalist extremism, their violent actions rightfully get condemned. But the silence at the violence that is structural and a pervasive consequence of the globalization of capital is rarely brought to anyone's attention.

All of us absorb this global reality into our unconscious, just as we absorb the violence, hatred, and demeaning of others. We tolerate the kind of endless put-downs that the "humor" magazines and even supposedly liberal comedians like Bill Maher perpetrate, not realizing how much damage all of this does to our souls. The spiritual consequences are all around us: people despairing of ever being understood by others, growing distrustful of others, and feeling that no one really can be trusted. A collective and global emotional depression makes so many people withdraw into themselves, sometimes in relatively harmless ways, but often in ways that undermine the possibility of any human community emerging that would be capable of dealing with the social and environmental problems that face the human race, thereby giving freedom for the global corporations and their hired guns in the media and politics to continue to run the world for their own narrow interests and without regard to the wellbeing of other people or the environment.

"But they ridicule everyone's religion, not just the Muslims'," we are reassured. But the reassurance isn't reassuring. That they ridicule everyone is exactly the problem—the general cheapening and demeaning of others is destructive to everyone. But of course not equally destructive, because people who are already economically and socially marginalized are in far greater danger of having this demeaning sting rather than feel funny.

"And shouldn't free speech and individual human liberties be our highest value? This value that is put into danger if you ask for some kind of responsibility from comedians." Two responses: 1. No, individual human liberties is not our highest value. Our highest value is treating human beings with love, kindness, generosity, respect, and seeing them as embodiments of the holy, and treating the earth as sacred. Individual liberty is a strategy to promote this highest value, but when that liberty gets abused (as for example in demeaning women, African Americans, gays in public discourse) we often insist that the articulators of racism, sexism and homophobia be publicly humiliated (not shut down, but using our free speech to vigorously challenge theirs). 2. Free speech is not defeated when we use it to try to marginalize hateful or demeaning speech. So let's call demeaning speech, including demeaning humor, what it really is—an assault on the dignity of human beings.

None of this is reason to stop mourning the horrific murders in Paris or to excuse it in any way. But it is reason to wonder why the media can never tell a more nuanced story of what is happening our world.

WHY I AM NOT CHARLIE!

Andre Vltchek

I am an atheist, but I am not Charlie Hebdo!

My disgust with Western imperialism and fascism is much stronger than my aversion towards religions. And I don't think that "all religions are equally evil." I mainly hold Christianity responsible for most of the crimes committed in modern human history. I hold it responsible for "derailing" and radicalizing traditionally much more peaceful religions, like Buddhism and yes, like Islam.

Therefore, I am definitely not Charlie!

I don't want to quarrel with dead people. Journalists at Charlie Hebdo should have never died in that terrible way. I actually don't know exactly who is responsible for their demise, although I am well aware of the fact that there are many sound theories, not only the official one.

What is clear and absolutely certain is that their deaths have been politicized by the Western regime, by the Empire. Politicized to a sickening extreme.

Their deaths became a rallying cry of the "liberals," of apologists who are once again ready to forget and forgive all the crimes committed by Western nations for those long centuries, all over the world.

They are ready to forgive their own crimes, the crimes committed by their own nations, crimes of their own religion, and of their own dogma. For many years the simple logic of Western liberals was: we are all human and humans are all equally violent. Which is thorough, absolute nonsense! The death of twelve people is not the same as death of one million! 2,000 victims are not the same as several hundreds of millions! Car brakes that fail ten times are much, much safer for people to use than those that fail several millions of times, and only a total idiot would claim otherwise!

These liberals, like Charlie Hebdo, have been extremely selective in their criticisms of the world. We hardly hear from them about the terror their Empire (consisting mainly of North America and the European nations) is spreading everywhere. They don't poke jokes at Western style "democracy" too often, or at the barbarity of Christianity, or at European colonialism, which has been enslaving almost the entire planet for hundreds of years, virtually destroying almost all alternatives for humanity.

We hardly hear them poking upsetting jokes at Zionism and Israeli apartheid. And where are their brave witty and provocative puns exposing genocides that are being committed by the Empire's allies: India and Indonesia? Why are we not rolling on the floor, laughing at those corrupt bandits in Jakarta and New Delhi, calling their servile, twisted regimes—

"democracies"? And where are Charlie Hebdo and others, confronting the funniest lies: those about so-called Western democracy?

Or are Charlie and his cohorts only brave where it pays and where it is not really risky at all?

I did some research, and realized that there was not one single essay or cartoon by Charlie Hebdo exposing Western responsibility for radicalizing Islam. Not one! And this is one of the main stories of the 20th and 21st centuries; the story about how Brits endorsed and helped to spread Wahhabism, the most appalling form of Islam, which is metastasizing radicalism all over the world. Or how the West literally liquidated all forms of socialist, secular, tolerant Islam!

That is exactly what Islam was becoming, at least after the WWII— secular, tolerant and socialist: in Indonesia, Iran, Egypt, and Afghanistan (allied to the Soviet Union) and in many other places.

Socialist Muslim countries: that would be, of course, thoroughly unacceptable to the West. The Empire needed yet another Rottweiler to fight socialism and Communism. A Rottweiler that could go, periodically, bananas, and would "have to be fought" by the West and its Christian fundamentalism, justifying insane and out of control "defense" budgets.

The Empire and its "brave satirists" like Charlie Hebdo saw (or were ordered to see) socially oriented, secular and tolerant Islam as a tremendous threat!

Eventually, all secular Muslim governments were overthrown directly by the West, at the cost of millions of human lives. And when great rulers of the Muslim world were murdered or sidelined, the common logic in the West proclaimed: "You see, these Arab niggers cannot rule themselves!"

And the brainwashed Western public ate up all these lies, that "intellectual shit," about the Muslim world, about Africa, Asia and Latin America—before Latin America rose again and broke its shackles!

What I have written about the Muslim world—that was, of course only the first, post-WWII wave. What followed decades later was total horror, genocide, in Iraq, Libya, Syria . . .

There were few half-hearted protests in several European public parks, but no decisive wave of resistance by the Western intellectuals, including the comedians and satirists.

Not a word from Charlie Hebdo on that account.

And that is why I am not Charlie!

To piss on Islam is an extremely safe undertaking. To do it, in the West, is unmistakable sign of "coolness" and "secularity." But deep down, it is nothing more than ignorance, bigotry and collaboration with the regime, a sign of cowardice!

If the trend continues, I will soon stop calling myself "atheist," because I do not want to be in "that" company.

True internationalists and sensible atheists want to liberate people from oppression, not to hurt, not to harm defenseless beings! And not to cover up crimes of the real villains and bandits!

Islam has already been ruined, humiliated, stripped of its socially oriented essence. Western demagogues, propagandists and academics usurped its achievements: from great accomplishments in medicine, science, and architecture, to enormous efforts to build egalitarian societies. Yes, the first free and public hospitals in the world were in the Muslim world, and the first universities were there as well. Now, most of them are for a fee, and have "American" in their names——Cairo, Amman, Beirut, everywhere!

Cultural Islam had been defeated: not in some open intellectual duel, but by brutal force and by the most effective weapons of Western "civilization"—by filthy tricks, by deceit!

As a result, all of humanity lost!

Of course, if you go "too far" in urinating on Islam, frustrated followers may chop you to pieces. But still, you will enjoy a great martyrdom after your death. You will be admired and commemorated by millions of brainwashed fellow Christian fundamentalists (yes, that is what most of them really are, even if they call themselves "secular," or even "atheists"). And if you are not killed (the great majority is not), you will be respected and embraced by the majority of your "oh so free countrymen" and glorified by mass media!

And that is why I am not Charlie! I don't want to be a collaborator. I don't want to be an official clown serving the fascist Empire. Forgive me, but no, seriously, fuck you!

Je Suis Chavez! Je Suis Lumumba! Je suis Salvador Allende, bordel! Not Charlie, oh no, not Charlie!

As I saw those multitudes marching in Paris, and as I saw their tears, I felt embarrassed and nauseated: yes, these people were Charlie! Yes, they were crying over their fallen men.

Those uncritical, brainwashed masses, are still reigning over the world. Not only the politicians and business tycoons (I don't buy the claim that Europeans and North Americans are "also victims") but also these people!

A few of their men falling evokes total national outrage, hysteria.

Millions that are being slaughtered because of French business interests, all over the world, particularly those millions in Africa, don't produce even one tear, or one major protest!

Hundreds of millions of Muslims who are forced to live under the yoke of the worst regimes imaginable, the shittiest rulers money can buy; rulers who are fully maintained by the Empire (of which France is an integral part) are of no interest to that selfish, horrifying crowd.

The crowd is naturally and fully responsible for its rulers. It is benefiting from global plunder; not as much as before the late 80's, but it is still benefiting, nevertheless!

The crowd desperately needs Charlies! It is insecure, intellectually and morally fucked, therefore it is longing for "symbols." It needs to feel that *it is* Charlie! It is cowardly, and therefore it needs heroes and martyrs.

The heads, dictators of the Empire, need Charlie, too. The crowd and the Empire are, on most accounts, one single entity, with similar goals: to fuck the world and do very little while living materially "great"—although arguably empty—lives.

That is why the Empire manufactures individuals like those who are willing to run bigoted magazines. That is why it is canonizing them, if they fall. That is why it makes sure that some of them do occasionally fall, in order to become martyrs . . .

This way the crowd can have its symbols, its "heroes."

And that is why I am not Charlie!

CHARLIE HEBDO, 9/11, AND THE SATANIC SACRED

Thaddeus J. Kozinski, Ph.D.

The modern nation-state, in whatever guise, is a dangerous and unmanageable institution, presenting itself on the one hand as a bureaucratic supplier of goods and services, which is always about to, but never actually does, give its clients value for money, and on the other as a repository of sacred values, which from time to time invites one to lay down one's life on its behalf. . . . It is like being asked to die for the telephone company.[245]

–Alasdair MacIntyre

For the general public is being reduced to a state where people not only are unable to find out about the truth but also become unable to *search* for the truth because they are satisfied with deception and trickery that have determined their convictions, satisfied with a fictitious reality created by design through the abuse of language.[246]

–Josef Pieper

Do not accept anything as the truth if it lacks love. And so do not accept anything as love which lacks truth! One without the other becomes a destructive lie.[247]

–St. Teresa Benedicta of the Cross

I. Freedom Isn't Free

Just four days after the Charlie Hebdo event, the world witnessed a march in Paris, in fact, the largest in French history, including two million people (with three million more Frenchmen marching in solidarity with the Parisians) and forty world leaders. The march was held to commemorate and mourn the sixteen people who were murdered at the *Charlie Hebdo* offices and at a Kosher deli, but it also had the purpose of emboldening and encouraging freedom-loving people, who must now risk their lives merely to exercise their right to free speech. *Nous sommes tous Charlie Hebdo maintenant.* The official government narrative of the event was that a few radical Muslim terrorists, and precisely those designated—quite immediately after the attack—by the authorities, murdered eleven employees of a newspaper simply because of the content of that newspaper, as well as five more Jewish people simply because they were Jewish. The official government-authorized meaning of the event was that violence employed against the free use of speech would not be tolerated in France. And any public utterance that did not fall perfectly in line with this authorized narrative and meaning met with the hostile force of the French state. Criticism of the blasphemous cartoons attacking the religious beliefs of millions of Christians and Muslims, and any hesitation in accepting with trust and gratitude the new French status quo of surveillance, suspicion, and censorship was considered intolerant, bigoted, and even criminal, for such could indicate only animosity toward free speech and thus solidarity with murderous terrorists.

In short, very soon after the largest free-speech march in European history—perhaps the *only* free-speech march in European history—there was a massive government crackdown on free speech, and precisely where that march took place. Included in the hundreds of the "dangerous enemies of free speech" that were arrested by the Paris police in the wake of " was an eight-year old French Muslim boy, detained and questioned by the police due to the dangerous content of his post-toddler speech. And only a month after this, a French citizen was sent to prison for two years merely for questioning the accuracy of certain episodes of another officially authorized narrative.[248] In short, the most obvious consequence of the Charlie Hebdo event was not the expansion and tolerance of free speech, but its radical suspicion and circumscription. Indeed, Charlie Hebdo was followed by an unprecedented escalation of government surveillance and the fanatical legal suppression of free speech. Daniel Spaulding from *Soul of the East* reports that:

> Over the past several decades, France has prosecuted numerous individuals for engaging in state-designated "hate speech." The French novelist and gadfly Michel Houellebecq, depicted in a satirical cartoon on the cover of *Charlie Hebdo* the same day of the terrorist attack, was at one time tried, and later acquitted, for making remarks derogatory toward Islam. And a mere few days after the Charlie Hebdo shooting, the comedian Dieudonné M'bala M'bala was arrested on the dubious charge of "glorifying terrorism" after decrying his previous persecutions at the hands of the French authorities for alleged "anti-Semitic" comments. If convicted he could spend several years in prison.[249]

In his book, *There's No Such Thing as Free Speech, and It's a Good Thing, Too*, Stanley Fish writes:

> "Free speech" is just the name we give to verbal behavior that serves the substantive agendas we wish to advance; and we give our preferred verbal behaviors *that* name when we can, when we have the power to do so, because in the rhetoric of American life, the label "free speech" is the one you want your favorites to wear. Free speech, in short, is not an independent value but a political prize, and if that prize has been captured by a politics opposed to yours, it can no longer be invoked in

the ways that further your purposes, for it is not an obstacle to those purposes.[250]

I would argue that the Charlie Hebdo event and the behavior that followed it provide solid evidence for the truth of Fish's words. There was an unmistakable Orwellian cast to the whole Charlie Hebdo event, suggesting the existence of an esoteric agenda underneath the exoteric one. If Fish is correct, and free speech is just the name given to verbal behavior that serves the agenda of capturing some political prize, *who* in Paris were seeking such a prize, and *what* was it? The who is easy: the French-Anglo-American-Israeli-European ruling classes, comprised of government, intelligence, technology, military, finance, academia, media, and entertainment, the organizers of the *Je Suis Charlie Hebdo* campaign and march, the budding Paris surveillance industry, the bureaucratic drafters and enforcers of France's version of the Patriot Act, the South Park-esque cartoonists of the *Charlie Hebdo* newspaper and their fans, and finally, every person wearing a Je-Suis-Charlie t-shirt (in spirit, if not on body). But what was the political prize? As we shall see presently, the *what* question is much more complex that the *who*.

When a narrative emerges whose explanation for a massively violent event and the meaning of the concomitant crisis becomes official, unquestionable, and authoritative; when it includes, and without empirical evidence or investigative inquiry, the assignation of innocence and exceptionalism to the victims, and utter depravity and terrifying power to the designated criminals; when dissent from this narrative is socially forbidden, even to the extent of legal harassment and prosecution; when it spawns behavior in contradiction with itself, such as the committing of acts of terror in the name of eradicating terrorism, or restricting and punishing free speech in the name of expanding and protecting it; when the narrative is immediately supported, echoed, and policed by the vast majority of the ruling classes, including both the mainstream and "alternative" (gate-keeping) left and right; when it successfully unites and synthesizes otherwise opposed factions of the populous—liberals with neoconservatives, libertarians with statists, humanists with Nietzscheans, theists with atheists; when rational scrutiny and frank discussion of obvious explanatory holes in the narrative are forbidden; and when the ritualistic, annual remembrance of an event and recitation of its hallowed story, particularly the harrowing portrayal of the demonic villains to which it assigns all blame for both the increasing domestic strife among citizens and the perpetual Manichean war against the newest "enemy," instills and evokes primordial fear and religious awe in the populous; when the narrative of an event or series of connected events possesses all of these attributes, or even just a few of them, we know we are dealing with no chance and ordinary phenomenon. Here we have something the apparent mystery and power of which strike at the very heart of the collective consciousness, searing it with something akin to the divine. What we are dealing with, in a word, is the *sacred*. And it just so happens that the Charlie Hebdo event and narrative bear all the aforementioned characteristics. But isn't the sacred an extinct relic of our benighted, superstitious, medieval past?

II. The Sacred (Secular) State

Secular modernity is neither secular nor modern. Of course, we no longer live under the medieval sacral regimes of throne and altar or post-Reformation confessional monarchies. And who can doubt the peculiarly modern rise of science and technology, the radically new kinds of political and economic institutions, the undisputed reign of democratic ideology, and our unprecedented religious pluralism? However, these obvious historical facts and features are not what are primarily signified by the words "secular" and "modern"; for, their inseparable concomitant is a "just-so" story of the genealogy of modernity: Only in secular modernity did man finally achieved his liberation from oppression and ignorance, from superstition, magic, tyranny, and priestcraft, from the dark forces of religious power, fanatical belief, and sectarianism. Man achieved this liberation primarily through the secularization of reason, morality and society, which was effected through the separation of religion from the political order, church from the state. Ever-increasing religious and ideological pluralism ensued as soon as previously oppressed men of good will were permitted to exercise freely their reason and act on their consciences. It is certainly the case that when Christendom was finally broken up in the wake of the Reformation, religiously intolerant, confessional, monarchical states emerged, but these evolved quite quickly, historically speaking, into the secular, tolerant-minded, pluralistic, democratic states we have today. The rise of secular society after the sixteenth and seventeenth-century "wars of religion" (to see why this phrase must be put in scare quotes, see the pioneering revisionist work of William T. Cavanaugh[251]) was rendered possible only by the removal of "religion" (a creation of the modern state, as Cavanaugh shows, being unprecedented in its newly depoliticized and privatized form[252]) from all positions of political significance and power. Good-willed, reasonable people were ready and willing to accept the desacralization of the state, so the story goes, after centuries of witnessing incessant bloodshed over religion. Sequestered, depoliticized, and privatized, religion and the sacred would now no longer cause war, divisiveness, and oppression, and the newly liberated, autonomous, politically secular individual could finally thrive. In the religiously tolerant, secular, pluralistic liberal democracy governed by the rights of men, not God, the sacred would still have a place, as well as a capacity to exert influence over politics, but now it would have to coexist with the many competing, private sacreds residing in the same city, now proliferating and dwelling together in peace precisely because none are permitted to obtain societal, cultural, and political power, let alone a monopoly on power.

In short, secular modernity was born at the moment when the archaic, violence-inducing *sacred* lost its public, political hegemony and influence, having been relegated to the sub-political, private sphere of men's fancies and hearts. What took its place in the public square is what should have always been there in the first place, the absolute right (restricted only by the equal rights of others) of the individual to self-determination, to freedom of thought, action, speech, property, and religion. Prescinding from the question of the ideological accuracy of this just-so narrative, it can be said with certainty that in modernity man attempted, for the first time in human history, to construct a political order *not* based upon the religious or the sacred. While not denying the right of every citizen to believe in a sacred, superhuman, cosmic, divine, transcendent power as the true ground of man's existence, both personal and social, the theoreticians of the modern paradigm, people such as Machiavelli, Hobbes, Locke, Rousseau, Kant, Madison, and Marx, justified, by appeals to reason, common sense and consent, historical inevitability, enlightened sentiment, or even the Will of God, the replacement of secular values and rights codified in a social contract, the general will, a constitution, or the party line for any supposed power or will higher than man.

Of course, the jury is still out on whether political power and unity can be derived from a purely immanent and secular source, from a contract made by humans with humans alone. Rémi Brague warns that, "Such a contract, precisely because it has no external point of reference, cannot possibly decide whether the very existence on this earth of the species *homo sapiens* is a good thing or not."[253] What the continual irruption and increasing proliferation of violent, crisis-making events that bear the sacred features described above—unimpeachable narratives, an ethos of fear and awe, the sudden unification of factions, etc.—indicates is that the phenomenon of the sacred is as publicly present, influential, and authoritative in secular modernity as it ever was in the ancient "religious" world. We need only think of other recent sacred events, such as Sandy Hook, the Boston bombing, the Aurora shooting, the ISIS beheadings, the Sydney chocolate-shop massacre, and all the other post 9/11, staged crisis-events that constitute the ongoing episodes in the "War on Terror," whose pilot episode was that most sacred of all American events, IX XI.[254] Can modern man really live without the sacred? And when he has repudiated the traditional sacred, or perhaps has just forgotten about it, is he bound to concoct sacreds of his own, in his own fallen and depraved image?

Must the political order be derived from a cosmic model (or, at any rate, from an external, transcendent reference point), or are there valid and effective substitutes? Can unaided humanity, through the mobilization of its faculties, create a sacred, or at least a myth, powerful enough to convey a model? If the answer to these questions is no, we must ask then: Can a community exist without the sacred component, by the mere power of rational decisions and intellectual discourse?[255]

No. A community cannot exist without a sacred component, and when the traditional sacred of monotheism was rejected in modernity, the shrine did not remain empty.

An objection might be raised here. Even if it were a delusional mistake to try entirely to desacralize politics and power, did not secular modernity bring us the freedom of religion, the rule of law, civil equality, and representative government, that is, unquestionably beneficial institutions and practices unheard of in the pre-modern world? We can say with certainty that modern liberal democracy, insofar as it has provided the political, legal, cultural, social, and psychological space for the free exercise of reason and conscience, and as it has helped men to flourish physically through its scientific, technological, and medical advances is a considerably good thing. But what is the price we have paid for all these secular advances? Was the dethronement of the traditional sacred from its rightful place at the heart of society, culture, and politics worth it?—"What profit a man if he gain the whole world but lose his very soul."

III.   Sacred Nihilism

One way to characterize the sacred is that which is considered absolutely *good*, under, around, in obedience to, and in pursuit of which men order their individual and corporate lives. Insofar as secular liberalism denies that such a metaphysical, ethical, and spiritual good, if it even exists, can or should have any public authority in civilized society, it is delusional and hypocritical. As Alasdair MacIntyre writes:

> Initially, the liberal claim was to provide a political, legal, and economic framework in which assent to one and the same set of rationally justifiable principles would enable those who espouse widely different and incompatible conceptions of the good life for human beings to live together peaceably within the same society. Every individual is to be equally free to propose and to live by whatever theory or tradition he or she may adhere to, unless that conception of the good involves reshaping the life of the rest of the community in accordance with it . . . And this qualification of course entails not only that liberal individualism

does indeed have its own broad conception of the good, which it is engaged in imposing politically, legally, socially, and culturally wherever it has the power to do so, but also that in so doing its toleration of rival conceptions of the good in the public arena is severely limited.[256]

Since secular liberal culture is, according to MacIntyre, founded upon a particular conception of the good, namely, the *sacral good* of the privatization and desacralization of all claims to truth, and a particular doctrine of truth, the irreducible plurality of conceptions of the good/sacred; and since the publicly authoritative rhetoric of liberal culture includes a denial of having any substantive sacred conceptions of its own, what liberalism amounts to is an institutionalized religious sacred—but one that indoctrinates citizens into disbelieving in its very existence as such. Just as the puppeteers in Plato's Cave must ensure that the shadows they cast on the wall in front of the shackled slaves are never seen by them *as shadows,* else the cave be identified as a *cave* and the prisoners break their chains in revolt, the "secular" state must never be exposed for what it really is, a sacred power exercising hegemony over all competing sacreds, which it has effectively privatized and neutered. Thus, its own sacred dogmas become unimpeachable, unquestionable, uncontestable, and, most importantly, invisible. It judges all beliefs and actions in accord with these dogmas, and executes its definitive judgments through its terrible liturgical violence and murderous ritual scapegoating, masked by the language of rights, democracy, freedom, security, diversity, equality, and tolerance. Orwell, eat your heart out.

All political orders require a mechanism for engendering and preserving unity, and the sacred has always been the source and engine of this unity. It is no different in our "modern" day. The Charlie Hebdo murders, though horrific and tragic, were exploited, and perhaps even orchestrated, through a kind of psychological and spiritual sorcery, the effect of which was to create a unified, regulated group-mind (to use the term of John McMurtry) in the French people and in the West at large. At the shrine of Charlie Hebdo, "free speech" became God, but a god with no substantive core, no divine identity, and no supernatural content. It is a cunning idol, nevertheless. It commands only toleration, and it promises only freedom. Yet it tolerates—and encourages—only blasphemy and ridicule of precisely those competing sacreds it seeks to vanquish, the God of Abraham, Issac, and Jacob, and the sacred personages of Mohammad and Christ—and it persecutes any who dare to critique its sacred nihilism. The desacralization, profanation, and degradation of Christianity and Islam is, since Charlie Hebdo, the official meaning of "free speech."

IV. 911 and the Satanic Sacred

Although Charlie Hebdo was quite a sacred spectacle, 9/11 was *the* exemplar of secular modernity's sacred. I have discussed this claim in more depth elsewhere[257], but for now it is sufficient to point out its uncanny resemblance to traditional sacred mythology, ritual, and sacrament. Sheldon Wolin writes:

> The mythology created around September 11 was predominantly Christian in its themes. The day was converted into the political equivalent of a holy day of crucifixion, of martyrdom, that fulfilled multiple functions: as the basis of a political theology, as a communion around a mystical body of a bellicose republic, as a warning against political apostasy, as a sanctification of the nation's leader, transforming him from a powerful officeholder of questionable legitimacy into an instrument of redemption, and at the same time exhorting the congregants to a wartime militancy, demanding of them uncritical loyalty and support, summoning them as participants in a sacrament of unity and in a crusade to "rid the world of evil." [258]

James Allison, an eminent theologian and expert on the thought of René Girard, the latter of whose oeuvre amounts to the complete unmasking of all non-Gospel-centered cultures as murderous, ritual scapegoating mechanisms, has given the most penetrating account of the 9/11 event as *the* nexus of satanic sacred power in the West. It is worth quoting in full:

> And immediately the old sacred worked its magic: we found ourselves being sucked in to a sacred center, one where a meaningless act had created a vacuum of meaning, and we found ourselves giving meaning to it. All over London I found that friends had stopped work, offices were closing down, everyone was glued to the screen. In short, there had appeared, suddenly, a holy day. Not what we mean by a holiday, a day of rest, but an older form of holiday, a being sucked out of our ordinary lives in order to participate in a sacred and sacrificial centre so kindly set up for us by the meaningless suicides . . . And immediately the sacrificial center began to generate the sort of reactions that sacrificial centers are supposed to generate: a feeling of unanimity and grief. Phrases began to appear to the effect that "We're all Americans now"—a purely fictitious feeling for most of us. It was staggering to watch the togetherness build up around the sacred center, quickly consecrated as Ground Zero, a togetherness that would harden over the coming hours into flag waving, a huge upsurge in religious services and observance, religious leaders suddenly taken seriously, candles, shrines, prayers, all the accoutrements of the religion of death. And there was the grief. How we enjoy grief. It makes us feel good, and innocent. This is what Aristotle meant by catharsis, and it has deeply sinister echoes of dramatic tragedy's roots in

sacrifice. One of the effects of the violent sacred around the sacrificial center is to make those present feel justified, feel morally good. A counterfactual goodness which suddenly takes us out of our little betrayals, acts of cowardice, uneasy consciences. And very quickly of course the unanimity and the grief harden into the militant goodness of those who have a transcendent object to their lives. And then there are those who are with us and those who are against us, the beginnings of the suppression of dissent. Quickly people were saying things like "to think that we used to spend our lives engaged in gossip about celebrities' and politicians' sexual peccadillos. Now we have been summoned into thinking about the things that really matter." And beneath the militant goodness, suddenly permission to sack people, to leak out bad news and so on, things which could take advantage of the unanimity to avoid reasoned negotiation . . . What I want to suggest is that most of us fell for it, at some level. We were tempted to be secretly glad of a chance for a huge outbreak of meaning to transform our humdrum lives, to feel we belonged to something bigger, more important, with hints of nobility and solidarity. What I want to suggest is that this, this delight in being given meaning, is satanic.[259]

All human beings "delight in being given meaning," but the meaning given to the masses through the 9/11 and Charlie Hebdo events is as meaningless as it is idolatrous and psychopathic. Charlie Hebdo informs us that those who aren't comfortable with public, state-supported mockery of other citizens' religious beliefs are equivalent to murderous terrorist fanatics. Through 9/11 and the War on Terror that followed, the United States, as the metonymic Twin Towers and the World Trade Center, was transformed into a suffering and resurrected God, scourged and crucified by the forces of pure evil that "hate our freedoms," but brought back to life by Bush, Rumsfeld, Cheney, et.al. as mediators of the immortal righteousness of the American people. Our priest/warriors inaugurated an endless "shock and awe" crusade against the demons of this world, one that not only "keeps us free" but also effectively manages to separate the sheep from the goats, the saved from the damned—"Either you are with us, or you are with the terrorists," the divinized oracle uttered. The meaning of 9/11, thus, is this: the definitive, once-and-for-all, divine confirmation of "our" exceptional righteousness, and, concomitantly, the inexorable, irredeemable wickedness of the "other," defined by magisterial fiat as anyone not willing to worship American power. Of course, Americans had some faith in the truth of this meaning before 9/11, but only on 9/11 was that faith confirmed and vindicated, seemingly by God Himself, using as his divine sign demonic planes crashing into our tallest shrines, while the *pontifix maximus* placidly meditated on his sacred scriptures, *The Pet* Goat, read upside down in an elementary school temple.

For Marvin and Ingle, death in war—what is commonly called the "ultimate sacrifice" for the nation—is what periodically re-presents the sense of belonging upon which the imagined nation is built. Such death is then elaborately ceremonialized in liturgies involving the flag and other ritual objects. Indeed, it is the ritual itself that retrospectively classifies any particular act of violence as *sacrifice*. Ritual gesture and language are crucial for establishing meaning and public assent to the foundational story being told. The foundational story is one of both creation and salvation. At the ceremonies marking the fiftieth anniversary of D-Day in 1994, for example, President Clinton remarked of the soldiers that died there both that "They gave us our world" and that "They saved the world."[260]

Charlie Hebdo was a satanic psychological-spiritual operation through which the French masses, already alienated from the true sources of meaning, truth, goodness, and beauty found in the beliefs and practices of traditional monotheism, were initiated into the satanic sacred, the worship of the empty shrine of nihilism. William Cavanaugh writes:

> The public shrine has been emptied of any one particular God or creed, so that the government can never claim divine sanction and each person may be free to worship as she sees fit . . . There is no single visible idol, no golden calf, to make the idolatry obvious . . . officially the shrine remains empty . . . The empty shrine, however, threatens to make a deity not out of God but out of our freedom to worship God. Our freedom comes to occupy the empty shrine. Worship becomes worship of our collective self, and civil religion tends to marginalize the worship of the true God. Our freedom, finally, becomes the one thing we will die and kill for.[261]

"You may confess on your lips any god you like, provided you are willing to kill for America."[262] And now France has officially joined itself to America's sacred War of Terror.

IV.   Two Cities

Since 9/11, individual liberty has been vastly curtailed, and global violence has exponentially increased. Wars and rumors of wars abound. Perhaps the next staged, false-flag terror event will trigger the final annihilation of our freedoms and the complete establishment of a global police state, if we aren't nuked out of existence first. The apocalypse seems to be upon us. So, what should we do—now? No doubt we should do all we can to restrict the scope and power of modern states and international institutions of global governance, as well as expose the machinations of the "deep state" that actually rules us. We must preserve what is left of the freedoms of speech, protest, and worship by non-violent means, and by self-defensive force if necessary. Moreover, if our analysis is correct and modernity is merely the replacement of one bloody sacred for another— we used to have bloody crusades and wars for Christ and Mohammad, now we have them for democracy and freedom—it would seem reasonable for us to turn our efforts towards banishing any semblance of the sacred from the public square so as to separate it from all corrupting, political, coercive, and violence-making power and thus corruption. This would protect both the sacred from profanation and the state from idolatry. In other words, if Western governments are indeed shrines and purveyors of satanic nothing-worship, then we need to strip them of all sacred authority and power.

While it cannot be denied that a more secular, less powerful, and more —much more—decentralized government-military-financial-educational-intelligence-media complex is the *sine qua non* of any solution, if we take the reality and power of the sacred as seriously as it deserves, we should be as discontented at seeing the sacred remain merely a private affair as we are seeing it counterfeited, mocked, and profaned. God exercises, whether we recognize it or not, social, cultural, and political reign over the world— we live now in a theocracy, always have, and always will, until the end of the world. And this rule is not just over individual hearts, but over institutions and states, over men organized collectively for the common good and for His honor, even if they dishonor Him and order the sacred commons to their monstrous, vampirish appetites. *He* is the ultimate common good, the ultimate ground for any human social contract, and if He is relegated to the private sphere of idiosyncratic and irrational fancy, something not-so-good will always take His place. Just as there is no such thing as free speech, there is no such thing as an empty shrine.

Thus, we must work not only to dethrone the satanic sacred, the Abomination of Desolation now residing in the Holy of Holies, but also to replace it with the authentic sacred, the worship of the Living, Holy, All-powerful, All-knowing, All-just, All-merciful God. We need to learn, practice, revitalize, and establish in our communities and states those Traditions that embody and transmit His existence and will, that embody and mediate the ultimate realities of man's existence, the transcendent origin, end, and meaning of all things that cannot be grasped by human reason alone, and which cannot be fully rationalized, defined, or articulated. Ultimate reality must be *experienced* and *obeyed* through and in its incarnations in authentic religious traditions. It is in this sense that genuine sacred traditions are the eyes that allow us desacralized men to see the spiritual, eternal, and transcendent meaning hidden in the physical, temporal, and mundane facts of everyday existence, to truly "delight in meaning" by being immersed in the True, the Good, and the Beautiful. We must replace the counterfeit and degrading meanings given to us by the satanic sacred with the truth.

To dethrone the satanic sacred that has usurped the seats of earthly power in Western society, we first must repent of our own complicity in its rites and ceremonies. What that complicity might look like would be the topic of another essay, but it has much to do with accepting the scapegoating status-quo because it flatters, protects, and keeps us feeling comfortable, and refusing to speak truth to power out of fear. After a thorough examination of conscience, we must unmask the satanic face hiding right out in the open so as to help those blinded to its existence and horrific nature through the unholy fear it engenders, the tortuous psychological and spiritual deceptions it incessantly enacts, and its totalitarian control of public discourse. As Neil Kramer describes, "For the ordinary person, the primary power of Empire rests not in its might or cunning, but in its invisibility. People who are not mindful of its presence do not comprehend their conscious and spiritual incarceration."[263]

The City of God is founded on a love of God that leads its citizens to contempt for themselves, counting all earthly things as worthless . . . Augustine argues that the temporal ought to be ordered to the eternal (Civ. Dei XIX,17), but that this ordering will never be achieved entirely harmoniously till the second coming of the Lord. For, there is a second city here on earth in addition to the city of God— the *civitas terrena*, the earthly city. This city is founded on a love of self to the contempt of God (Civ. Dei XIV,28). And these two cities are in conflict . . . The earthly city is always opposed to true religion . . . Justice consists in giving each his own, thus no society is just that does not give God the worship due to Him.[264]

The city of man has always been opposed to true religion, to the truly sacred, and this opposition has only increased in our "secular age," and exponentially since 9/11. At the heart of every culture is always the sacred, and at the heart of our post-9/11, pathocratic, imperial culture of death and deception is a terrible—but entirely vincible—sacred power in mortal conflict with the *Logos*, the merciful, loving, and truly sacred Person who protects, guide, and saves those who are willing to recognize, adore, and trust in Him.

CHARLIE HEBDO AND THE WEST'S CULTURAL WAR ON ISLAM

By Zafar Bangash

Every time Islam, Muslims and their revered personalities and books are insulted, the argument of "freedom of expression" is trotted out. This mantra has become something of an absolute in Western society that, we are told, must be upheld regardless of the consequences as was demonstrated by the *Charlie Hebdo* affair. The pro-Zionist Islamophobic magazine has for years published insulting cartoons of the Prophet of Islam (upon whom be peace. This is an expression Muslims use whenever the Prophet is mentioned) totally disregarding the concerns of Muslims and whether such conduct is appropriate even for the larger good of society. Its editor, cartoonists and workers insist that they have the "right" to do what they like regardless of the consequences.

Following the January 7th attack on the Paris weekly's offices, not only France but virtually the entire Western world and their puppets in the Muslim world went into a frenzy of grief. It was interesting to see rulers that brutally suppress any freedom of expression in their own societies were walking hand in hand for freedom of expression in Paris!

For the record, let us state that Islam does not permit the killing of innocent people. In the Qur'an, the divinely revealed Book that Muslims follow, there is a verse that categorically forbids the killing of innocent people (Chapter 5, verse 32). Such killing is equated with the murder of the whole of humanity. So before people accuse Islam or Muslims of such conduct, they ought to know what the Islamic position is on such matters. Further, even if someone is guilty of a crime, that person must be tried in a court of law and punishment administered by a legally constituted authority, not individuals taking the law into their own hands.

It is important, however, to properly investigate who the perpetrators of this crime were. We have had far too many false flag operations to accept the official version of events in Paris at face value.

The French government called for a march on January 11th. An estimated one to two million people marched through the streets of Paris and perhaps a million and a half in other French cities, according to corporate media reports. It was revealing that a government called for this march; not members of civil society groups. The Paris march was attended by such "upholders of press freedom" as David Cameron of Britain and Benjamin Netanyahu, the Prime Minister of Zionist Israel. Accompanying them were a number of Arab potentates whose regimes do not allow any freedom of expression. They have never held any elections either. Cameron's regime does not allow Julian Assange, holed up in the Ecuadorian Embassy in London for more than a year, the freedom of passage out of the country. What was Assange's crime? He leaked diplomatic cables about American spying operations worldwide. Where is his freedom of expression and why are people not marching in his support?

The Zionist war criminal Netanyahu came to Paris with his hands still dripping with the blood of innocent Palestinian children. He was accompanied by fellow Zionist war criminals as if they were not guests in Paris but conquerors. And he kicked the French in the teeth by telling French Jews to migrate in even larger numbers to Occupied Palestine (a.k.a. Israel) because they were not "safe" in France.

On January 10th, French Prime Minister Manuel Valls said his government had declared war against "radical Islam" because its practitioners had attacked "our values, which are universal." Hubris is not confined to American warmongers; the French, British and Zionists are just as susceptible to flights of fancy. The formal declaration of war, however, has come a little late. France has been at war with Muslims for decades and if we consider its colonial history (Algeria, other parts of Africa and Indo-China) we are talking about centuries. The French and indeed Western colonial legacy is long, horrible and gory.

Let us, however, consider France's claim to having "universal values." Did France not participate in the slaughter of millions of innocents in Iraq, Afghanistan, Libya and Syria in recent years? What about Algeria where more than a million people were killed before the North African country gained independence in 1961, or Indo-China (Vietnam) between 1946 and 1954? Are the lives of millions of Vietnamese, Algerians, Iraqis, Libyans, Syrians and Afghans not worth anything? Is mass murder, even if perpetrated in conjunction with other Western warmongers, something to be proud of? And why are seventeen—yes a grand total of seventeen—French lives more important than the millions of people, almost all of them Muslims slaughtered elsewhere? Are these the kind of values people can or should be proud of?

Let us first examine the Islamophobic magazine's track record. Founded in February 1969 under the original name, Hara-Kiri Hebdo, it espoused leftwing causes associated with the oppressed. In November 1970, the French Interior Ministry banned the magazine (no freedom of expression there) because it insulted the memory of Charles de Gaulle when it published a cover upon his death, with the headline: "Tragic prom in Colombey [de Gaulle's city of origin], one dead."

In 2000, the magazine now renamed, Charlie Hebdo, under its new editor Philippe Val, shifted direction to the right and became extremely hostile to Muslims and Palestinians. It fully supported the Zionist aggression against Lebanon in 2006 where the invading Zionist army murdered more than 1100 Lebanese civilians and destroyed $12 billion worth of infrastructure, most of it in South Beirut. Perhaps this was the magazine's way of exercising "freedom of expression," more like freedom of aggression.

There are other anomalies as well. In 2008, one of its cartoonists, Siné made fun of President Nicolas Sarkozy's son. The junior Sarkozy converted to Judaism in order to marry a Jewish woman. Siné ran a caption under the cartoon, "This lad will go far in France," hinting at the inordinate influence Jews enjoy in the country. While the joke reflected the reality of French society, the editor of Charlie Hebdo considered this "anti-Semitic" and fired Siné.

When asked whether he would make fun of Jews in the same manner as he has consistently done of Muslims, the magazine's recently dead editor, Stephane Charbonnier (a.k.a. Charb), said he would not because this would be politically unacceptable. So the issue is not one of freedom of expression per se, although it is most often touted as a cherished value, but one of what is politically acceptable. Nicolas Sarkozy promoted Charlie Hebdo's editor Philippe Val to executive editor of France-Inter (a public radio station).

It is also revealing that "freedom of expression" is invoked only when the powerful, especially among the whites, insult and abuse others. There is no freedom of expression for the weak and the oppressed. This was most graphically illustrated by the arrest of black French comedian Dieudonné M'bala M'bala in the wake of the *Charlie Hebdo* affair. On his Facebook page, he wrote: "I feel like Charlie Coulibaly." (Amedy Coulibaly was the alleged kidnapper of people in a Jewish store in Paris where four people died. He was shot and killed by the police. We say "alleged" because he was not charged or convicted in a court of law and it is not clear who killed the four persons there). Dieudonné referred to both *Charlie Hebdo* and Amedy Coulibaly but this was unacceptable in France which had just held a million-strong rally in defense of "freedom of expression." He was accused of supporting terrorism! One would be hard pressed to find a more accurate definition of hypocrisy.

Freedom of expression is not an absolute and never has been, although some journalists try to push the limits as much as possible, not to support freedom of expression but to advance their pre-determined agenda. There are always limits to freedom of expression and even retreat in the face of social pressure and consequences. At a time when Muslims are facing extreme right-wing attacks in France, Britain, Germany and many other countries and marches by fascist neo-Nazi groups are growing throughout Europe (think Dresden), *Charlie Hebdo's* attacks against the Prophet of Islam are only adding fuel to fire.

It is dishonest to claim that the press enjoys absolute freedom or that there are no restrictions on attacking religion. In Britain, there is a law against blasphemy but it only covers the Protestant Church. This has now been extended to Judaism as well but Islam is excluded. The Jews did not always enjoy this privilege. In fact, Europe has a long terrible history of persecution of the Jewish people. In most European countries today, however, it is illegal to deny the Holocaust.

Even more fundamental to the discussion about media responsibility is the case of the Nazi publication *Der Sturmer* that carried vehemently anti-Semitic caricatures of Jewish people both before and during the Second World War. *Charlie Hebdo* indulges in the same obscene depiction of Muslims and the Prophet to incite hatred and ridicule. The French government's support of such publications and their policy of Islamophobia, and by extension of those Frenchmen that support them, put them in the same category as the Nazi newspaper during the Second World War.

What happened to the editor of *Der Sturmer*, Julius Streicher when the war ended? He was put on trial, convicted of crimes against humanity and executed. In light of this and the fact that the French resisted the Nazi occupiers of their country, it is hypocritical of the French government to now support *Charlie Hebdo's* campaign of spreading hatred against Muslims. Unfortunately, this is part of Western policy: to demonize and, therefore, marginalize Muslims. The neo-Nazis in Germany are calling for the expulsion of Muslims; and the French and British are vilifying them. The French regime of Francois Hollande went further: it announced a grant of one million euros to *Charlie Hebdo*! Western hypocrisy about "freedom of expression" is further exposed by their ban on Iran's Press TV and the Lebanese satellite channel Al-Manar. The latter is linked with Hizbullah. Unlike *Charlie Hebdo*, these two channels do not spread hatred against anyone; they simply provide news and analysis that the Western corporate media refuses to provide.

The French conduct in support of *Charlie Hebdo* is also in violation of article 19 of the International Covenant on Civil and Political Rights (ICCPR) to which it acceded in 1980 with the following reservation: The Government of the Republic [of France] declares that articles 19, 21 and 22 of the Covenant will be implemented in accordance with articles 10, 11 and 16 of the European Convention for the Protection of Human Rights and Fundamental Freedoms of 4 November 1950.

Francis Boyle, a leading International Law professor in the world today (he teaches at the University of Illinois, in Champaign-Urbana,

Illinois, US), has provided the text of Article 10 of the European Convention on Human Rights as set forth below:

ARTICLE 10
1: Everyone has the right to freedom of expression. This right shall include freedom to hold opinions and to receive and impart information and ideas without interference by public authority and regardless of frontiers. This article shall not prevent States from requiring the licensing of broadcasting, television or cinema enterprises.

2: The exercise of these freedoms, since it carries with it duties and responsibilities, may be subject to such formalities, conditions, restrictions or penalties as are prescribed by law and are necessary in a democratic society, in the interests of national security, territorial integrity or public safety, for the prevention of disorder or crime, for the protection of health or morals, for the protection of the reputation or the rights of others, for preventing the disclosure of information received in confidence, or for maintaining the authority and impartiality of the judiciary.

From the above it is clear that freedom of expression comes with responsibilities and that it "may be subject to such formalities, conditions, restrictions or penalties as are prescribed by law and are necessary in a democratic society, in the interests of national security, territorial integrity or public safety, *for the prevention of disorder or crime, for the protection of health or morals, for the protection of the reputation or the rights of others*, for preventing the disclosure of information received in confidence, or for maintaining the authority and impartiality of the judiciary." (*emphasis added*).

Professor Boyle states: "Strangely, there may be a perverse correlation between how much blood is shed and our eventual moment of self-examination. It took two world wars to produce such documents as the Universal Declaration of Human Rights. How much blood has to be shed before we actually honor them? The International Covenant on Civil and Political Rights . . . is considered to be international implementing legislation for the Universal Declaration of Human Rights."

The learned professor then gives his legal opinion on the issue of *Charlie Hebdo*'s insulting cartoons about the Prophet of Islam. He writes:

. . . The cartoons degrading Mohammed [peace be upon him] fit within the exception to the right of freedom of expression set forth in the [ICCPR]. It turns out that when France acceded to the terms of the Covenant it made a Reservation to Article 19 on the basis of Article 10 of the European Convention on Human Rights of 1950 . . . Certainly the cartoons degrading Mohammed [pbuh] clearly fit within this exception to Freedom of Expression under both the International

Covenant on Civil and Political Rights and the European Convention on Human Rights.

The French government is not constrained by its legal obligations or the covenants it has signed. The same goes for its allies. They are obsessed with targeting Muslims—the most vilified people in the world today—and they want to do it in the most degrading manner by publishing insulting cartoons of the Prophet of Islam. Forgotten in this modern-day Crusade is the fact that Muslims are forced to migrate to the country of their former colonial masters because their own societies were so horribly deformed by centuries of colonialism.

While direct colonialism may have ended in a formal sense, it continues in the form of Western puppets ruling Muslim societies. Thus, even while nominally independent, Muslim societies remain in bondage. Western colonial powers refuse to accept responsibility for their conduct and the manner in which they ravaged colonized societies. They insist that colonized people must accept Western cultural norms but refuse to treat them as equal. The five million Muslim French citizens lead marginalized and abused lives. They face racism and discrimination in employment, housing and education and constant harassment at the hands of the police. In 2005, this exploded into fury leading to several days of rioting. Muslim girls are banned from wearing the hijab in French schools since 2004 (no freedom there!).

The situation in other Western societies is hardly different. Additionally, they continue to attack in the most brutal manner Muslim majority societies killing hundreds of thousands of innocent people but insist their lives do not matter. These are mere "collateral damage." Drones continue to kill innocent people in Afghanistan, Pakistan, Yemen and Somalia. Western occupation forces remain in Afghanistan and are now re-entering Iraq. They are trying to find an excuse to attack Syria directly as well.

There is bound to be reaction against such racism and Islamophobia. Instead of blaming Muslims, rulers in the West should look inward and see what their policies have created: resentment among ordinary Muslims.

FRANCE'S WAVY LINE ON "FREE SPEECH"

Lawrence Davidson

On January 7th, two heavily armed men walked into the Paris offices of a satirical magazine called *Charlie Hebdo (Charlie Weekly)* and methodically murdered twelve people, including the magazine's editor Stephane Charbonnier (aka Charb), four cartoonists, a columnist, a proofreader, a maintenance worker, two policemen stationed inside the building, and one outside.

The killers were Muslim extremists associated with al-Qaeda, but their actions were praised by the Islamic State (also known as ISIS) as well. Almost everyone else, including most Muslim commentators, condemned the attack for the horrible crime it certainly was.

Why *Charlie Hebdo?* The immediate reason for the attack seems to have been the repeated satirization of the Prophet Mohammed in cartoons that were, to put it mildly, of questionable taste. Of course the magazine had satirized others as well but gave disproportionate attention to Muslims and their Prophet.

All of this was done under the cover of freedom of speech. As Charb said in a 2012 interview, "Our job is not to defend freedom of speech but without it we're dead. We can't live in a country without freedom of speech. I prefer to die than to live like a rat."

I think everyone with a progressive outlook can agree that freedom to criticize governments and other centers of power is an absolute necessity if we are to have a free society. But we must also recognize that the notion of unimpaired free speech is an ideal that is constantly approached and retreated from. In practice its limits tend to be culturally and politically determined. Further, when we move beyond the critique of power there are good arguments for the position that freedom of speech should be coupled with a promulgated definition of social responsibility.

It seems to me that Charb and his magazine had little concern for these issues and, by concentrating their ridicule on Muslims with occasional jabs at the Catholic Church, had accommodated themselves to France's selectively censored environment. Consider the following:

• *Charlie Hebdo* was founded in 1970 after its predecessor magazine, called the *Hara-Kiri Hebdo,* had been shut down by the French government. Why? It had insulted the memory of the then recently deceased Charles de Gaulle.

• If *Charlie Hebdo* had satirized the Jews in the same way it did the Muslims, its director and staff would have likely been hauled into court and charged with anti-Semitism, expressions of which are illegal in France.

• As the political scientist Anne Norton points out, while "casting itself as the defender of free speech … the Paris prosecutor's office is investigating [and subsequently has taken into custody] comedian Dieudonne M'bala M'bala for 'defending terrorism' after his Facebook post, 'I feel like Charlie Coulibaly.'" Coulibaly was the terrorist involved in the recent Paris violence against Jews.

Charbonnier and his fellows at *Charlie Hebdo* were aware of the first two facts. Thus, Charb was telling the truth when he said that the magazine was not defending free speech. He knew that the *Charlie Hebdo* approach would work only as long as its ridicule was seen as politically acceptable by both most French people and their government. Defaming national heroes or Jews was out of bounds, but ridiculing Muslims was and is acceptable, and maybe that is why they became *Charlie Hebdo's* preferred target. That, in turn, made the magazine's staff targets of Muslim extremists.

The Larger Context

Whatever Stephane Charbonnier's actual motives and aims, he and his fellow workers at *Charlie Hebdo* died in the course of promoting them. At that point their motives were co-opted by the French government in what was soon declared as a war of values. On January 10th, French Prime Minister Manuel Valls declared war against "radical Islam" because its practitioners had attacked "our values, which are universal."

That last claim is an example of French hubris getting in the way of reality. For better or worse, French values are definitely not universal. They are just another version of culturally determined practices which, in terms of speech, set the limits of what the powers-that-be find permissible. These limits may be broader than the ones promoted by Islamists but, as we have seen, they are not open-ended.

Nonetheless the illusion of universal values was used by Prime Minister Valls to rally his fellow citizens. On January 11th, a reported two million French men and women, with some forty world leaders (most notably half the Israeli cabinet) at their head, marched through Paris to protest the attack on *Charlie Hebdo*. It was said to have been the largest public rally France has seen since the liberation of Paris at the end of World War II.

Most of those who attended this historic rally probably knew little or nothing of the context of the crime they protested. And, while the magazine's demeaning cartoons might have been the immediate cause of the murders, they were certainly not the only cause. Prime Minister Valls publicly declared war just a few days ago, but in truth France has been acting as if it was at war with Muslims and their values for a very long time.

During their 130-year occupancy of Algeria, the French segregated most Muslims from European colonists and adopted policies that undermined the indigenous Arab lifestyle. Since then they haven't been very welcoming toward Muslim immigrants in France, insisting that they give up their traditional ways and integrate into French culture. However, as riots in 2005 suggested, very little effort has been made on the part of the French government or its people to accommodate such integration.

Finally, France has been promoting intervention in Syria. In an ill-advised effort to undermine the secular regime of Bashar al-Assad, French governments (all of which have had a misplaced and certainly racist sense of *mission civilisatrice* toward Syria) have helped finance and equip Syrian rebels. This threatens to be a repeat of the U.S. mistake made in Afghanistan back in the 1980s, because a good number of these Syrian rebels hate the French (and other Western powers) as much as they do al-Assad.

A Vicious Cycle

Under the present circumstances, and by this I mean given longstanding foreign policies of the Western powers, there is no end in sight for terrorist attacks such as that in Paris or, for that matter, in New York on Sept. 11th, 2001. They will come again and again because they are ripostes to even more violent actions coming from the West.

In other words, what we have going here is a vicious cycle. It began with modern imperialism and has been sustained by frankly counterproductive Western policies in the Muslim world—often in support of brutal Arab dictators and racist and expansionist Israelis. What goes around comes around.

This conclusion is usually dismissed by Western leaders as blaming the (Western) victims. However, to take this position one must ignore the myriad number of victims in the Middle East and North Africa. So, sadly, it really is a matter of which victims one gives priority to: the ones in the Twin Towers or the ones in Gaza; the ones in the offices of *Charlie Hebdo* or the ones killed by French-backed rebels in Syria.

Then there are the dead and injured members of the wedding parties that Western drones afflict with uncanny regularity; the million dead Iraqi civilians; the dead Afghan civilians; the victims of the French-promoted chaos in Libya. There are our victims and there are their victims. It is victims all around and everyone is out for revenge.

A Possible Way Out

Is there a way out of this vicious cycle—one that might also uphold a broad and truly universal standard for freedom of speech? Ideally, there is —it is called international law. This is not just any set of laws, but ones that reflect human and civil rights.

After World War II there were so many victims of war and terror that international laws and conventions were created to prevent, or at least ameliorate, the practices and policies that victimized millions of innocent people. Updated Geneva Conventions and the Universal Declaration of Human Rights (Article 19 of which supports a broad interpretation of freedom of speech) are examples of these efforts.

These are very good precedents which, in theory, have many endorsers among the world's nations. Unfortunately, their influence on practice has always been marginal and even that much has been waning. Particularly in the last fifty years these rules of behavior have been undermined by fading memories of the mid-Twentieth Century horrors that once made them seem so necessary.

In the place of those memories has come a resurgence of narrow-minded nationalism, delusional racism, outright bigotry, and increasingly unchecked instances of brutality. Some might say that is the true nature of human beings at work—their fallen nature. However, I don't believe this. The Geneva Conventions and Universal Declaration of Human Rights are every bit as much a product of human decision-making as are the criminal acts they seek to prevent.

So, ultimately, we have to ask what sort of a world we want to live in. If part of that answer is a world without terror attacks, then we have to honestly investigate why those attacks take place. And, if that investigation reveals (as it surely will) that Western popular ignorance and intolerance, and the governmental policies these conditions allow, have helped motivate those attacks, then it behooves us to reconsider our attitudes and actions and set new standards for our behavior. The progressive international laws and conventions cited above can serve us as good standards in such an effort.

Strangely, there may be a perverse correlation between how much blood is shed and our eventual moment of self-examination. It took two world wars to produce such documents as the Universal Declaration of Human Rights. How much blood has to be shed before we actually honor them?

"JE NE SAIS PAS QUI JE SUIS" :
MAKING SENSE OF TRAGEDIES LIKE THE CHARLIE HEBDO INCIDENT WHEN THE GOVERNMENT NARRATIVE DOESN'T MAKE SENSE

Cynthia McKinney

Abstract

This paper seeks to establish that for citizens to turn their bellicose state into one that espouses peace, they must be aware of the operation not only of their Public State, but also of their Deep State. Moreover, this paper establishes that The Deep State acts for reasons that are not always readily apparent and in ways that are not always apparently legal. On some occasions, The Deep State even acts in ways that could be considered treasonous. The Public State then lies to cover up the actions of The Deep State. Insightful citizens understand government lies, but may not be aware of the operation of The Deep State. This paper argues that in order for citizens to turn belligerent governments into peaceful ones, they must understand that a powerful clue has been emitted whenever the government narrative doesn't make sense. Therefore, under these circumstances, the patriotic act is disbelief of the government narrative thereby rendering the actions of The Deep State dysfunctional. Finally, this paper examines the Charlie Hebdo tragedy in light of past "Deep Events" that include the 1963 assassination of President John F. Kennedy and the 2005 London Bombing.

Charlie Hebdo Incident Details

According to a recent internet search, at least five major mainstream media outlets produced a timeline of the Charlie Hebdo events. On January 7th, the date of this murderous event, the Canadian Broadcasting Corporation (CBC) produced a timeline of events complete with a map and audio of an English-speaking witness.[265]

The CBC article includes that the gunmen shouted "Allahu Akbar" as they entered the Charlie Hebdo office. The *Telegraph* Newspaper in London and the *International Business Times* in New York City followed suit on January 8th with their timelines.

The *Guardian*, The *Independent*, *EuroNews*, and CNN all also published timelines. This is the most basic set of events in all of the timelines:

• Just before 11:30 a.m. a car arrives in front of the Charlie Hebdo office and two masked and hooded individuals get out. They are given access to the office by an employee just arriving for work.

• Just after 11:30 a.m. gunmen depart and engage in three police encounters that include gunfire and result in the death of one police officer lying on the ground. They carjack a car and make their getaway.

• By 2:00 that afternoon, the hashtag (#), "Je suis Charlie," had become a global social media trend.

Curiosities and Inconsistencies in the French Government Narrative Begin to Emerge

While Muslims all over the planet began to apologize for what had happened, already, citizen journalists and members of the global Truth Movement found inconsistencies in the details of the French Government's official narrative of the Charlie Hebdo events. At first, the video of the shooting of the police officer was blacked out. But later, un-blacked-out footage emerged that clearly showed that the police officer was not shot at all by the gunmen in the footage that had been circulated on most media websites. Even today, when we know that un-blacked-out footage exists and is widely available elsewhere, on the *International Business Times* website, the black-out video is labeled with a caution: "Graphic footage: Police officer shot by Paris gunmen."[266]

Paul Craig Roberts, Ph.D., former Assistant Treasury Secretary for Economic Policy under Republican President Ronald Reagan, was among the first to publish his own compilation of inconvenient findings in his column, "Suspicions are growing that the French shootings are a false flag operation" (the initial version of his essay for this book). Roberts noted that the effect of the tragic events was to bring France back into line after French President Hollande had spoken against Washington-inspired sanctions against Russia and to stop Europe's slide toward support of Palestinian aspirations for self-determination through a real and viable state. Roberts lists the following questions, originally raised by members of the Truth Movement, and unanswered by the official narrative:

A) The suicide of the police chief in charge of the Charlie Hebdo investigation;
B) Youtube's removal of the un-blacked-out video footage due to "shocking and disgusting content";

C) An analysis and display of the un-blacked-out video footage of the shooting of the police officer showing no blood, no recoil, no head fragments splattering.

On January 13th, Jonathan Cook, a prize-winning journalist based in Nazareth, cited the same un-blacked-out video as Roberts that seems to show that the police officer the French government and media say was shot in the head, was, in fact, not shot in the head. After reviewing the video, Cook drew two conclusions: that the authorities lied about the cause of the policeman's death and the media simply "regurgitated an official story that does not seem to fit the available evidence."[267]

On January 18th, 2015, the blog Panamza.com published an article that listed several inconsistencies. The article is entitled, "Fuite des terrorists de Charlie Hebdo: un trajet impossible."[268] This article describes the flight of the Charlie Hebdo attackers as "an impossible route." This story is based on yet another video showing their departure as one that contradicts the official narrative. Finally, addressing this thorny issue, Panamza reports that Paris's Chief Prosecutor, François Molins, at a press conference on January 9th, 2015 ascribed an impossible getaway route to the perpetrators.

It was reminiscent of the Warren Commission's Theory of the Magic Bullet that struck Texas Governor John Connally and killed President Kennedy, but was substantially unscathed when found on a hospital stretcher.

Utilizing Google Maps, members of the public are seeking to answer the question, "Which way did they go?"

On yet another citizen analysis blog, appears the following commentary: "I made an itinerary of the place where the first car was abandoned and the place where the attackers supposedly hijacked one of the witnesses. It is impossible. The witness lies."

On January 13th, 2015, Reuters published a video, republished by Panamza, that directly contradicted the official getaway version. In fact, the official getaway version caused more people, familiar with the neighborhood, to join the Charlie Hebdo Truth Movement.

Finally, there was the revelation—just a reminder, really—of a chance encounter between French President Sarkozy and Amedy Coulibaly, where the latter asked the former for a job and then years later terrorized a Kosher grocery store![269]

Making Sense of the Nonsensical: The Rise of The Truth Movement

In my lifetime, the Truth Movement began the day everyone in the government subscribed to "The Magic Bullet Theory" in the murder of President Kennedy. At that time, people who later impacted me deeply asked important questions of a government that was not forthcoming. For example, in 2013, I had the opportunity to interview Dr. Cyril Wecht, who investigated the President's autopsy report on behalf of the American Medical Association. He did not believe the official government narrative of what happened to President Kennedy after studying that report and did not believe it when I interviewed him fifty years later. Dr. Cyril Wecht became a member of the Truth Movement only after he had been entrusted to study important information as a result of many objections to the government's narrative. Dr. Wecht became a source of information and inspiration for many important others.

Inspection of the government's official narrative of the murder of Dr. Martin Luther King, Jr. also reveals certain anomalies that just don't add up. For example, a jury found in the 1999 trial that there was a government conspiracy to murder Dr. Martin Luther King, Jr., and that the order was given by Jesse Jackson to have the local armed group, The Invaders, to leave the Lorraine Motel only minutes before the assassination. In order to make sense of all of the puzzle pieces individually and as a whole, each bit of information must be put into perspective by devising a completely new way of looking at it, even questioning "conventional wisdom"—whatever that is.[270]

This questioning of conventional wisdom or even what is taken to be the prevailing "common sense" at the time is what can produce break-throughs in understanding. Like connecting the dots in that famous photograph of the Black person touching Dr. King on the balcony of the Lorraine Motel after he had been shot. According to testimony in the trial, that person was Merrell McCullough, then-Officer with the Memphis Police Department, and infiltrator of the group, The Invaders, later, at the time of the 1999 trial, employed by the Central Intelligence Agency (CIA).[271] Thus, yet another Truth Movement emerged around the murder of Dr. King. One of the popular street researchers in this area was Steve Cokely who proclaimed at one of his lectures that his job was to translate the tedious minutiae of the 1999 trial into people-speak so that the average ordinary person who was impacted by the murder of Dr. King could understand what had happened and why it mattered. Truth Warriors like Steve Cokely are never rewarded by the state—or for that matter, the public at large—and suffer like the whistleblowers that they are for their dedication to getting the truth out about these tragic events. At best, ignored by the special interest press, their daily labor is without recognition or award.

A powerful Truth Movement moment occurred when JFK researchers joined with MLK researchers and then began delving into the facts of two other important assassinations of the decade: Malcolm X and President Kennedy's brother, Robert Kennedy, who himself was poised to become the next President of the United States. The COINTELPRO Papers provided a treasure trove of information on the government's orchestrated attacks on peace activists during the Anti-Vietnam War era, as well as social movement activists working the streets of the U.S. for social and economic justice for African-Americans, Puerto Ricans, American Indians, Mexican-Americans and their supporters. The Church Committee went further and exposed assassination attempts on foreign leaders and the infiltration of every aspect of social, religious, and academic life by U.S. intelligence, including breaches of the U.S. Constitution.

After September 11th, 2001, all Members of Congress were told that we were hit because we were free and that we should tell that to our constituents. All over the U.S., Members of Congress dutifully repeated that official narrative. But not me. I couldn't stoop so low when I understood that the United States had invested trillions of dollars in an intelligence and military infrastructure that on one day failed four times— including at the Pentagon itself! September 11th, 2001 created a new generation of Truthers because the U.S. government's official narrative was so unbelievable. And as September 11th is the excuse for draconian legislation that snatches civil liberties from U.S. citizens and creates an illusion of support for U.S.-led wars all over the world, more and more people are heeding Paul Craig Roberts' plea to people to just use their brains and think.

The Truth Movement as a Complex Adaptive System

A complex adaptive system (CAS) is a type of human organization and activity that produces new leadership and new knowledge. Complexity Leadership Theory seeks to explain new ways of acquiring knowledge in the 21st century. Uhl-Bien calls it "shifting leadership from the industrial age to the knowledge era."[272] According to Uhl-Bien, leadership models in the past were top-down, but now, leadership is more organic, adaptive, and emergent. According to Uhl-Bien, leadership today takes place in a more interactive and dynamic context: the Complex Adaptive System. Actors within the CAS have common goals and common needs. The individuals inside the CAS are linked in a kind of social system where they "solve problems creatively and are able to learn and adapt quickly."[273]

I propose that The Truth Movement has become a complex adaptive system, brought into existence for the purpose of cutting through government lies on important and oftentimes tragic events. This Truth CAS seeks to make sense of the nonsense that has been put forward by The Public State and it produces new leaders who exercise a new kind of citizen leadership, not associated with position inside a bureaucracy or authority gained from a position. Thus, the members of the Truth CAS also represent something new: They are activated and empowered by the very fact that the Public State lies.

CAS adapt quickly to environmental conditions. Members of the CAS are interdependent and able to interact with each other and with the outside environment—in this case, the Public State. CAS also engage in a creative problem-solving process (trying to find the truth) which Uhl-Bien defines as annealing. This annealing is enhanced by interactions with a deceptive Public State that create the need for more creativity and more problem-solving. According to Uhl-Bien, "the annealing process does however find solutions that individuals, regardless of their authority or expertise, could not find alone."[274] According to Complexity Leadership Theory, this "knowledge movement" is more capable of producing innovations and advances far more rapidly than what emerges "from the isolated minds of individuals."[275] I suggest here that Truth Movements that arise as a result of government lies are, in essence, CAS that operate as knowledge movements. I also posit here that, not only are these movements inevitable as all of the people are not willing to drop their critical analytical skills at the threshold of government propaganda, but that these movements represent the exercise of citizenship and patriotism due to their demand for truth in governance and the return to rule of law. In other words, "you can fool some of the people all of the time and all of the people some of the time, but you can't fool all of the people all of the time." And thus, a Truth Movement CAS is born.

"Je ne suis pas Charlie; je suis Jean Charles de Menezes:" A London Execution on 7/7

After Jean Charles de Menezes was shot dead by three bullets to the head in a 2005 gross "mistake," an emotional officer apologized to the victim's family, according to The Telegraph.[276] However, that error did not stop Scotland Yard from spying on the grieving family members, as was disclosed by The *Daily Mail* on July 23rd, 2014.[277] According to Tom Cook, a Visiting Professor of Broadcast Journalism at Birmingham City University, "Britain's rights to basic freedom of expression which writers, journalists, and free speech activists fought for over centuries have been sacrificed and abandoned in the space of a few short disastrous years."[278]

Cook chronicles police hacking of journalists' e-mail, what he calls "fearful self-censorship," and creeping powers of the state that exhibit signs of authoritarianism.

The Deep State Reveals Itself

Peter Dale Scott, Ph.D. theorized The Deep State when researching certain U.S. events and popularized the concept in his eponymous book, *The American Deep State*. He noticed, when researching four Deep Events in U.S. history—the assassination of President Kennedy, Watergate, Iran-Contra, and 9/11—that the events all bore certain common characteristics. In the U.S. setting, these events all shared the fact of involvement of individuals who had access—either from the top or somewhere down the line—to the Continuity of Government (COG) apparatus for the United States. COG planning concerns itself with what happens in the U.S. when/if a catastrophic event takes place. Scott discovered that each of the investigated events were carried out by individuals who had access to this COG apparatus. Moreover, many of these events were carried out by the same individuals—whether they were in the government nominally or not! COG were the extreme measures that would be carried out even if they violated the Constitution because the Constitution would be suspended under this regime. Scott found that in the Iran-Contra scandal, the COG secret communications network was used to evade a Congressionally-mandated prohibition on the sale of weapons to Iran as well as financial support of the *Contras* who were, at that time, organized by the U.S. to fight the Sandinista government of Nicaragua, headed by Daniel Ortega. Scott explains that "a very small group had access to a high-level secret network outside government review, in order to implement a program in opposition to government policy."[279] The COG planning was begun decades ago by Dick Cheney and Donald Rumsfeld and, according to Scott, they implemented COG officially "for the first time" on 9/11/01.[280]

According to Scott's research, Iran-Contra and 9/11 were not the only Deep Events in which the U.S. government's secret communication channel was utilized. In fact, this particular feature characterizes the environment in which the assassination of President Kennedy, Watergate, Iran-Contra, and 9/11 took place. Scott highlights a powerful aspect of a Deep Event for the Truth Movement to research: the use of the government's secret communication channel. An important question for intrepid Charlie Hebdo truthers is whether or not any French government secret communications channels were activated prior to or during the Event.

Scott also identified three other characteristics of Deep Events that are worth bearing in mind as we digest the Charlie Hebdo tragedy: 1) a ready-made government explanation that is parroted by the press; 2) self-incriminating "evidence" implicating the "protected" individual(s) blamed by the government for causing or carrying out the tragedy; and 3) a small group of insiders able to control Deep Events and their aftermaths, including the narrative, the investigation, and the cover-up. Citizen journalists have been able to poke a considerable number of holes through the official French government narrative that has been expounded *ad nauseum* by the press. The fact that neither the government narrative nor the line of the parroting press change in spite of new and contradictory evidence is alarming to citizens who trust their critical analysis skills more than they trust the utterances of their own governments. Therefore, it should not be surprising that more and more video evidence eventually becomes available, "on the street" as it were, that does not conform to that official narrative. In the case of 9/11, the government still refuses to release photographic and video evidence that might contradict its official narrative, leaving citizens to speculate about government intentions as well as what else the government has lied about. With as little as a cell phone, or easily-available tools of social media—like Google Maps, for example —anyone can put their analytical skills to the test, record historic events, or deconstruct government propaganda. All of this aids the task of citizen activists and alternative journalists, who have discovered many holes in the official Charlie Hebdo story. I will now discuss just a few of those holes.

True to form, the ID card left behind in the vehicle is as curious a piece of government evidence as was the passport that refused to burn amid the rubble of New York's evaporated World Trade Center buildings. This ID card bolsters the French government's explanation of who did what on that fateful January day, but it also conforms to Scott's prediction that Deep Events will provide self-incriminating evidence for the named patsy(ies). In the case of the murder of President Kennedy, it was Lee Harvey Oswald's own U.S. intelligence activities, intended to bolster his persona as a pro-Cuban Communist, that became his undoing during his public scapegoating as the government's designated guilty party.

From *Paris Match*, we have the story of one of the last men to have seen *Charlie Hebdo* cartoonists Cabu and Wolinsky alive. He is a market stand owner in one part of town who sold newspapers to the cartoonists on the morning of their deaths, but who also just happened to be the same person who was in the same and distant part of town as the Kouachi brothers after their deadly attack. This market stand owner was reportedly told by the Kouachi brothers, "If the media ask you any questions, we are Al Qaeda Yemen."

A French citizen observer notes that while the much-celebrated identity card of Said Kouachi was found in their hijacked getaway car, the driver's license of Cherif Kouachi, Said's brother and accomplice, was also left behind in the very same car! But even more than that, this very same witness, the market stand owner, was the owner of the car hijacked by the Kouachi brothers to make their getaway out of Paris. And it was in this witness's car that the lost IDs were found! Yet another French citizen observer asks how could the market stand owner travel from one part of Paris to another so quickly and have such fortuitous encounters with both the *Charlie Hebdo* cartoonists as well as their killers in the same day, all within a matter of minutes.[281] Where is there no traffic at all at 11:30 in the morning in a major French city? The Eleventh Arrondissement in Paris is the most densely populated in the city—almost twice the density of Manhattan in New York City. How did the Kouachi brothers flee unimpeded against traffic in the most densely populated neighborhood in all of France?

Yet another "witness" by the name of "Eric," who lived next door to the Kouachi brothers, was interviewed by the press and was found to have known Wolinski "very well" and Cabu, "somewhat." This situation is similar to the 9/11 incident where an FBI informant actually lived with two of the alleged hijackers!

And then, we have the prior terror event in France involving an alleged terrorist (Merah) who happened to be an agent with France's now-disbanded anti-terrorism outfit.[282] The links between Al Qaeda, Islamic States (IS) also known as Da'esh, and the United States government are inconvenient, well-known, and not denied. They're just never mentioned in either the official narrative or that handed to us by the mainstream media. I label that media "the special interest media" so that it becomes patently clear whose interest that media serves—not the public's or the people's. In fact, the special interest media are part and parcel of The Deep State, which could not operate its deceptions without media complicity. As Jonathan Cook writes, "one would expect 'professional' journalism to respond by engaging with these concerns,"[283] but instead, professional journalists meet these inconvenient facts with either silence or ridicule for those raising them.

Critical information, such as David Headley's connection to U.S. intelligence in the Mumbai blast, is never mentioned and left to swirl only in the realm of the "coincidence evidence" cited by Truth Movements.[284] Likewise ignored is the inconvenient presence of war games or training exercises at the very moments of the September 11th hijackings and the disappearance of the Malaysian Airlines plane MH117 over the Pacific Ocean, as well as the London Tube bombing and the Boston Marathon Bombing.[285]

Mapping the route, questioning the accounts of the witnesses, studying publicly available video of the tragic events, remembering the magic passport and the connections to intelligence in previous recent terror tragedies are all activities of a healthy state investigation and a healthy media. This is exactly the kind of activity which, while unfortunately ignored by public institutions, thrives within a Truth Movement CAS. Truth Movements flung across our globe come together by way of social media and the internet, in the midst of the chaos of the moment, helping us unmask and understand what is actually going on. These Truth Movements, then, are our last great hope to thwart the plans of the Deep State and reassert citizen rights to governance that respects rule of law and the human rights of all, including environmental rights of nature that nurtures and sustains us all.

Unmasking the Deep State is the best way to thwart its accelerating merger with the Public State—a circumstance that could render the political process and the operation of the Public State irrelevant. If politics is the authoritative allocation of values in a society, then, in such a situation, the policies adopted by the Public State would bear no resemblance at all to the values of the citizens who elect it. Sadly, that is exactly the situation that many inside the U.S. Truth Movement describe. The peace movement largely agrees. Activists inside these movements believe that halting the global slide toward fascism is a matter of the political survival of the international rule of law and, in the U.S., of Constitutional governance. I agree with them. Therefore, there are hardly more important urgencies than this. While not necessarily embracing each others' causes, it is imperative that disparate groups coalesce for this particular cause. The Deep State operating under official color of the United States government once wrote that misdirecting the public was one of its chief aims. This objective was announced in the FBI's COINTELPRO papers. The people's continued division is the Deep State's victory.

Preventing the Merger of The Deep State and The Public State in Order to Make A Peace State

As a sitting Member of Congress, I was the first of 535 to demand an investigation of 9/11 and ask, "What did the Bush Administration know and when did it know it." That simple question, coming from me, was too much for our political system—or rather for The Deep State—to countenance. Thanks to Dr. Peter Dale Scott's important theoretical formulation, I can now make sense of the downward spiral that I was subjected to from all sides, including the hate message delivered over the public airwaves by a "journalist" who, at the time, was on the FBI payroll. The Deep State won as I was put out of office and replaced by someone who would reliably vote for war while hypocritically espousing "peace." The war machine rolls on, destroying individual lives and entire countries in its wake. My questions, almost fourteen years later, have never been officially answered. And still the events of 9/11 are used to justify every illegal U.S. policy from the wars against Iraq, Afghanistan and Pakistan, Somalia and Yemen, to the wars at home against the Bill of Rights and the U.S. Constitution. Yet it is only the Truth Movement that has come close in assessing what happened on that fateful day and the global consequences of its aftermath. Most of the current crop of Congresspersons know from my example that the Deep State is riddled with landmines of self-protection. Best to say nothing, do nothing, and know nothing—for any motion at all could set off a deadly device. And so, except for a few brave voices from unexpected places of power, Officialdom is no closer to understanding what happened on 11 September 2001 and how it happened than on that sorrow-filled day. However, for true peace, the world must know how September 11th came to happen and then engulfed it in war.

Our goal is peace. Yet there are powerful individuals with access to state power who thwart that goal. My personal formulation is that the bedrock foundation for peace lies in truth. For without truth, there can be no justice. And without justice, there can be no peace. Going further, without peace there can be no dignity for human beings or for the Earth that gives us life. In 1963, President John F. Kennedy spoke at the graduation ceremony of American University—and used the word "peace" over thirty times in a speech lasting less than thirty minutes. President Eisenhower, before Kennedy was sworn in as President, warned the people of the United States against the machinations of the Military-Industrial Complex. Today, that Complex has also absorbed Wall Street, which in turn has swallowed Congress and the media. Instead of turning back the Deep State, the people of the U.S. have allowed the Deep State to encroach further and further into the public sphere. Some of this is caused by the collaboration of activists inside the Truth Movement, knowingly or unknowingly, with the mechanisms of the Deep State. Yet, far more important is the fact of public lack of awareness of this aspect of governance. With access to illicit proceeds from drug trafficking and other illegal activities, the Deep State of the U.S. has almost unlimited funds with which to co-opt and corrupt officials in the Public State all over the world.

Jonathan Cook concludes that "We have to trust that the officials haven't lied to the journalists and that the journalists haven't misled us. And yet there are no grounds for that trust apart from blind faith that our officials are honest and not self-interested, and that our journalists are competent and independent-minded."[286] I agree with him. And part of the importance of Scott's research is how he demonstrates that a very small group of insiders can implement a program "in opposition to government policy." I do believe that the other side of that coin is also operative: that is, that a very small group of courageous insiders or individuals like the activists who broke into the FBI office in order to expose the excesses of COINTELPRO, can make a huge difference in saving our government from its current cabal of controllers.

I encourage the Truth Movements around the world to continue their brave questioning of official narratives that seem ready-made in the face of tragedies. While I have nothing to offer them except the knowledge that there is life after whistleblowing, whistleblowers even while suffering greatly under the Administration of President Barack Obama must continue to act on their consciences—and we must support them in every way that we can. For, today, we are on the path of a fusion between the Deep State and the Public State.

If we are successful, we will be able, finally, to stop the wars and the immobilizing madness of hatred and division and place the U.S. squarely on the path of truth, reconciliation, and peace. If the Deep State is able to beat back our truth and knowledge movements, I shudder to even contemplate what our future holds.

JE SUIS SÉMITE! (I AM SEMITIC)

Ibrahim Soudy, introduction by Kevin Barrett

In the wake of the Charlie Hebdo affair, the French government is defending free speech by cracking down on . . . .free speech. As National Public Radio reports, "scores have . . . been arrested for condoning terrorism and inciting racial and religious hatred."[287] Virtually all of those arrested have either been Arabs or Muslims themselves, or people who support the Arab-Muslim cause.

Many victims of the French crackdown have been charged with anti-Semitism. Dieudonné Mbala-Mbala, the well-known comedian, was arrested and fined 30,000 euros for joking that he has been hounded so much that he feels like a terrorist. His persecutors have called the comedian "anti-Semitic" for defending Semites against Zionism—a movement led by non-Semites, namely Jews of European, not Semitic, background.

George Orwell must be rolling over in his grave. Those who defend Semites are called "anti-Semitic"; while those who invade, occupy, rob, mass-murder, and ethnically-cleanse Semites must never, ever be criticized, because anyone who dares speak out will be attacked as an anti-Semite.

It is long past time to drop this Orwellian use of the term anti-Semite. All of us who have some claim to being called Semites—along with everyone who supports the real Semites in their legitimate self-defense against the faux-Semite invaders, occupiers, robbers, mass-murderers, and ethnic-cleansers—must stand up and proudly declare: JE SUIS SÉMITE!

Yes, I too am a Semite, even though I have no discernible Middle Eastern ancestry.

The word Semitic refers to a group of Middle Eastern languages, and secondarily to people who speak those languages. By far the most prominent living Semitic language is Arabic, which is the first language of nearly 200 million people, and a second language of more than a billion non-Arab Muslims.

I speak Arabic. I watch TV news in Arabic and read Arabic newspapers. I read the Qur'an, in Arabic, every day. I have taught Arabic at the University of Wisconsin-Madison (where I was once attacked as an anti-Semite, and issued an official letter of reprimand by the administration, simply for writing a letter to the editor defending the Palestinians). That gives me more Semitic credentials than any European or American Jew who does not speak a Semitic language.

Admittedly, I am of European ancestry—just like the European Jews who claim to be victims of "anti-Semitism." (My ancestors were mostly from Western Europe, while theirs were from Eastern Europe.) Genetically, I am no more closely related to the historically Semitic-speaking peoples than are the Ashkenazi Jews. But my wife is a native speaker of Arabic, which would make my children half-Semites, biologically speaking. So I have the family ties, as well as the language. I'm a Semite through and through.

Well, sort of.

But enough about me. Let's hear from someone whose claims to Semitism are even more impeccable than mine.

Je Suis Sémite: Jews, Stop Being Anti-Semitic and Tell the World to Stop Using the term "Anti-Semitism"!

By. Ibrahim Soudy, PhD, PE, SE, P.Eng.

The vast majority of Jews use the term *anti-Semitism* very effectively to attack anyone who would dare criticize anything related to THEM. Talk all you want about how many Jews are Nobel Laureates or how Jews make good doctors, lawyers, and merchants and they will not want you to stop. But say that AIPAC is manipulating US foreign policy to the advantage of Israel and you will very quickly be called "anti-Semitic"; you might even lose your job and career altogether. Just ask Helen Thomas, who remained White House correspondent for decades till she said something that some Jews thought went too far. So much for freedom of speech!

Let me tell you something: Jews who use the term "anti-Semitism" are arrogant, racist, bigoted, and anti-Semitic THEMSELVES. Did you read what I just wrote?! Let me say it again, Jews who use the term "anti-Semitism" are arrogant, racist, bigoted, and anti-Semitic THEMSELVES. Non-Jews who use the term are simply IGNORANT people who do not pay attention to the words they say or do not even know what they mean. Let's start by examining how the term is used and its origins.

Open a dictionary or an encyclopedia and search for the term anti-Semitism and here is a sample of what you will find (notice what I underlined):

> **anti-Semitism:** Hostility toward or discrimination against Jews as a religious or racial group. The term *anti-Semitism* was coined in 1879 by the German agitator Wilhelm Marr to designate the anti-Jewish campaigns under way in central Europe at that time. Although the term now has wide currency, it is a misnomer, since it implies a discrimination against all Semites. Arabs and other peoples are also Semites, and yet they are not the targets of anti-Semitism as it is usually understood. The term is especially inappropriate as a label for the anti-Jewish prejudices, statements, or actions of Arabs or other Semites. Nazi anti-Semitism, which culminated in the Holocaust, had a racist dimension in that it targeted Jews because of their supposed biological characteristics—even those who had themselves converted to other religions or whose parents

were converts. This variety of anti-Jewish racism dates only to the emergence of so-called 'scientific racism' in the 19th century and is different in nature from earlier anti-Jewish prejudices.[288]

Anti Semitism: Not etymologically restricted to anti-Jewish theories, actions, or policies, but almost always used in this sense. Those who object to the inaccuracy of the term might try Hermann Adler's Judaeophobia (1882).[289]

Anti-Semitism Has its origin in the ethnological theory that the Jews, as Semites, are entirely different from the Aryan, or Indo-European, populations and can never be amalgamated with them. The word implies that the Jews are not opposed on account of their religion, but on account of their racial characteristics. As such are mentioned: greed, a special aptitude for money-making, aversion to hard work, clannishness and obtrusiveness, lack of social tact, and especially of patriotism. Finally, the term is used to justify resentment for every crime or objectionable act committed by any individual Jew.

Its recent origin is proved by the fact that David Kaufmann, in 1874, speaks of the ethnic theory of Semitism as "allerneueste Weisheit" ("Magazin für die Literatur des Auslandes," 1874, No. 44), and Ludwig Bamberger, in his essay, "Deutschtum u. Judentum ("Unsere Zeit," 1880, i. 194), says, "The war-cry against the Semites is, as the word indicates, of very recent date." In his memoirs, too, referring to 1858 or shortly before, Bamberger says that the word "Semitism" had not then been invented ("Erinnerungen," ii. 311, Berlin, 1899). In February, 1881, a correspondent of the "Allgemeine Zeitung des Judenthums" speaks of "Anti-Semitism" as a designation which recently came into use ("Allg. Zeit. d. Jud." 1881, p. 138). On July 19, 1882, the editor says, "This quite recent Anti-Semitism is hardly three years old" (*ib.* 1882, p. 489). So far as can be ascertained, the word was first printed in 1880. In that year W. Marr published "Zwanglose Antisemitische Hefte," and Wilhelm Scherer used the term "Antisemiten" in the "Neue Freie Presse" of January."

It is, however, impossible to trace with certainty the first use of the word. It does not appear to have been coined before the end of the seventies, when the German empire entered upon a course widely different from its former policy. The nature of the word implies the preexistence of the word and idea of Semitism, which has itself a history that must be traced. August Ludwig von Schlüzer (1735-1809) and Johann Gottfried Eichhorn (1752-1827), both professors in Göttingen, were the first to use the term "Semitic nations" (Eichhorn, "Historisch-Kritische Einleitung in das Alte Testament," 2d ed., 1787, p. 45; *idem,* "Repertorium," 1781, i. 61; "Ausland," 1872, p. 1034) in a philological sense; but the ethnical distinctness of Semitic nations was not a generally accepted theory until Franz Bopp (1791-1867), in his "Comparative Grammar" (1833-52), had created the correlative term of "Indo-Germanic languages," called by the French school "Indo-

European," and by the English "Aryan." What was originally a merely linguistic term soon became an ethnical designation based on the results of comparative philology. The first who attempted to draw a picture of the ethnical character of the Semites as contradistinguished from the Aryans seems to have been Christian Lassen (1800-76), professor at Bonn, who, in his "Indische Altertumskunde," Bonn, 1844-61, i. 414, says:

> Civilization has been the gift of but a few nations. Of other races only Egyptians and Chinese, and of the Caucasian only Semites and Aryans, have built up human civilization. History proves that Semites do not possess the harmony of psychical forces which distinguishes the Aryans. The Semite is selfish and exclusive. He possesses a sharp intellect which enables him to make use of the opportunities created by others, as we find it in the history of the Phenicians and, later on, of the Arabs.[290]

You see, using the term exclusively for "Jews" is equivalent to telling all other Semites that they do NOT exist or exist but do not matter. Can you imagine a bigger insult? The other Semites are the people who speak any of the following languages "Arabic, Aramaic, Amharic, or Syriac." In other words, there are more Semites in Cairo, Egypt alone than there are Jews in the whole world!!

As a Semite myself, I do exist and I do matter and I do not accept at all the use of the term exclusively when people mean to refer to Jews. It is about time for the Jews to stop being the most ANTISEMITIC people in the world.

JE SUIS CONFUSED

Yvonne Ridley

For weeks after the horrific killings of the Charlie Hebdo staff, headlines around the world were dominated by fallout from the incident. In truth, though, each day left me more confused about France's position on free speech, which we are all being led to believe can be used and abused without restriction.

Defending their position on attacking Prophet Muhammad, peace be upon him, white French intellectuals insist that they attack every single religion without fear or favour; and with impunity. It then emerged that Maurice Sinet, aged 80, who works under the pen name Siné, faces charges of "inciting racial hatred" over a column he wrote in Charlie Hebdo.

The piece ignited a debate among the Parisian intelligentsia and ended in the dismissal of the left-wing cartoonist who has since been charged with anti-Semitism for suggesting that Jean Sarkozy, the son of the former French president, was converting to Judaism for financial reasons. With obvious hindsight, being sacked probably saved Sinet's life.

Meanwhile, as more than a million people rallied in Paris in support of the magazine, many holding placards with the Twitter hashtag #JeSuisCharlie, world leaders also joined hands and marched at their head; or so we were told. Some of the political big names who took part were British Prime Minister David Cameron, German Chancellor Angela Merkel, Spanish Prime Minister Mariano Rajoy, Malian President Ibrahim Boubacar Keïta, Palestinian leader Mahmoud Abbas and former French President Nicolas Sarkozy. It has emerged since, however, that most of them gathered in Boulevard Voltaire with the victims' families, and the road was then sealed off. The leaders' "protest march" was a photo opportunity in a well-guarded, near-empty street.

Israeli leader Benjamin Netanyahu was also there despite presiding a few months earlier over a war against the people of Gaza in which seventeen journalists were killed by his soldiers; hardly an act by a state whose prime minister went to Paris to promote free speech. Marching near him was a representative of Saudi Arabia who kept silent about the plight of Raif Badawi; the imprisoned blogger had by then already received the first 50 of 1,000 lashes, part of his punishment for running a liberal website devoted to, er, yes, you've guessed it, freedom of speech in the kingdom.

The day after the rally we heard that Netanyahu was demanding an apology from the London-based *Sunday Times* for a cartoon by Gerald

Scarfe which was published in the Murdoch-owned newspaper. It depicted the Zionist leader as a bricklayer cementing Palestinians into a wall using blood red cement; Scarfe's work is brutal, bloody and brilliant when it comes to satire, and it has appeared in the paper every week since 1967.

Accusations that the cartoon was anti-Semitic are nonsense. It didn't mock Judaism, target Jews or depict the object of its attack with any religious symbolism at all. Nevertheless, the drawing exposed just how sensitive Israel and Netanyahu are when it comes to satire and free speech. Rupert Murdoch called the cartoon "offensive and grotesque" and then apologized for the caricature. The media mogul made his apology days after sending out an unrelated tweet attacking the world's 1.8 billion Muslims and inferring that we are all somehow to blame for the horrific killings at Charlie Hebdo and the kosher supermarket which was also attacked a couple of days later.

Back in London, just hours after marching alongside Netanyahu in Paris in the name of liberté and a good photo opportunity, David Cameron was helping to revive the Snooper's Charter. It seems that the prime minister will only support free speech when it can be accessed and reviewed by the state security services.

While all of this was going on, back in France "anti-Semitic" comedian Dieudonné M'Bala M'Bala was arrested after he appeared to compare himself with one of the armed gunmen who murdered four people at the Jewish supermarket in Paris. After mocking the media superlatives scattered about liberally to describe the #JeSuisCharlie march, the comedian declared, "As for me, I feel I am Charlie Coulibaly." He was referring to Amedy Coulibaly, the man who took hostages and killed people in the supermarket before being killed himself by police officers. The French police say that M'Bala could face charges of making an "apology for terrorism" and state prosecutors opened a formal investigation on Monday night into remarks he made on his Facebook page. What he said was, in my opinion, in poor taste and showed a distinct lack of judgement; which just about sums up my feelings about the cartoons in the latest issue of Charlie Hebdo.

After the killings, the circulation of the "satirical" magazine soared to around five million copies in a number of languages, including English and Arabic. It is being funded by donations from other media organizations, including Britain's Guardian Newspaper Group, and the French government. This would be unthinkable for the British Private Eye, which is merciless in lampooning the government and any public figures which enter its crosshairs.

As for free speech in America, some confuse that with pure invention, like daft Steven Emerson. The so-called terrorism expert on the right-wing Fox News channel claimed that Birmingham, Britain's second largest city, is "a totally Muslim" city "where non-Muslims just simply don't go." The discussion, on the back of the Paris killings, was about supposed no-go zones in Europe where Muslims are apparently in complete control. More apologies followed.

While the Parisian deaths are indeed a tragedy, no one mentions the former French colony of Syria where dozens of innocent civilians are killed every hour at the hands of the brutal Bashar Al-Assad regime. Not to be outdone—and to cap it all—Assad joined in with some crocodile tears of his own along with a few double standards and a liberal dose of hypocrisy when he extended his sympathy to the people of France. "We are against the killing of innocent people anywhere in the world," he said without a hint of irony. "At the same time, we want to remind people in the West that we have been talking about such consequences since the beginning of the Syrian crisis."

More than 200,000 people have been killed since a rebellion against the Assad family's four-decade rule began in March 2011, triggering a brutal crackdown that is tearing the country apart. Bashar Al-Assad made his statement in an interview with Czech publication Literarni Noviny. Some might call his interview the ultimate in satirical journalism.

After all of this, the issue of freedom of speech is, I'm afraid, still as clear as mud. Je suis definitely confused.

MODERN ISRAELI GENESIS

Barry Chamish

Editor's note: On February 24th, 2015, Barry Chamish interviewed me for his radio show.[291] During the interview, he volunteered to contribute an article to this book. The article he submitted, "Modern Israeli Genesis," does not explicitly refer to the Charlie Hebdo shootings. So in order to help the reader understand what Barry is getting at, I have prepared a transcript of some of his remarks during that interview.

Barry Chamish (remarks made during 2/24/15 interview with Kevin Barrett)

Well, I read your stuff, and by the way, I've got the same suspicions (that the Charlie Hebdo affair was a false flag). I'm not sure if it's the same conclusions. But I certainly share the suspicions.

The perpetrator, Said Kouachi, left his wallet in the getaway car. What does that say to you?

. . . There's plenty fishy about this . . . The fact that that wallet was in the stolen getaway car shows (quoting from Barrett's article) that he (Kouachi) was an "innocent patsy framed by the real perpetrators."

I want to make one point. I've got to work out how to write this. (I think) the real Charlie Hebdo victims were the Jews. And without diving into it, because you don't know, Zionism is very divided, there are good guys and bad guys. And labor Zionism is the bad guy. For me to write this won't be simple.

Like if he isn't busy enough, the Prime Minister of Israel, Benjamin Netanyahu, was in France the next day after a synagogue was hit and four Jews killed. Now same thing in Denmark. No, in France it was a Jewish grocery store, in Denmark a synagogue. It doesn't matter. There's always a Jewish tie. And it's a lot of effort to go to to prepare a Jewish tie. But every time . . . two in a row anyways. And not just those two. It goes back further. And it bothers me a whole heck of a lot . . .

Netanyahu showed up with a magic message at the funeral. Actually it was at the synagogue, where he invited all French Jews to emigrate to Israel. Now, most Jews don't want to leave. They'll wait it out if they can. Well, he considers them stupid. But most potential migrants are going to the United States, they're not going to Israel. But he was there, giving that message. It bothered me a whole lot. It didn't look good. It really didn't . . . You have to understand, Israel's losing population—an awful lot to the (United) States. You have a few attacks in France, Denmark—Denmark's minor, 12,000 Jews. France has got 450,000. You can repopulate your country...*if it works*. Okay? I'm not saying—It's looking like it's not going to work terribly well. But if that's the idea . . . there's a background to this.

MODERN ISRAELI GENESIS

by Barry Chamish

Israel: How much longer can I live in truth by living a lie? If Israel is to survive, we need an immediate survival manifesto, one that somehow we can all objectively accept. Here is the genesis of our nation forming, as simple as any two year old can buy into. Believe me, I'm simplifying our dreadful recent past but twenty-two year olds on are hiding from it. They can't much longer.

In 1933, Chaim Arlozorov was the negotiator of a treaty with the Nazis called The Transfer Agreement. So immoral was this agreement with thugs that Arlozorov was murdered, a crime never solved, but which a few Right Wing innocent Jews were briefly arrested for. This was just enough time to throw the right and religious out of the Jewish Agency, the unofficial Jewish leadership of Palestine, and ultimately send the European Jews to their doom on the too famous Ships Of Fools.

Less than 1% of the German Jews supported Zionism. Many later tried to escape from Naziism by boat to Latin and North American ports but the international diplomatic order was to turn them back. Any German Jew who rejected Palestine as his shelter would be shipped back to his death.

By 1934, some German Jews got the message and turned to the only Jewish organization allowed by the Nazis, the Labour Zionists. For confirmation of the conspiracy between them and Hitler's thugs read *The Transfer Agreement* by Edwin Black, or *Perfidy* by Ben Hecht. The deal cut worked like this. The German Jews would first be indoctrinated into Bolshevism in Labour Zionism camps and then, with British approval, transferred to Palestine. Most were there by the time the British issued the White Paper banning further Jewish immigration. The Labour Zionists got the Jews they wanted, and let the millions of religious Jews and other non-Labour Zionists perish in Europe without any struggle for their survival.

By 1935, the head of the Jewish Agency, Chaim Weizmann, was bragging about what was coming up for Europe's Jews: "An upcoming Holocaust will devastate Europe's Jews. Perhaps only 2 million will survive. But they will be strong and good for Palestine."

But Weizmann was very wrong. Wherever the Nazis conquered, about 100,000 Jews survived and six million were slaughtered. This opposed his sick calculations and there was no way to create a nation or an army without people. Desperate for cannon fodder, the Labor Zionists stirred up the same anti-semitism in nearby nations. From Morocco to Yemen, vicious attacks were launched against Jews but with a difference; Israel sent "wings of eagles," to every Middle East nation to ship the hapless Jews to Israel.

Now why would the leaders of the Mid-East agree to create an armed enemy? Fine, they got their assets. Sure, greedy leaders bought into that deal. Now blind Jews, look at the nightmare that was done to to EVERY single Sephardic child to have them shipped to the new nation of Israel. Look at the big picture:

Ringworm Children: https://www.youtube.com/watch?v=8nsOpLcSDFo

In the '50s, a young psychopath, Shimon Peres, chief of the Israeli Atomic Energy Commission, offered a whole race, Sephardim Jews, as guinea pigs to be blasted with massive doses of x-rays through their brains in exchange for nuclear secrets. I vowed not to delve into my research this time, but I worked personally with the spokesmen for 4500 kidnapped Yemenite kids and/or the other 110,000 Sephardic children, And I won't this time. But...

OH GOD!!!

As for the delusions of Palestinians: In 1844 the Ottomans, and in 1862 the British, conducted censuses showing Jews the majority of such major centers as Jerusalem, Haifa, Tsfat and Tiberius. After 1918, when the British job opportunities lured Arabs from throughout the Middle East to Palestine, which nearly doubled Palestinian population, the conflict began in earnest. But you Arabs face your own truth, if you're mature enough. I have profound doubts that you are. But do your best.

Meanwhile, our truth ain't so hot. I was on Bill Deagle's radio show recently and we discussed American and Israeli creation of ISIS and today's war throughout the Middle East. I quoted an Israeli source:

> This appeared to contradict a fact which Israel has kept very dark: The Syrian rebel offensive to wrest Quneitra would have stood no chance without Israel's aid—not just in medical care for their injured, but also in limited supplies of arms, intelligence and food. Israel acted as a member, along with the US and Jordan, of a support system for rebel groups fighting in southern Syria. Their efforts are coordinated through a war-room which the Pentagon established last year near Amman.

The US, Jordanian and Israeli officers manning the facility determine in consultation which rebel factions are provided with reinforcements from the special training camps run for Syrian rebels in Jordan, and which will receive arms.[292]

Bill told me, "We call it after a chain store, 'Terrorists Are Us.'"
I told him, "No Bill. We call it, 'Goys Are Us.'."

CHARLIE HEBDO AND THE MANIPULATIVE MEDIA MASTERS

Ashahed M. Muhammad

Mainstream media narratives must be challenged at every opportunity. Daily, we receive misleading reports fashioned by manipulative media masters containing spurious claims: propagandized "truths" coming from so-called "authoritative" media outlets. There are numerous examples in which the deceptive influence of those media controllers swiftly and successfully moved entire nations to action based on information later proven to be false.

I am an investigative journalist. I take on taboo topics. I challenge accepted truths. I am not afraid to ask the difficult questions, even if it makes some feel uncomfortable. This also involves challenging time-honored versions of historical events since I believe they should be revised as new data becomes available or is revealed. To me, this seems to be the best way to ensure accuracy.

That is something altogether different from definitively declaring something a False Flag Operation straight out the gate. False Flag Operations are covert campaigns designed to deceive the public and conceal the true intentions and identities of those responsible for a particular event or crime. Typically, atrocities (or crimes) committed by military or security forces are blamed on terrorists in order to justify or aid in promoting an agenda that is not readily apparent. Governments throughout history have used such tactics to sway elections, to aid in the establishment or furtherance of foreign or domestic policies, and to take nations to war.

Was Charlie Hebdo a false flag operation? I don't know. It often takes decades before it can definitively be declared that something was in fact a false flag operation. Sources must be cross-referenced, dots need to be connected, and there must be a gathering of all available facts.

Keep in mind that there is something known as circumstantial evidence. Circumstantial evidence is very valid, and in many cases can be used to reach a conclusion.

I saw the video, which lacked the presence of blood and brains, when French Muslim Ahmed Merabet was shown being shot with a high-powered rifle, reportedly by one of the gunmen. I questioned the likelihood of a "highly trained assassin" leaving behind his national identification card in a getaway vehicle, especially if he went through such great lengths to conceal his identity by wearing a mask. It certainly sounded strange to me, and obviously, many others found it strange as well. I had also wondered where their desire to "die as martyrs"—which was so reliably reported by the mainstream media—came from.[293] Such a convenient and tidy narrative; especially since they were both killed before being able to speak for themselves.

Whether it was a false flag operation or not, the events surrounding the Charlie Hebdo deaths cannot be viewed properly unless viewed comprehensively in terms of their aftermath. We are witnessing a severe and heavy-handed crackdown on Muslims and an increasingly hostile and xenophobic climate has been created for followers of Islam in Western Europe.

I watched the hypocritical show of "unity" between world leaders locked arm in arm January 11th in the streets of Paris. Incidentally, the advocacy group Reporters Without Borders criticized the presence of leaders who severely restrict press freedoms in their own lands. In fact, they referred to them as "representatives of regimes that are predators of press freedom." Egypt is ranked 159th out of 180 countries in RWB's press freedom index, Russia, 148th, Turkey, 154th, and the United Arab Emirates, 118th. All were represented at the Paris march.

And then there was the odious presence of Israeli Prime Minister Benjamin Netanyahu, who elbowed his way to a forward and visible position on the day of the rally. In my view—and in the view of many others—he is a war criminal. Did you know that seventeen journalists were killed in Gaza during their merciless bombing campaign in the summer of 2014?[294] Killing journalists and media personnel is a violation of international law.

While it was clear there was a large groundswell of support after the Charlie Hebdo incident, I wasn't surprised when the photographed image beamed across the globe of the so-called "courageous world leaders" was revealed to have been a staged public relations photo op.[295] No one should be surprised when politicians use emotional ploys and tragedy to polish their image and capitalize on events. President François Hollande's approval ratings have in fact jumped from historic lows hovering in the mid to upper teens at the end of 2014, to 40 percent as of January 19. Presumably, the nation has come together in a show of solidarity in the aftermath of the attacks.

When Lutz Bachmann, a prominent leader within Germany's intensifying anti-Islam movement posted a picture of himself on Facebook styled as Adolph Hitler, it was met with scorn and derision. The public relations gaffe resulted in him being forced to resign from his position as leader of PEGIDA (Patriotische Europäer Gegen die Islamisierung des Abendlandes, or Patriotic Europeans Against the

Islamization of the West), an organization he co-founded in October 2014.

Despite being what writers from Der Spiegel classified as "a collection of right-wing rogues," the group rapidly expanded their presence by holding weekly marches protesting what they declared to be "the Islamization of the West," and appealing to working middle class German citizens fearful of the influx of Muslims and other immigrants. PEGIDA's largest march reportedly drew nearly 25,000 to Dresden, a metropolitan area serving as a cultural and political center with a population of 2.4 million.

In France, Marine Le Pen is the right wing's most visible and influential figure. The National Front (NF), which she leads, currently holds 24 of 74 seats in France's European Parliament. Le Pen wrote an op-ed appearing in the New York Times making it clear that in her view, the problem is Islam and "massive waves of immigration, both legal and clandestine."[296]

"Let us call things by their rightful names, since the French government seems reluctant to do so. France, land of human rights and freedoms, was attacked on its own soil by a totalitarian ideology: Islamic fundamentalism. It is only by refusing to be in denial, by looking the enemy in the eye, that one can avoid conflating issues," Le Pen wrote.

The Charlie Hebdo incident—while throwing France into a state of fear and instability—may have in fact boosted Le Pen's chances of becoming president when French elections are held in 2017. French polling data late last year actually had NF leader Le Pen beating Hollande 54-46 percent.

In the meantime, everyday life has been disrupted for many Muslims in France, Germany, the United Kingdom, and other European nations such as Belgium. Anti-terrorism tactical officers are rounding up activists while mosques and gathering places frequented by followers of Islam have been threatened and attacked.

The decision by Charlie Hebdo to publish what is being called the "Survivor's Edition" and reprinting offensive depictions of Prophet Muhammad, predictably caused another wave of anger in Muslim lands, and in a strange twist, the popular French comedian Dieudonné was arrested for exercising his right to freedom of speech and expression in a Facebook posting that was viciously mischaracterized as "incitement of terrorism" or "defending and glorifying terrorism." Reportedly dozens— including four minors—were arrested and or detained on similar charges.[297] A clear double standard and an example of selective enforcement.

For very good reasons, some topics are considered "taboo" or "off limits" and it is understood that for your own good, you might want to carefully consider your words and actions because your words and actions will generate an immediate and powerful response. There are consequences for all spoken and written words. There are consequences for all actions. This is a Universal Law, the Law of Cause and Effect.

Considering questioning any aspect of The Holocaust in spoken or written form? Prepare to be targeted, dehumanized, disrespected, and a climate will be created which could ultimately lead to your physical harm. I have seen it. Elderly Jews who can barely walk will stand up, shout, and aggressively respond to whoever is speaking, whether it is in a public place or a controlled environment. The topic is painful for them and considered "taboo" or "off limits" as far as they are concerned.

This is clearly an example of political favoritism easily observable by all fair-minded and clear thinking individuals.

Whether it is in media, politics, academia, or social activism, the world is bullied into compulsory obedience by the muscular Israel first lobby. It has proven to be an effective strategy for decades.

As we've seen in America and with Charlie Hebdo, there are no particular sensitivity considerations when dealing with Muslims. The staff members of Charlie Hebdo—and many Islamophobic opinion shapers in Europe and America—have an intense and deeply ingrained hatred of Islam and Muslims. They are using the noble sounding principles of freedom of speech and freedom of expression as crafty covers to express and spread that hatred.

According to the Pew Research Center's Forum on Religion and Public Life, there are over 4.1 million Muslims in Germany outnumbered in Europe only by France, with 4.7 million. It is estimated that by 2030, Germany will have over 5.5 billion Muslims and in France, over 6.8 million. The United Kingdom has 2.8 million Muslims, projected to grow to over 5.5 billion by 2030.

Looming demographic threats always seem to torment those who have used their power and influence to exploit others. They seem to fear retaliatory justice caused by their own malevolent words and actions.

COPENHAGEN FALSE FLAG:
SEQUEL TO CHARLIE HEBDO?

Ole Dammegard

An edited transcript of interviews with Ole Dammegard conducted on March 11th and 16th, 2015, concerning the reported shootings in Copenhagen on February 14th–15th, 2015.[298]

Ole, what have you discovered about what really happened in Copenhagen?

Well, I have spent thirty years looking into false flag operations and major assassinations, acts of terror, so-called acts of terror. And in early January I came across what seemed to be a possible agenda that they were carrying out. When I say "they" I mean the power structure behind the New World Order. And it seemed like they were aiming at Dublin first, then Paris, then Copenhagen, and then Italy.

When I first heard about that, I didn't take it seriously. But then there was a bomb scare at the Irish Intel plant just outside Dublin. That, as far as I know, was defused. Nothing happened. But ISIS took responsibility. I'm sure most of your listeners know that ISIS is not what people think it is. It's just an upgrade of al-Qaeda; it's a hoax, a total hoax.

And I would also suggest that these false flag operations are being carried out by the same team that's being transported from country to country. So people are running around in police uniforms looking very official in Paris, might very well be the same people running around in police uniforms in the streets of Sydney or Ottawa or Copenhagen. If you look at the normal way they do these things, they would be transported in military planes, landing on military bases, and then be transferred from there to the site of the false flag. So people living nearby air bases, especially US air bases or NATO air bases, please be observant of vehicles, maybe busloads of people. If you see them, film them. Take photos. Upload them. They might be very important.

I spent a lot of time working as an extra on film sets. I spent many hours in the background, just sitting and waiting. So I've had a lot of time to see from the inside how they set these things up. And when it comes to false flag operations nowadays, many of them are just film sets. They're filmed events that are there for media, to be pumped out by media to create this reaction from us, this freak-out—"oh my God, we need to be saved"—so that they can serve us the solution. And the solution, every single time, is something we would not have accepted had it not been for the problem they themselves created.

And they love to repeat the same dates, for some reason. There's a ritualistic thing with that. Also, they're very aware of the location, the names of the streets, the area. When you look into sites where somebody was assassinated, often it will be an old place where they used to execute people, or a freemasonry site, and so on.

Let's just go quickly through the official story of the Copenhagen attack, and then get into the details (that contradict it). The official story is that there was a meeting at a cultural cafe in central Copenhagen. It went under the title of "Art, Blasphemy, and Freedom of Expression." And it was attended by a controversial cartoonist, a Swedish man named Lars Vilks. The French Ambassador to Denmark was also there, François Zimeray. It's not a big café at all; it's quite small. And officially, at 3:30 p.m. on the 14th of February, a gunman came out of nowhere and suddenly opened fire, shooting through the windows of this café. He killed one fifty-five year old man and wounded three police officers. Then he carjacked a vehicle, using it as a getaway car. Later he was observed taking a cab through Copenhagen. And then in the early hours of Sunday morning around 1 a.m., a Jewish man was killed outside a synagogue in central Copenhagen, and two police officers were wounded there.

So it was just like Charlie Hebdo: First they target cartoonists and freedom of expression; then they target Jews.

You're spot on. This is why you can predict these things, because they do the same thing again and again and again.

At 5 a.m. a suspected gunman was shot dead after the police had been stalking an address in the airport district of central Copenhagen.

It ends with the perpetrators shot dead. Very tidy. That's like Charlie Hebdo too.

But it's not just Charlie Hebdo. We're looking at hundreds of these types of events over the last hundred years. There are so many of them.

Recently we've had Canada, Australia, Paris, and now Denmark.

It's the same, it's the same, it's the same. I also wanted to say that I warned about this exactly one month before (the shooting), that something was going to happen in Copenhagen. I thought it was going to happen the night before the 14th and 15th of January, because they had a major drill at a train station in Central Copenhagen. I went out big time on Facebook and other social media and said, "Please, anyone nearby, go there, film these people. Maybe it's a drill, it's for our security. Or maybe it's something more sinister. Go there, film them, make it very, very obvious to them that they are being observed. Stream it live on youtube. Get it out there. And if there is a darker agenda behind this thing, maybe we can defuse it before it happens. Give them cold feet and make them take a step back so we can stop this madness.

So people went down there, they filmed, and nothing happened. I thought afterwards, "Thank God, at least nothing happened. Maybe I was paranoid, I don't know." Then exactly on the hour one month later, on the exact same night between the 14th and the 15th, boom! It happened. And it followed all the different steps that are part of a normal false flag operation.

So if it's okay with you, I'll start picking it apart bit by bit. There is an audio recording from the Art, Blasphemy and Freedom of Expression meeting. It's copyrighted by BBC News. And BBC has an incredible way of popping up everywhere.

Twenty minutes before (World Trade Center) Building 7 came down they reported it happening, even though it hadn't happened yet.

That's one, yes. And also in Paris, you have the BBC reporter who said "Here's the blood that has been put on the pavement." *Put* on the pavement. A Freudian slip. And also in Peshawar (at the school massacre) you had the BBC showing the memorial wall where one of the victims from the Peshawar school shooting was Noah Posner, one of the victims from Sandy Hook, almost exactly two years earlier. And here in Copenhagen, the BBC had the copyright of this audio recording. When you listen to the audio recording, which you can find on youtube, there's a woman giving a speech. And then suddenly you hear the gunfire—*bam bam bam*! A normal reaction when somebody suddenly opens fire, is people start screaming. They panic, they throw themselves under the tables, they knock over glasses, all of these things.

But listen to the sound here. As soon as the shots start, there's no screaming, you hear no voices, there is no noise of tables being knocked over, nothing like that. Just a lot of footsteps. And then . . . it's like the sound of an iron bar dropped on what sounds like a concrete floor. But if you look inside the café, it's a beautiful wooden floor. The sound would be different. And what is a metal bar doing there at all? It sounds like it's at least a meter or two, one of these big heavy things.

There's also raw footage from outside the coffee shop. It's only a few seconds, and it keeps getting taken down from youtube. But it's called "raw footage."[299] And you will see the shot being fired, you see the bullet holes appear in the windows. You cannot see any people in there. And there are no people outside. Compare the shooting patterns from the recording of the speech and the bullet holes appearing in the coffee shop windows. It is not the same shooting pattern. And witnesses reported two shooters, which somehow later morphed into one.

The woman who gave the speech was later interviewed. She said, "Well, I didn't want a thing like this to interrupt our event. We shouldn't let this affect us." So even though somebody was dead outside, shot point blank with a head shot on the pavement outside, officially anyway, it was like "the show must go on." She said that she called everyone back, finished her speech, and then they put on a video. Does that sound likely to you?

It's very odd.

It's like George Bush Jr. who didn't want to interrupt his reading *My Pet Goat* (to schoolchildren) during 9/11. And the man who was said to be the target for this, the Swedish artist, was hiding in the back, not being wounded, not being shot at. And nobody noticed the person whom they said was killed outside. He was a fifty-five year old Danish filmmaker who had done documentaries. So a normal investigation would straightaway look at the victim and say "why was this guy shot?" But there's nothing about that. There have been no interviews with the driver whose car the shooter supposedly hijacked. And the whole focus is on the Swedish guy who got a death threat in 2007 because of him drawing Muhammad with the body of a dog. 2007 to 2015 seems quite a long time-span.

I also want to point out that this café is named The Gunpowder Barrel Café, referencing the Gunpowder Plot of 1605.

That was the first big modern false flag operation, the one that launched the British Empire. It sent the British to war against Spain and Portugal.[300]

Yes, and the 15th of February is another very important date. That was when the USS Maine was blown up in Havana Harbor. The US used that to start a totally unjust war of aggression against Spain. As a result, the US stole Guam, the Philippines, Cuba, and Puerto Rico.

That was the false flag that launched the American Empire. So this is very interesting. The Copenhagen shooting occurred in a café named for the false flag that launched the British Empire, on the anniversary of the false flag that launched the American Empire— almost exactly one month after the Charlie Hebdo shooting.

They love playing with the dates. So anyway, if this was a false flag, they wouldn't want any interruptions with vehicles from outside. They need to control the area. And they also need an area for logistics: Where to park the vehicles, the trucks, the car for the director and the cameramen— whatever they need. Explosives, weapons. And it mustn't be obvious for people in the surrounding areas.

So take a look at this café. A hundred meters down the road there's a big stadium. That stadium would be the perfect place to get the vehicles in. You would have a cafeteria, you would have dressing rooms, and all of these things would be on location. Also, the street in front of the café has no auto traffic; they closed it off so it's only for bicycles. So they won't have a problem with automobiles getting in the way. And then right in front of the café is a big area with bushes and trees, almost like opposite where Martin Luther King was shot from. There's a big park area, blocking the view. So they don't have a problem with nosy people who can see what's going on.

So the location was perfect. And somebody was filming when the shots were fired. To me it looks like the bullets were coming from the inside going out. The bullets were coming out around the level of the chest and stomach area, not at the level of the legs. But the police officers that were wounded were all hit in the legs. You look at photos from inside the café—there are a few I've been able to get hold of—there is a series of photos, though the big TV channels didn't show up for more than an hour after the shooting, which is very strange, though typical of false flag operations. There were helicopters circling in the area, but no news media.

And there's one photo of a police officer lying on the floor, just lying there with a bandage around his leg, and nobody's attending to him! Nobody talks to him. They're all attending to their own business. And another police officer there in civilian clothes has just had his leg bandaged as well. He's just walking around, talking on his mobile phone, very calmly. There's no furniture damaged or anything like that. Also, the gunman said to have been standing outside fires into this crowd, between twenty and forty shots they said at first, now they're talking about two hundred. The only ones wounded were police officers. Two of them were PET officers, Danish secret police. So the shooter apparently missed the target, the Swedish artist, and instead the people he wounded were all police officers. I would say, why police officers? Because these are people that the perpetrators control. The identities of police officers do not have to be given out because of national security, police security. So they never have to come forward with their identities.

We should also note that police officers are sometimes actually intelligence officers using the role of police officer as cover. Jesse Ventura has discussed how he was debriefed by CIA officers disguised as state government officials including, I believe, state police officials, after he was elected Governor of Minnesota.[301] This is completely illegal, since the CIA is prohibited from operating domestically, but they do it anyway. There are countless other cases showing how police departments are routinely infiltrated by intelligence services and their organized crime affiliates. So I wouldn't be surprised if the Danish officers they claim were wounded were actually actors that they control.

I love your comments. You are, in my opinion, spot on. So we go to the next event, which is at 1 a.m. on Sunday the 15th of February. According to the official story, the shooter was checking out people going to a bar mitzvah. And there were supposed to be eighty people inside the synagogue. I don't know, I'm not Jewish, but . . . is that normal, to hold a Bar Mitzvah at one o'clock in the morning? So what happened, they say, was that a Jewish man who was standing guard outside was shot dead, and two police officers were wounded in the leg. Both of their guns supposedly were defective, did not work. I find that highly strange. So they go down, and the guy takes off again.

Now take a look at this address, this synagogue, which is the center of the Danish Jewish community, on Crystal Street. Remember Kristallnacht, the Night of Broken Glass, before the Second World War? The Nazis went berserk, smashing thousands of windows of synagogues, Jewish-owned shops and houses.

The people who script false flag events like to hit our subconscious to get us going emotionally. So here we have a Jewish synagogue, and the street name is Crystal Street. It could be a coincidence.

Kristallnacht was of course the big symbolic event that told Germany's Jews that it was time to go. And the wealthy elite Jews got out with no problem, while poorer Jews without resources ended up staying and facing horrible persecution. It sounds like the Kristallnacht reference could be part of Netanyahu's propaganda ploy to convince European Jews to flee to Israel. The Israelis have a history of using false flag terrorism to make Jews to flee to Israel.

And that is the exact message that Netanyahu came out with hours after this happened.

So if I can take you to the Boston bombing, which not-so-coincidentally happened on Patriot's Day . . . just a few minutes before the bombs went off, the Boston Globe tweeted "there's going to be a bomb drill right outside the Main Library." Bullhorns blared "this is a drill." And a few minutes later, BOOM![302] If you look at where the supposed bombs went off, it was right across the street from the entrance to the main library. They needed the logistics sorted out. They needed bathrooms, catering, dressing rooms, a communication center with all the technical stuff set up. So I think it was carried out from the library in Boston.

Now let's look at Copenhagen. Get on Google Maps, look at the synagogue, do a 180 degree turn, and you're looking straight into the back entrance of Copenhagen's main library.

So after the shooter disappears, the police come and block off the area with crime scene tape. But there's a news team filming, and one of the things they film—remember, this is two or three o'clock in the morning—the police officers clear the street because there is a big vehicle coming down the street and it's too wide for the narrow street. The vehicle turns out to be a big bus. What is a big bus doing on that small, narrow back street at two or three o'clock in the morning? It wasn't one of the normal buses that run in Copenhagen. I suspect this was the bus that carried out the people and the equipment from the library staging area. There was a big sign painted on the top front of the bus. Do you know what it said? "Evacuation." This could be a double-meaning that works on the subconscious. On the one hand, it was evacuating the actors and equipment from the false flag command center in the library. But it was also hinting at getting the Jews out of Europe, evacuating them to Israel. They're playing with our minds here, again. They're trying to get to us at a subconscious level.

And also, the guy who was accused of having done this was from a Palestinian family. A key part of these false flag operations, for decades, has been a patsy with a Muslim background. In the old days, the boogieman was the communist Russians. Then the Berlin Wall came down. So they needed a new type of patsy. So enter on stage the Muslims, the "Muslim terrorists." In so many of these false flag operations, totally innocent Muslim people have been blamed. The perpetrators love patsies with Muslim-sounding names, faces with big black beards and dark eyebrows. So who is it this time? It's Omar Abdel Hamid El-Hussein. He fits the patsy template perfectly.

So how did the police catch him? They supposedly staked out his residence, he returned, opened fire, and was shot dead by police right outside his front door. This is very, very close to the same train station where they held the drill exactly one month earlier—the drill that led me to predict that there would soon be a false flag attack in Copenhagen, which by the way is a very big city. What are the odds that this would take place at the exact location, exactly one month later?

Then there are the fake witnesses. Very often with these false flags, the people interviewed on-site by the media are part of the game. They're just following scripts. Their job is to amplify what happened—"oh my God, it's awful, it's awful"—and then the reporter will come with the agenda. Just like the guy they interviewed in the street on 9/11, "Harley guy," who told Fox News: "I saw this plane come out of nowhere and just ream right into the side of the Twin Towers, exploding through the other side. And then I witnessed both Towers collapse, one first and then the second, mostly due to structural failure, because the fire was just too intense."[303]

He recited his lines so badly he's become the poster child for these "bad actors" in false flag operations.

Often they'll interview many supposed witnesses who use almost the same words, such as "lone, crazy" or "crazy and alone" or "alone and crazy."

Lone wolf Muslim terrorists are the latest rage.

Yes. And the reason they want a lone crazy guy as patsy is that if he's alone, by law there's no conspiracy, so they don't have to investigate. If he's dead, they can close the case right away. And if he's crazy, there's no rational motive. Just close up the case, nothing to see here, goodbye and go home.

And the official story is set in stone immediately and forever.

This guy, Omar Abdel Hamid El-Hussein, was just an ordinary guy. No violent or extremist background. Not into drugs. But then the media started portraying him as a madman. They interviewed a psychiatrist who said this man was "totally fucked up." Those are the words he used. How can you say a thing like that, especially if he's not your patient? It's done to create media impact and paint the patsy as a totally disturbed individual.

And then the Danish Queen and Prime Minister stood up and said "This is an attack on Denmark." Just like the Charlie Hebdo event in Paris: It's an attack on liberty, free speech, and so on. And also what they love to say, for subliminal impact, is "we have to unite the nation." They love these words. "We have to stand united as a nation." And they wanted people to stand united with NATO. "If you're not with us, you're with the terrorists."

I try to come at these things with an open mind, without predetermined opinions. It's too easy to start shouting "false flag" as soon as something happens. But in the case of the Copenhagen attacks, I think this is what we're looking at. And one of the ingredients of false flags is that they love doing them on very specific dates. They also love using drills. That's one of the main elements in false flag operations.[304] I think the reason they use drills is to be able to get vehicles, explosives, extras, all of these things in place in such a way as that normal people won't notice anything.

The Copenhagen event that was targeted was all about the theme of free speech, and that somebody had attacked the Muslim population by doing cartoons. I think we have to look at these things as propaganda or marketing operations. The more times you mention something like Coca-Cola, the more you keep repeating it, it just goes into the subconscious. And this theme of attacking cartoonists for having drawn cartoons of Muhammad is nothing new. The first chapter was when Ayatollah Khomeini put out his fatwa on Salman Rushdie on February 14th, 1989—the exact same date, February 14th, as the attack on the Copenhagen café. I believe the word fatwa was also used in the title of the Copenhagen event. And February 14th, Valentine's Day, is a major day on the satanic calendar.

Leading up to the Copenhagen attack was the 2005 Jyllands-Posten Muhammad cartoons controversy. Then in 2007 the Swedish cartoonist Lars Vilks made a very ugly cartoon of Muhammad with the face of Muhammad and the body of a dog. He is said to have had bodyguards since 2007. Then came Charlie Hebdo, with the exact same theme. And then back to Denmark, where Lars Vilks was at the event with the French ambassador.

With this Copenhagen attack it's almost as if they've taken it to the next level. This is seventy years since the liberation of Auschwitz, and coming up on seventy years since the end of World War II and the liberation of Denmark and other occupied countries. I think they're going for the emotional impact, following the problem-reaction-solution template. And the emotion this time is for us to feel sorry for the Jewish population and blame someone else, take the pressure off the state of Israel so they can continue doing what they're doing.

The people who orchestrate these things are very much into numerology, numbers and dates and so on. And just a few days before the event happened in Denmark, on the 9th of February, one of the major newspapers in Denmark, called Politiken, devoted about 30% of the whole front page was the number 666 in red on a black background. This

666 had nothing obvious to do with the article underneath it, which upon closer inspection turns out to be about how 666 million were hidden in Swiss bank accounts. And on top of the gigantic 666 were two staring eyes, the all-seeing eye, the eye in the pyramid. To the right of the eyes there is a pyramid shaped form with a radioactive sign inside it. And then to the left it says "let the people draw the prophet the way they want."

This was published five days before the Copenhagen attack. And then the same 666 recurs inside the newspaper a few days later, before the attack happened. It was in a very strange cartoon. Normally a cartoon at least attempts to be funny. This one is not funny at all. It shows a man behind a desk reading the newspaper with the huge 666 image, not drawn by hand but a photo of the actual front page from a few days earlier. Next to him, there's someone standing with glasses—he looks like a politician. And in between them is a dragon with goat's horns, and a quote from the Bible talking about the Beast.

It sounds like they're advertising for the Antichrist, which (in Shaykh Imran Hosein's eschatology) is the Zionist false-flaggers.

That's also my interpretation. It's difficult for me to interpret it in any other way.

MESSAGE OF THE AYATULLAH SEYYED ALI KHAMENEI, LEADER OF THE ISLAMIC REPUBLIC OF IRAN, TO THE YOUTH OF EUROPE AND NORTH AMERICA

In the name of Allah, the Beneficent the Merciful,

Recent events in France and similar ones in some other Western countries have convinced me to talk to you directly about them. I am addressing you [the youth], not because I overlook your parents; rather it is because the future of your nations and countries will be in your hands, and also I find that the sense of quest for truth is more vigorous and attentive in your hearts.

I don't address your politicians and statesmen in this message because I believe they have consciously separated the route of politics from the path of righteousness and truth.

I would like to talk to you about Islam, particularly the image that is presented to you as Islam. Many attempts have been made over the past two decades, almost since the disintegration of the Soviet Union, to place this great religion in the seat of a horrifying enemy. The provocation of a feeling of horror and hatred and its utilization has unfortunately a long record in the political history of the West.

Here, I don't want to deal with the different phobias with which Western nations have thus far been indoctrinated. A cursory review of recent critical studies of history would bring home to you the fact that the Western governments' insincere and hypocritical treatment of other nations and cultures has been censured in new historiographies.

The histories of the United States and Europe are today full of shame for practicing slavery, embarrassed by the colonial period and the oppression of people of color and non-Christians. Your researchers and historians are deeply ashamed of the bloodshed wrought in the name of religion between Catholics and Protestants or in the name of nationality and ethnicity during the First and Second World Wars. This approach is admirable.

By mentioning a fraction of this long list, I don't want to reproach history; rather I would like you to ask your intellectuals as to why the public conscience in the West awakens and comes to its senses after a delay of several decades or centuries. Why should the revision of collective conscience apply to the distant past but not to current problems? Why is it that attempts are made to prevent public awareness regarding an important issue such as the treatment of Islamic culture and thought?

You know well that humiliation and spreading hatred and illusionary fear of the "Other" have been the common base of all those oppressive profiteers. I would like you to ask yourself why the old policy of spreading "phobia" and hatred has targeted Islam and Muslims with unprecedented intensity. Why does the power structure in the world want Islamic thought to be marginalized and remain latent? What concepts and values in Islam disturb the programs of the super powers and what interests are safeguarded in the shadow of distorting the image of Islam?

Hence, my first request is: Study and research the incentives behind this widespread tarnishing of the image of Islam.

My second request is that in reaction to the flood of prejudgments and disinformation campaigns, try to gain a direct and firsthand knowledge of this religion. The right logic requires that you understand the nature and essence of what they are scaring you about and want you to keep away from.

I don't insist that you accept my reading or any other reading of Islam. What I want to say is: Don't allow this dynamic and effective reality in today's world to be introduced to you through resentments and prejudices. Don't allow them to hypocritically introduce their own recruited terrorists as representatives of Islam.

Receive knowledge of Islam from its primary and original sources. Gain information about Islam through the Qur'an and the life of its great Prophet. I would like to ask you whether you have directly read the Qur'an that Muslims follow. Have you studied the teachings of the Prophet of Islam and his humane, ethical doctrines? Have you ever received the message of Islam from any sources other than the media?

Have you ever asked yourself how and on the basis of which values has Islam established the greatest scientific and intellectual civilization of the world and raised the most distinguished scientists and intellectuals throughout many centuries?

I would like you not to allow the derogatory and offensive image-buildings to create an emotional gulf between you and the reality, taking away the possibility of an impartial judgment from you. Today, the communication media have removed the geographical borders. Hence, don't allow them to besiege you with fabricated and mental borders.

Although no one can individually fill the gaps thus created, each one of you can construct a bridge of thought and fairness over these gaps to illuminate yourself and your surrounding environment. While this preplanned challenge between Islam and you—the youth—is undesirable, it can raise new questions in your curious and inquiring minds. Attempts to find answers to these questions will provide you with an appropriate opportunity to discover new truths.

Therefore, don't miss the opportunity to gain proper, correct and unbiased understanding of Islam so that hopefully, due to your sense of responsibility toward the truth, future generations would write the history of this current interaction between Islam and the West with a clearer conscience and lesser resentment.

Seyyed Ali Khamenei

21st January 2015

AFTERWARD: A LIST OF CHARLIE HEBDO SUSPECTS

Kevin Barrett

When a detective investigates a murder, he or she draws up a list of suspects. These are people who might have had the means, motive, and opportunity to commit the crime. The first question in compiling such a list is *cui bono (who* benefits)?

Most contributors[305] to this book suspect the Charlie Hebdo crimes were not properly investigated. The apparent murder of Helric Fredou, the policeman pursuing a possible connection between the Charlie Hebdo killings and an organized crime network linked to intelligence agencies, may have sent a message to police and prevented further serious inquiry along non-official-story lines.

Since the official investigation appears to have been blocked, the only alternative is a citizens' investigation. To that end, I have compiled a list of names of possible suspects (including some who were blamed, presumably falsely, by the authorities). Note that not all contributors to this book agree with my views on this or other subjects. Please keep in mind that all of these people should be presumed innocent until proven guilty. Also keep in mind that, as Ashahed Muhammad notes, the truth about murky events like Charlie Hebdo often emerges slowly, over many years or decades. We must, as the Qur'an says, "persist in (pursuing) truth, and persist in patience."

Feel free to post comments referencing new information about this case, or other pertinent reactions to this book, at www.WeAreNotCharlieHebdo.blogspot.com.

List of Suspects for Further Investigation

Bellaïche, Martine Bismuth and Patrick Bellaïche Owners of Patistory, 45 rue de Meaux, a Paris business linked to the Zionist association Migdal, the terrorist group Jewish Defense League (JDL) and the Israeli Defense Forces (IDF). Alleged Charlie Hebdo shooters Cherif and Saïd Kouachi reportedly abandoned a getaway car and carjacked another vehicle directly in front of Patistory—the exact center of Jewish Paris, a seemingly odd place for Islamic extremists to switch cars. Investigators believe the "car switch" may have been a staged event.[306]

Bougrab, Jeannette Self-described "companion" of slain Charlie Hebdo editor Charb (whose family denies the relationship: someone is lying).[307] Member of French Council of State under Sarkozy; arch-Zionist and islamophobe. Police officer Helric Fredou appears to have been murdered for investigating Charb's relationship to Bougrab. Investigators suspect the Charb-Bougrab "relationship" may be linked to the mysterious sources of funding that kept the bankrupt Charlie Hebdo magazine afloat, and that the magazine may have been paid to publish ultra-obscene anti-Islam cartoons in order to prepare the way for the January 7th Gladio-style false flag operation.

Cazeneuve, Bernard. Minister of the Interior. Worked closely for two years (2010–2012) and had an "excellent relationship" with police officer Helric Fredou, who appears to have been murdered for refusing an order to stop investigating family and financial relationships surrounding *Charlie Hebdo* magazine. Despite the close relationship, Cazeneuve pointedly refused to pass condolences to Fredou's surviving family.[308]

Coulibaly, Amedi. Blamed for hostage taking and deaths in Hyper-Kosher market. Unavailable for questioning. Killed in what appears to have been a pre-planned execution-style slaying by police, not a shootout. (Videos show he was executed by police while handcuffed.)[309] Apparently a long-term pawn of Deep State forces, he met former French President Sarkozy, a suspected agent of NATO and Israel, in a mysteriously well-publicized incident in 2009.[310]

Dassault, Laurent. See Janek.

Emsalem, Michel Edmond Mimoun. Sold the Hyper-Kosher market the day before the shooting there—an extremely lucky move, since the incident caused a huge downturn in business. Moved to New York after sale/shooting. Emsalem's wife Dinah is an executive at SMCP Fashions, owned by KKR investments, whose owners and co-founders are two extremely rich Jewish Zionists, Henry Kravis and George Roberts. KKR hired former CIA Director David Petraeus in 2013.[311]

Friedman, Gil. Director of the Regional Criminal Police, Limoges. The direct superior of police officer Helric Fredou, ordered off the case on the night of the Charlie Hebdo shooting (January 7th, 2015) then found dead later that night with a bullet in the head. Fredou's death was ruled a suicide, but family members are skeptical. The police violated French law by denying Fredou's family access to the autopsy.[312]

Hollande, François. President of France. Popularity rating doubled due to Charlie Hebdo incident.[313] While there is no evidence implicating Hollande personally in the attacks, abundant circumstantial evidence points toward individuals in the French intelligence services, whose nominal boss is the President. President Hollande's post-attack campaign against people questioning the official version of Charlie Hebdo, which implicates him in the cover-up if not the crime itself, singled out two contributors to this book, Kevin Barrett and Webster Tarpley.[314]

Janek. Supposedly a Polish worker who miraculously found himself in a perfect position to film the Charlie Hebdo terrorists' escape from the magazine's offices. Janek somehow gained access to the roof of a building owned by Geoffroy Sciard, a wealthy man with intelligence agency connections who is a close associate of Netanyahu's friend Laurent Dassault, a DSGE (French Intelligence) partner and a pillar of Israel's ultra-right and its military-industrial complex.[315]

Kouachi, Cherif. Blamed for shooting in Charlie Hebdo offices. Unavailable for questioning. Killed in what appears to have been a pre-planned execution-style slaying by police, whose commanders apparently had no interest in interrogating him. Arrested by police for possession of child pornography in 2010 but not prosecuted, presumably due agreeing to serve as intelligence informant and eventual patsy.[316] Had brown eyes and thus could not have been the Charlie Hebdo killer identified by a witness.[317]

Kouachi, Saïd. Also blamed for shooting in Charlie Hebdo offices. Unavailable for questioning. Killed in what appears to have been a pre-planned execution-style slaying by police, whose commanders apparently had no interest in interrogating him. Arrested by police for possession of child pornography in 2010 but not prosecuted, presumably due agreeing to serve as intelligence informant and eventual patsy. Had brown eyes and thus could not have been the Charlie Hebdo killer identified by a witness.[318]

Lieberman, Avigdor. Ultra-radical Israeli Foreign Minister who advocates the violent ethnic cleansing of non-Jewish people from historic Palestine, including the more than two million non-Jewish citizens of Israel (25% of the Israeli population). Secretly visited Paris on December 25th, 2014, less than two weeks before the Charlie Hebdo killings.[319] The purpose of his clandestine trip to Paris was a "confidential" meeting with

Mossad officials.[320] Responded to the Charlie Hebdo killings by falsely blaming Hamas, then used Charlie Hebdo propaganda in his election campaign more than any other Israeli official or candidate.[321]

Mourad, Hamyd. 18-year-old French citizen falsely accused of being the getaway driver and "third man" in the Charlie Hebdo attack, even though videos showed there was no such driver. Turned himself in to local Charlesville-Mezieres police on the night of the attack, which may have saved him from being gunned down and silenced like the Kouachi brothers. Had a strong alibi supported by many witnesses. So why did the authorities invent a nonexistent getaway driver? And why did they falsely identify Mourad as that driver? Those questions have not been answered —perhaps because the true answer is that Mourad was blamed but not silenced due to a glitch in the false flag operation's script and/or execution.[322]

Netanyahu, Benjamin. Israeli Prime Minister and credibly-accused war criminal. Responsible for killing more than 2000 people, most of them civilians, during Israel's assault on Gaza in the summer of 2014. Announced (or threatened) in August 2014 that if France recognized the existence of Palestine, terrorists would attack France. Explicitly disinvited by President Hollande from the big Charlie Hebdo march in Paris on January 11th, 2015, Netanyahu nonetheless crashed the event—reminding observers of the way mafia chieftains make uninvited appearances at the funerals of their victims.

de Rothschild, Eduard Baron. Bought bankrupt Charlie Hebdo magazine in December, 2014, one month before the attacks, according to his nephew Philippe Baron de Rothschild.[323] The magazine had been in decline for years and losing increasingly large amounts of money. After the January 7th attack, the magazine's print run increased from 60,000 to seven million copies, an all-time record for the French press and a 120-fold increase over the pre-shooting print run.[324] Backing by the Rothschild fortune facilitated the huge print run, which in turn further enriched the world's richest and most powerful family—which also happens to be the founding family of the State of Israel.

Sciard, Geoffroy. See Janek.

CONTRIBUTORS

Zafar Bangash is Director of the Institute of Contemporary Islamic Thought and on the Editorial Board of Crescent International newsmagazine. He is the author of several books including the recent *Power Manifestations of the Sirah: Examining the Letters and Treaties of the Messenger of Allah*. His latest book is titled: *The Doomed Kingdom of the House of Saud*.

Kevin Barrett, an American Muslim and PhD Arabist-Islamologist, is one of America's best-known critics of the War on Terror. He has authored and edited several books, appeared on Fox, CNN, PBS and other broadcast outlets, and inspired feature stories and op-eds in the New York Times, the Christian Science Monitor, the Chicago Tribune, and other mainstream publications. A former teacher of French, Arabic, Islamic Studies, and Humanities, he currently works as nonprofit organizer, editor at Veterans Today, and pundit at Press TV, Russia Today, al-Etejah and other international channels. His website is TruthJihad.com.

Barry Chamish is a bestselling Israeli author and world-class investigative journalist. The author of *Who Murdered Yitzhak Rabin?*, *Shabtai Tzvi, Labor Zionism and the Holocaust*, *Israel Betrayed*, *Bye Bye Gaza*, *The Last Days of Israel*, *Save Israel*, and other books, he was harassed, threatened, and violently attacked by the corrupt forces behind the Rabin assassination, and finally had to flee to the USA, where he continues to write and host a radio show. His website is BarryChamish.com.

John B. Cobb, Jr. is professor emeritus of the Claremont School of Theology. He is founding director of the Center for Process Studies and co-founder of Progressive Christians Uniting, for which he edited *Progressive Christians Speak* (2003). He is an ordained minister of the United Methodist Church. Among his books are *The Liberation of Life* with Charles Birch (1984) and *For the Common Good* with Herman Daly (1989), as well as *Christ in a Pluralistic Age* (1975) and *Postmodernism and Public Policy* (2001).

Ole Dammegard is a journalist who has authored six books, including the classic *Coup d'Etat in Slow Motion* on the murder of Swedish Prime Minister Olaf Palme. His website is LightOnConspiracies.com.

Lawrence Davidson is a retired professor of history from West Chester University in West Chester PA. His academic research focused on the history of American foreign relations with the Middle East. He taught courses in Middle East history, the history of science and modern European intellectual history. Hailing from a secular Jewish background, he has published many works on Islam, Zionism and US foreign policy, including *Islamic Fundamentalism: An Introduction* (1998), *America's Palestine: Popular and Official Perceptions from Balfour to Israeli Statehood* (2001), *A Concise History of the Middle East* (2006) and *Cultural Genocide* (2012).

Laurent Guyénot is an Engineer (National School of Advanced Technology, 1982) and medievalist (PhD in Medieval Studies at Paris IV-Sorbonne, 2009). He has authored numerous books; the latest is *JFK-9/11: 50 Years of Deep State*.

Anthony Hall is Professor of Globalization Studies at University of Lethbridge in Alberta Canada. His been a teacher in the Canadian university system since 1982. Dr. Hall has recently finished a big two-volume publishing project at McGill-Queen's University Press entitled *The Bowl with One Spoon*. The second volume, *Part II, Earth Into Property: Colonization, Decolonization and Capitalism* was selected by The Independent in the UK as one of the best books of 2010, and the Journal of the American Library Association called it "a scholarly tour de force." One of the book's features is to set 9/11 and the 9/11 Wars in the context of global history since 1492.

Barbara Honegger, M.S., is a former White House Policy Analyst and Senior Military Affairs Journalist at the Naval Postgraduate School, the premiere science, technology and national security affairs graduate research university of the Department of Defense. Her book *October Surprise* exposed the treasonous secret deal with Iranian leaders, negotiated by George H.W. Bush and William Casey, that denied President Jimmy Carter a second term. She is also well-known for her research on the Pentagon and anthrax components of the 2001 9/11-anthrax operation.

Imran N. Hosein was born in the Caribbean island of Trinidad in 1942 from parents whose ancestors had migrated as indentured laborers from India. He is a graduate of the Aleemiyah Institute in Karachi and has studied at several institutions of higher learning including the University of Karachi, the University of the West Indies, Al Azhar University and the Graduate Institute of International Relations in Switzerland. A former Director of Islamic Studies for the Joint Committee of Muslim Organizations of Greater New York, he is widely regarded as the world's leading Islamic eschatologist and has published many books including *Jerusalem in the Qur'an*, *Gog and Magog in the Modern Age*, and *The Prohibition of Ribah in the Qur'an and Sunnah*. His website is ImranHosein.org.

Ayatollah Seyyed Ali Khamenei is the Supreme Leader of the Islamic Republic of Iran.

Thaddeus J. Kozinski is Associate Professor of Philosophy and Humanities at Wyoming Catholic College. A teacher of humanities, the Trivium, and philosophy for over ten years, he is the author of The *Political Problem of Religious Pluralism: And Why Philosophers Can't Solve It.*

Rabbi Michael Lerner is editor of Tikkun magazine (tikkun.org), chair of the interfaith and secular-humanist-welcoming Network of Spiritual Progressives (spiritualprogressives.org), rabbi of Beyt Tikkun Synagogue (beyttikkun.org) and author of eleven books including two national best sellers: *The Left Hand of God: Taking Back our Country from the Religious Right* and *Jewish Renewal: A Path to Healing and Transformation.* He welcomes your involvement in building a Love and Justice movement in Western societies. RabbiLerner.tikkun@gmail.com

Cynthia McKinney was elected in 1992 as the first African-American Congresswoman from Georgia. She has served six terms in the House of Representatives and gained national and international renown as a tireless advocate for human rights, voting rights and holding government accountable. The Green Party Candidate for President of the United States in 2008, she is nearing completion of a Ph.D. under the supervision of leading Deep State expert Peter Dale Scott.

John Andrew Morrow (Ph.D. Islamic Studies, University of Toronto) has a Native American background and is a member of the Metis Nation. He is not just a Western-trained Islamologist, but has also completed the full cycle of traditional Islamic seminary studies both independently and at the hands of a series of Sunni, Shi'i, and Sufi scholars, making him a respected 'alim holding the titles of ustadh, duktur, hakim, and shaykh. Director of The Covenants Foundation and editor of The *Covenants of the Prophet Muhammad,* he travels widely and incessantly to support the Foundation's efforts to disseminate traditional, civilizational Islam; promote Islamic unity; protect persecuted Christians; and improve relations between Muslims and members of other faiths.

Ashahed M. Muhammad is executive director of the Truth Establishment Institute and Assistant Editor of the influential Black weekly The Final Call. A specialist in advocacy and investigative journalism, he has been widely published in a variety of outlets worldwide, appears as a news analyst and pundit on global broadcast outlets, and hosts a talk radio show on KNOW Radio. His website is ashahed.blogs.finalcall.com.

Yvonne Ridley is a British journalist and Vice President of the European Muslim League. She had worked in written and broadcast journalism for news outlets including The Sunday Times, The Independent on Sunday, The Observer, The Mirror, The News of the World, Wales on Sunday, the Sunday Express, al-Jazeera, Islam Channel, and Press TV. As an activist she has worked with CagePrisoners.org, the Free Gaza movement, and the Respect Party. She is the author of *In the Hands of the Taliban* (2001) and *Ticket to Paradise* (2003).

Paul Craig Roberts served as Assistant Secretary of the Treasury under President Reagan, and was later associate editor and columnist for the Wall Street Journal. He has held academic appointments at Virginia Tech, Tulane University, University of New Mexico, Stanford University where he was Senior Research Fellow in the Hoover Institution, George Mason University where he had a joint appointment as professor of economics and professor of business administration, and Georgetown University where he held the William E. Simon Chair in Political Economy in the Center for Strategic and International Studies. He is the author of many books including *How America Was Lost: from 9/11 to the Police/Warfare State* (2014).

Alain Soral is politically-engaged philosopher, essayist, journalist, filmmaker and actor, and founder of the Egalité et Réconciliation (Equality and Reconciliation) political-cultural party, which advocates a "left for the workers, right for traditional values" position as a response to capitalist globalization. His books include *Comprendre l'Empire* (2011), *Chroniques d'avant-guerre* (2012) and *Dialogues désaccordés, combat de Blancs dans un tunnel* (interviews with Éric Naulleau) (2013).

Ibrahim Soudy (Ph.D., Structural Engineering) holds ten different structural engineering licenses, and thus is one of the most highly-qualified analysts of the 2001 World Trade Center demolitions among the thousands of professionals at Architects and Engineers for 9/11 Truth (AE911Truth.org).

Webster Tarpley is a philosopher of history who seeks to provide the programs and strategies needed to overcome the current world crisis. His Ph.D. in early modern history from the Catholic University of America analyzes the role of Venice in the origins of the Thirty Years' War (1618-

1648). He is the author of many books including *9/11: Synthetic Terror: Made in USA* and *Surviving the Cataclysm: Your Guide to the Worst Financial Crisis in Human History*, as well as groundbreaking investigative biographies of George Bush, Barack Obama and Mitt Romney. His website is Tarpley.net.

Andre Vltchek is a novelist, filmmaker and investigative journalist. He has covered wars and conflicts in dozens of countries. The result is his latest book: *Fighting Against Western Imperialism*. Pluto published his discussion with Noam Chomsky: *On Western Terrorism*. His critically acclaimed political novel *Point of No Return* is re-edited and available. *Oceania* is his book on Western imperialism in the South Pacific. His provocative book about post-Suharto Indonesia and the market-fundamentalist model is called *Indonesia—The Archipelago of Fear*. His feature documentary *Rwanda Gambit* is about Rwandan history and the plunder of DR Congo. After living for many years in Latin America and Oceania, Vltchek presently resides and works in East Asia and Africa. He can be reached through his website AndreVltchek.weebly.com or his Twitter.

NOTES

1   Ali Abunimah, "Who's a Charlie? France cracks down on free speech in order to defend it." *Electronic Intifada* Jan. 14, 2015. (http://electronicintifada.net/blogs/ali-abunimah/whos-charlie-france-cracks-down-free-speech-order-defend-it).

2   "Charlie Hebdo: plus de 100.000 personnes rassemblées en hommage," nouvelobs.com (in French), January 7, 2015.

3   Elizabeth Dias, "Pope Francis on Charlie Hebdo: 'One Cannot Make Fun of Faith.'" *Time*, January 15, 2015 (http://time.com/3668875/pope-francis-charlie-hebdo/).

4   *Financial Times*, "Russian and Turkish Conspiracy Theories Swirl After Paris Attacks." Cited at http://www.zerohedge.com/news/2015-01-13/turkish-presidents-stunning-outburst-french-are-behind-charlie-hebdo-massacre-mossad, archived at http://m911t.blogspot.com/2015/01/turkish-presidents-stunning-outburst.html.

5   ibid.

6   The subject of another article of mine in this book.

7   Hicham Hamza, "Charlie Hebdo bombshell! Suicided officer's family denied access to autopsy" (http://www.veteranstoday.com/2015/01/26/fredou/).

8   I am not arguing that Boisseau was not killed, simply that the corporate media assertion that he was shot in the head with an AK-47 as seen in the video is false. The video depicts actors staging a fake killing; it is not an authentic record of an actual killing.

9   "De Rothschild's Print Charlie Hebdo: 'We Doubted Whether We Should Buy Newspaper Libération.'" *Quote* 13:23 January 22, 2015. (http://www.quotenet.nl/Nieuws/De-Rothschild-s-print-Charlie-Hebdo-We-doubted-whether-we-should-buy-newspaper-Liberation-144350).

10 John Lichfield, "Paris attacks: Jean-Marie Le Pen says French terror attacks were work of Western intelligence." The *Independent*, January 17, 2015. (http://www.independent.co.uk/news/world/europe/paris-attacks-jeanmarie-le-pen-says-french-terror-attacks-were-work-of-western-intelligence-9985047.html).

11 Rory Mulholland, "Jean Marie Le Pen injured in house fire." The *Telegraph*, January 26, 2015. (http://www.telegraph.co.uk/news/worldnews/europe/france/11370225/Jean-Marie-Le-Pen-injured-in-house-fire.html).

12 Peter Dale Scott, *The American Deep State: Wall Street, Big Oil, and the Attack on U.S. Democracy* (NY: Rowman & Littlefield, 2014).

13 Nafeez Ahmed, "Why was a Sunday Times report on US government ties to al-Qaeda chief spiked?" *Ceasefire*, May 17, 2013. (https://ceasefiremagazine.co.uk/whistleblower-al-qaeda-chief-u-s-asset/).

14 Paul Moses, *The Saint and the Sultan: The Crusades, Islam, and Saint Francis of Assisi's Mission of Peace* (NY: Doubleday, 2009).

15 Karen Armstrong, *Muhammad: A Biography of the Prophet* (NY: Harper Collins, 1991, 1993), p. 26.

16 Maria Menocal, *The Ornament of the World: How Muslims, Jews, and Christians Created a Culture of Tolerance in Medieval Spain* (NY: Little, Brown, 2002), p. 70.

17 Menocal, p. 71.

18 Qtd. in Alan Levine, "Skepticism, Self, and Toleration in Montaigne's Political Thought." In Allan Levine, ed., *Early Modern Skepticism and the Origins of Toleration* (Lanham, Maryland: Lexington, 1999), p. 65.

19 West-östlicher Divan

20 Edward Said, *Orientalism* (NY: Vintage, 1978, 1979), p. 5.

21 "Developing economies to eclipse west by 2060, OECD forecasts." *The Guardian,* Nov. 9, 2012 (http://www.theguardian.com/global-development/datablog/2012/nov/09/developing-economies-overtake-west-2050-oecd-forecasts).

22 Gen. Wesley Clark has revealed that 9/11 was designed to "take out seven countries in

five years." All seven were Muslim-majority countries with governments unfriendly to Israel. See Joe Conason, "Seven Countries in Five Years." Oct. 12, 2007. (http://www.salon.com/2007/10/12/wesley_clark/) .

23 Lisa Erdmann, "The power of TV images: What's the truth?" *Der Spiegel*, Sept. 21 2001. (http://www.spiegel.de/politik/ausland/die-macht-der-tv-bilder-was-ist-die-wahrheit-a-158625.html).

24 Sources of Bin Laden's statements deploring 9/11 and denying involvement include: "Osama Bin Laden claims terrorist attacks in USA were committed by some American terrorist group," *Pravda*, Sept. 12 2001; "Taliban says Bin Laden denied role in attacks," *Yahoo News*, Sept. 13 2001; statement to al-Jazeera television, reported by CNN on September 17th, 2001; interview with *Ummat*, Sept. 28 2001, Karachi, Pakistan.

25 Ed Haas, "#16 No Hard Evidence Connecting Bin Laden to 9/11." *Project Censored*, April 28, 2010. (http://www.projectcensored.org/16-no-hard-evidence-connecting-bin-laden-to-9-11/) .

26 "Were Israelis Detained on Sept. 11 Spies?" ABC News *20/20* program, June 21, 2000. (http://abcnews.go.com/2020/story?id=123885&page=1).

27 World Public Opinion poll, "Muslims Believe US Seeks to Undermine Islam." April 24, 2007.
(http://www.worldpublicopinion.org/pipa/articles/brmiddleeastnafricara/346.php).

28 Peter Gottschalk and Gabriel Greenberg, *Islamophobia: Making Muslims the Enemy* (Plymouth, UK: Rowman & Littlefield, 2008).

29 George Lakoff, *Don't Think of an Elephant* (White River Junction, Vermont: Chelsea Green, 2004).

30 Chomsky, Noam and André Vltchek, *On Western Terrorism: From Hiroshima to Drone Warfare* (London: Pluto Press, 2013).

31 Lt. Col. Dave Grossman: *On Killing: The Psychological Cost of Learning to Kill in War and Society* (Boston, NY: Little, Brown, 1995).

32 Grossman, p. 4.

33 ibid.

34 ibid, p. 35.

35 Denver Nicks, "Report: Suicide Rate Soars Among Young Vets." *Time* Magazine, Jan. 10th 2014. (http://time.com/304/report-suicide-rate-soars-among-young-vets/).

36 Robert Pape, *Dying to Win: The Strategic Logic of Suicide Terrorism* (NY: Random House, 2005) p. 4.

37 "Study: Threat of Muslim-American terrorism in U.S. exaggerated." CNN, January 6, 2010. (http://edition.cnn.com/2010/US/01/06/muslim.radicalization.study/).

38 Charles Kurzman, *The Missing Martyrs: Why There Are So Few Muslim Terrorists* (NY: Oxford UP USA, 2011).

39 Investigative journalist Dave Lindorff has written several excellent essays calling into question the official narrative of the Boston bombings, including "Official Story has Odd Wrinkles: A Pack of Questions about the Boston Bombing" (http://whowhatwhy.com/2013/05/20/official-story-has-odd-wrinkles-a-pack-of-questions-about-the-boston-bombing-backpacks/) and "Dark Questions About a Deadly FBI Interrogation in Orlando" (http://www.counterpunch.org/2014/03/24/dark-questions-about-a-deadly-fbi-interrogation-in-orlando/).

40 Charles Kurzman, "Muslim-American Terrorism in 2013." Durham, NC: Triangle Center on Terrorism and Homeland Security, February 5, 2014. (http://sites.duke.edu/tcths/files/2013/06/Kurzman_Muslim-American_Terrorism_in_2013.pdf).

41 US Department of Justice, Federal Bureau of Investigation, "Terrorism 2002-2005." (http://www.fbi.gov/stats-services/publications/terrorism-2002-

2005/terror02_05#terror_05sum).

42 Danios, "Europol Report: All Terrorists are Muslims…Except the 99.6% that Aren't."
    (http://www.loonwatch.com/2010/01/terrorism-in-europe/).

43 Europol, "EU Terrorism Situation and Trend Report: TE-SAT 2013."
    (https://www.europol.europa.eu/sites/default/files/publications/europol_te-
    sat2013_lr_0.pdf).

44 Kevin Barrett, *Questioning the War on Terror* (Madison, WI: Khadir Press, 2009). p. 21.
    Statistics about lightning strikes and bathtub drownings were provided by
    LightningSafety.com and the National Safety Council.

45 Patrick Buchanan, *The Death of the West: How Dying Populations and Immigrant Invasions
    Imperil Our Country and Civilization* (NY: St. Martin's Griffin, 2002).

46 Lawrence Davidson, *Cultural Genocide* (New Brunswick, NJ: Rutgers UP, 2012).

47 "Muslims Believe US Seeks to Undermine Islam." April 24, 2007.
    (http://www.worldpublicopinion.org/pipa/articles/brmiddleeastnafricara/346.php) .

48 "Remarks by the President Upon Arrival." Archived at http://georgewbush-
    whitehouse.archives.gov/news/releases/2001/09/20010916-2.html.

49 John Vinocur. "Politicus: Bush might be heading for tangle with neocons." *International
    Herald Tribune.* January 11, 2005.

50 "Learned helplessness is a mental state in which an organism forced to endure aversive
    stimuli, or stimuli that are painful or otherwise unpleasant, becomes unable or
    unwilling to avoid subsequent encounters with those stimuli, even if they are escapable,
    presumably because it has learned that it cannot control the situation." J.L. Nolen in
    Encyclopedia Britannica, cited in Wikipedia, "Learned Helplessness" (retrieved April 5,
    2014).

51 Robert Fisk, "The re-writing of Iraqi history is now going on at supersonic speed." *The
    Independent*, May 26, 2004.

52 "Israeli Interrogators 'in Iraq'." BBC News, July 3, 2004.
    (http://news.bbc.co.uk/2/hi/middle_east/3863235.stm).

53 Rumy Hasan, *Dangerous Liasons: The Clash Between Islamism and Zionism* (London: New
    Generation, 2013).

54 Stephen Sniegoski, *The Transparent Cabal: The Neoconservative Agenda, War in the Middle
    East, and the National Interest of Israel* (Norfolk, VA: Enigma, 2008) p. 351.

55 Dr. Maria Yellow Horse Braveheart, PhD, "Welcome to Takini's Historical Trauma."
    http://www.historicaltrauma.com/ .

56 Stephen T. Newcomb, *Pagans in the Promised Land: Decoding the Doctrine of Christian
    Discovery (*Golden, CO: Fulcrum, 2008).

57 Anthony Hall, *Earth Into Property: Colonization, Decolonization, and Capitalism* (Montreal:
    McGill-Queens UP) p. 454.

58 Javed Jamil, *Muslims Most Civilized But Not Enough* (Saharanpur, Uttar Pradesh, India:
    Mission Publications, 2013).

59 Suzana Nabil Saad, "Why Is Divorce on the Rise Among US Muslims?" *On Islam*,
    February 17, 2013. (http://www.onislam.net/english/reading-islam/living-islam/islam-
    day-to-day/family/461407-divorce-on-the-rise-among-us-muslims.html).

60 "Looking back at Salman Rushdie's The Satanic Verses." *The Guardian*, September 14,
    2012. (http://www.theguardian.com/books/2012/sep/14/looking-at-salman-rushdies-
    satanic-verses).

61 Christine Victoria Brown, "The Satanic Verses and the Debate Over Great Britain's
    Blasphemy Laws: How a Fictional Novel Caused a Western Society to Re-Evaluate Its
    Identity." Thesis Submitted to Vanderbilt University, April, 2009, p. 4.
    (http://discoverarchive.vanderbilt.edu/bitstream/handle/1803/2981/BrownCVthesis0
    9.pdf?sequence=1) .

62 *Schenck v. United States*, 249 U.S. 47 (1919).

63   "Looking back at Salman Rushdie's The Satanic Verses." *The Guardian*, September 14, 2012. (http://www.theguardian.com/books/2012/sep/14/looking-at-salman-rushdies-satanic-verses).

64   Gilad Atzmon, *The Wandering Who?: A Study of Jewish Identity Politics* (Winchester UK: John Hunt, Zero Books, 2011) p. 162.

65   Nafeez Ahmed, *The War on Truth: 9/11, Disinformation, and the Anatomy of Terrorism* (Northhampton, Massachussetts: Interlink, 2005) pp. 3-6.

66   Lynn Margulis, Statement to PatriotsQuestion911.com website, August 27, 2007. (http://www.patriotsquestion911.com/professors.html#Margulis).

67   "Effects of the Internet on politics: Research roundup." *Journalist's Resource,* March 15, 2013. (http://journalistsresource.org/studies/politics/citizen-action/research-internet-effects-politics-key-studies#sthash.AceONIzs.dpuf).

68   Alan Cowell, "West Beginning to See Islamic Protests as Sign of Deep Gulf." *New York Times*, February 8, 2006. (http://www.nytimes.com/2006/02/08/international/europe/08islam.html?ref=danishcartooncontroversy&_r=0).

69   Gwladys Fouché, "Danish paper rejected Jesus cartoons." *The Guardian*, February 6, 2006. (http://www.theguardian.com/media/2006/feb/06/pressandpublishing.politics).

70   Christopher Bollyn, "Why the European Press is Provoking Muslims." *American Free Press*, February 3, 2006.

71   Cited in Bollyn.

72   Patricia Cohen, "Yale Press Bans Images of Muhammad in New Book." *New York Times*, August 12th, 2009. (http://www.nytimes.com/2009/08/13/books/13book.html?_r=0).

73   "Cartoons 'part of Zionist plot.'" *The Guardian*, February 7th 2006. (http://www.theguardian.com/world/2006/feb/07/muhammadcartoons).

74   I am using the term *conspiracy* both in its common sense of "working together in secret to do something illegal or harmful," and in the sense of the term's roots which mean "to breathe together." Much Zionist activity in service to dubious ends, such as the consistently deceptive nature of Zionist discourse, seems to be as unconscious and "natural" as breathing.

75   Thomas Dalton, *Debating the Holocaust: A New Look At Both Sides* (Chicago: Theses and Dissertations Press, 2009).

76   Gordon Duff, "VT's 30 Day Old Story on Benghazi Had it Right." *Veterans Today*, September 22, 2012. (http://www.veteranstoday.com/2012/10/22/vts-30-day-old-story-on-benghazi-had-it-right/).

77   David Brock and Ari Rabin-Havt, *The Benghazi Hoax* (Media Matters for America, 2013).

78   David Brock, "The Benghazi Hoax." *Huffington Post*, October 21, 2013. (http://www.huffingtonpost.com/david-brock/the-benghazi-hoax_b_4136492.html).

79   ibid.

80   Duff, op. cit.

81   Tom Hussain, "Pakistani government minister offers bounty for killing Innocence of Muslims makers." The London *Telegraph*, September 22, 2012. (http://www.telegraph.co.uk/news/worldnews/asia/pakistan/9559842/Pakistani-government-minister-offers-bounty-for-killing-Innocence-of-Muslims-makers.html).

82   Todd Starnes, "WH Silent Over Demands to Denounce 'Piss Christ' Artwork." *Fox News Radio*, September 21, 2012. (http://radio.foxnews.com/toddstarnes/top-stories/wh-silent-over-demands-to-denounce-piss-christ-artwork.html).

83   "Putin signs 'gay propaganda' ban and law criminalizing insult of religious feelings." *Russia Today*, June 30th, 2013. (http://rt.com/politics/putin-law-gay-religious-457/).

84   Mujahid Kamran, *9/11 and the New World Order* (Lahore, Pakistan: University of the

Punjab, 2013).

85 Shaykh Imran Hosein, "World War III and Muslim Alliance." Youtube video uploaded Dec. 2, 2011. (https://www.youtube.com/watch?v=opJd1FGPE3g).

86 *Truth Jihad Radio* interview with Bishop Richard Williamson. April 22, 2013. (http://truthjihadradio.blogspot.com/2013/04/bishop-richard-williamson-dr-nick.html).

87 Jytte Klausen, "The Danish Cartoons and Modern Iconoclasm in the Cosmopolitan Muslim Diaspora." Harvard Middle Eastern and Islamic Review 8 (2009), 86–118.

88 Patrick Goodenough, "US Tries to Break 'Religious Defamation' vs. Free Speech Deadlock at UN." CBS News, October 4, 2009.

89 Robert Evans, "Islamic bloc drops U.N. drive on defaming religion." *Reuters*, March 25, 2011. (http://in.reuters.com/article/2011/03/24/idINIndia-55861720110324).

90 Austin Dacey, "United Nations Affirms the Human Right to Blaspheme. *Religion Dispatches*, August 11, 2011. (http://www.religiondispatches.org/archive/politics/4985/united_nations_affirms_the_human_right_to_blaspheme_|_politics_|_/).

91 A.N. Wilson, *God's Funeral: The Decline of Faith in Western Civilization* (NY: W.W. Norton, 1999).

92 Patrick Buchanan, *The Death of the West: How Dying Populations and Immigrant Invasions Imperil Our Country and Civilization* (NY: St. Martin's Griffin, 2002).

93 John Perkins, *Confessions of an Economic Hit Man* (NY: Plume, 2005).

94 Zbigniew Brzezinski, *The Grand Chessboard: American Primacy and Its Geostrategic Imperatives* (NY: Perseus/Basic, 1997).

95 Karen Armstrong, *Fields of Blood: Religion and the History of Violence* (NY: Knopf, 2014).

96 Terry Melanson, *Perfectablists: The 18th-Century Bavarian Order of the Illuminati* (Walterville, Oregon: Trine Day, 2009).

97 http://www.bridgestocommonground.org/

98 John Andrew Morrow, *The Covenants of the Prophet Muhammad with the Christians of the World* (Hillsdale, NY: Sophia Perennis, 2013).

99 http://www.covenantsoftheprophet.com/

100 Sükran Vahide, qtd. in Ian S. Markham, *Engaging with Bediuzzaman Said Nursi: A Model of Interfaith Dialogue* (Farnham, Surrey, UK: Ashgate, 2009) p. 15.

101 Webster G. Tarpley et al., *Chi ha ucciso Aldo Moro* (Roma: Partito Operaio Europeo, 1978). Reprints available from author.

102 Webster G. Tarpley, "Norway Terror Attacks a False Flag: More Than One Shooter on Island; Oslo Police Drilled Bomb Blasts; Was It NATO's Revenge for Norway's Decision to Stop Bombing Libya?," Tarpley.net, July 24, 2011.

103 Spengler [David P. Goldman], "Terry Jones, asymmetrical warrior," *Asia Times*, September 14, 2010.

104 Webster G. Tarpley, "The Mohammed Cartoons—Recruiting Europe For Bush's War On Iran," February 9, 2006, online at Tarpley.net.

105 And indeed the papacy benefitted immensely in religious legitimacy from the end of its temporal power in the Papal states after 1870.

106 J. Bowyer Bell, *Terror Out of Zion* (Transaction Publishers, 1996).

107 *International Terrorism: Challenges and Response,* Proceedings of the Conference on International Terrorism, Jerusalem, July 2-5, 1979.

108 "A Day of Terror: The Israelis," *New York Times*, September 12, 2001. (http://www.nytimes.com/2001/09/12/us/day-terror-israelis-spilled-blood-seen-bond-that-draws-2-nations-closer.html).

109 Interview with Ehud Barak, BBC World "Hard Talk," September 11, 2001. (https://www.youtube.com/watch?v=gA00sKASfBo).

110 *A Clean Break: A New Strategy for Securing the Realm* (http://www.iasps.org/strat1.htm).

111 *Rebuilding America's Defenses*, Project for a New American Century, September 2000, (http://www.newamericancentury.org/RebuildingAmericasDefenses.pdf).

112 It was especially the Pentagon attack that made 9/11 the long-desired New Pearl Harbor. The destruction of private property at the WTC might not have been sufficient to turn even such a huge crime into "war," but an attack on an iconic national military facility like the original Pearl Harbor—the Pentagon—definitely was. See *Behind the Smoke Curtain: What Happened at the Pentagon on 9/11, and What Didn't, and Why It Matters.* (http://tinyurl.com/smokecurtain).

113 Ashton Carter, Philip Zelikow and John Deutsch, "Catastrophic Terrorism: Tackling the New Danger.." *Foreign Affairs*, November/December 1998. (http://www.foreignaffairs.com/articles/54602/ashton-b-carter-john-deutch-and-philip-zelikow/catastrophic-terrorism-tackling-the-new-danger).

114 Human Rights Watch and Columbia Law School Human Rights Institute, July 22, 2014, "All of the high-profile domestic terrorism plots of the last decade, with four exceptions, were actually FBI sting operations." (http://reason.com/blog/2014/07/22/human-rights-watch-all-of-the-high-profi).

115 "What We Know About the Alleged 9-11 Hijackers," by Jay Kolar. In *The Hidden History of 9-11*, Paul Zarembka ed. (Seven Stories Press, 2008). Part I, pp. 3-44.

116 "Symbolic vote in France Backs Palestinian State," *New York Times*, Dec. 3, 2014. (http://www.nytimes.com/2014/12/03/world/europe/france-vote-recognize-palestine.html).

117 "French Police Say Suspect in Attack Evolved from Petty Criminal to Terrorist," *New York Times*, Jan. 11, 2015.

118 "Disputed Claims over Qaeda Role in Paris Attacks," *New York Times*, Jan. 15, 2015. (http://www.nytimes.com/2015/01/15/world/europe/al-qaeda-in-the-arabian-peninsula-charlie-hebdo.html?emc=edit_th_20150115&nl=todaysheadlines&nlid=63905770).

119 a) "In New Era of Terrorism, Voice From Yemen Echoes," *New York Times*, Jan. 11, 2015 (http://www.nytimes.com/2015/01/11/world/middleeast/in-new-era-of-terrorism-voice-from-yemen-echoes-as-france-declares-war.html ? emc=edit_th_20150111&nl=todaysheadlines&nlid=63905770). b) "Paris Attackers Funded by Pentagon Dinner Guest." Jan. 11, 2015. (http://landdestroyer.blogspot.com/2015/01/opps-paris-attackers-funded-by-pentagon.html) ; and c) Jeremy Scahill, "The Paris Mystery: Were the Shooters Part of a Global Terrorist Conspiracy?" Jan. 12, 2015 (http://linkis.com/kQu1g).

120 "Zionist hand revealed: Rothschild family had purchased Charlie Hebdo in December 2014'." Jan. 22, 2015 (http://medhajnews.com/article.php?id=NjAwMA). The purchase of the Paris satirist publication shortly before the shootings that massively increased its revenues parallels Larry Silverstein's leasing of the WTC complex shortly before the 9/11 attacks, as well as negotiating a change in his insurance policy so that twin terrorist attacks would result in doubled payouts.

121 Jonathan Cook. "What Hebdo Execution Video Really Shows." (http://www.informationclearinghouse.info/article40699.htm).

122 Interview with Ole Dammegard, by Kevin Barrett, Truth Jihad Radio, Feb. 2015, (http://noliesradio.org/archives/95385).

123 "Paris Silence: Charlie Hebdo Attack Lead Investigator Found Dead While Writing Report." January 11, 2015. (http://cut2thetruth.wordpress.com/2015/01/11/paris-silence-charlie-hebdo-attack-lead-investigator-found-dead-while-writing-report/).

124 Hicham Hamza, "Suicided officer's family denied access to autopsy," translated by Kevin Barrett. *Veterans Today*, Jan. 26, 2015. (http://www.veteranstoday.com/2015/01/26/fredou/).

125 "Hollande asked Netanyahu not to attend Paris memorial march." *Haaretz* [Israel],

Jan. 12, 2015. (http://www.haaretz.com/mobile/.premium-1.636557?
v=D9B18F0B6D785F827EDA7137FD551BC6).

126 "France Deploys Troops to Guard 'Sensitive Sites." *New York Times*, Jan. 13, 2015.

127 "Emotion Mixes With Politics as 4 Killed at Paris Market are Buried in Jerusalem."
New York Times, Jan. 14, 2015.
(http://www.nytimes.com/2015/01/14/world/middleeast/paris-terror-attacks-
funeral-jerusalem.html?emc=edit_th_20150114&nl=todaysheadlines&nlid=63905770).

128 "France Fights Call for Mass Migration of Jews." *USA Today*, Feb. 17, 2015.

129 Ali Abunimah, "French President's Holocaust Day Speech Presages Crackdown on
Palestine Supporters." Jan. 27, 2015.
(http://www.informationclearinghouse.info/article40824.htm).

130 Tony Cartalucci, "Paris Shooters Just Returned from NATO's Proxy War in Syria."
January 8, 2015. (http://landdestroyer.blogspot.com/2015/01/paris-shooters-just-
returned-from-natos.html).

131 Tom Secker, "The Origins of NATO's Secret Islamist Terrorist Proxies."
March 11, 2013. (http://wideshut.co.uk/gladio-b-the-origins-of-natos-secret-islamic-
terrorist-proxies/); b) Operation Gladio document collection,
http://www.investigatingtheterror.com/documents/Operation_Gladio_Document_Co
llection.htm; c) Daniele Ganser, *NATO's Secret Armies*; and d) Richard Cottrell, *Gladio:
NATO's Dagger at the Heart of Europe.*

132 http://www.helpfreetheearth.com/news1149_FF.html

133 "Paris Terror, the Smell of False Flag," *Veterans Today*, Jan. 15, 2015.
(http://www.veteranstoday.com/2015/01/15/neo-paris-terror-the-smell-of-false-
flag/).

134 Lance deHaven-Smith, *Conspiracy Theory in America* (Austin: U of Texas P, 2013) p. 14.

135 ibid.

136 See Architects and Engineers for 9/11 Truth (www.ae911truth.org) and the *Journal of
9/11 Studies* (www.journalof911studies.com).

137 Michael Dorman, "Hijackers' lost luggage conveniently solves so many 9/11
mysteries." *Newsday*, April 17 2006. Republished with acerbic commentary at
http://www.unknownnews.org/0604180417lostluggage.html .

138 Jay Kolar, "What We Now Know About the Alleged 9/11 Hijackers." In Paul
Zarembka, Ed., *The Hidden History of 9/11* (NY: Seven Stories Press, 2011) pp. 3 - 44.

139 Charles Kurzman, "Al-Qaeda as Fringe Cult: 12 Years Later, Heretical Text of 9/11
Hijackers Still Withheld by FBI." (http://www.juancole.com/2013/09/heretical-
hijackers-withheld.html).

140 The *New Yorker* 10/8/2001, cited at http://www.historycommons.org/context.jsp?
item=a0901deliberatetrail .

141 On 9/11-anthrax as a single false flag operation, see Graeme MacQueen, *The 2001
Anthrax Deception* (Atlanta, GA: Clarity Press, 2014).

142 Project for a New American Century (PNAC), "Rebuilding America's Defenses:
Strategy, Forces, and Resources for a New Century." September, 2000.
(http://www.informationclearinghouse.info/pdf/RebuildingAmericasDefenses.pdf).

143 Ashton Carter, Philip Zelikow and John Deutch, "Catastrophic Terrorism: Tackling the
New Danger." *Foreign Affairs*, November-December 1998.
(http://www.foreignaffairs.com/articles/54602/ashton-b-carter-john-deutch-and-
philip-zelikow/catastrophic-terrorism-tackling-the-new-danger).

144 "Thinking about Political History", Miller Center Report, Winter 1999, pp. 5-7.

145 Ralph Blumenthal, "Tapes Depict Proposal to Thwart Bomb Used in Trade Center
Blast." *New York Times*, October 28, 1993, p.A1.
(http://www.nytimes.com/1993/10/28/nyregion/tapes-depict-proposal-to-thwart-
bomb-used-in-trade-center-blast.html?pagewanted=all&src=pm).

146 ibid.

147 Ralph Schoenman, "Who Bombed the U.S. World Trade Center?—1993 Growing Evidence Points to Role of FBI Operative," Prevailing Winds, Number 3, 1993.

148 Peter Lance, *Triple Cross: How bin Laden's Master Spy Penetrated the CIA, the Green Berets, and the FBI* (NY: William Morrow, 2009). Summarized by the author, reported at http://www.washingtonsblog.com/2009/06/triple-cross-or-inside-job.html.

149 Peter Dale Scott, "How the FBI Protected al-Qaeda's Hijacker Trainer." Global Research, October 8th 2006. (http://www.globalresearch.ca/how-the-fbi-protected-al-qaeda-s-9-11-hijacking-trainer/3422).

150 ibid.

151 Hyman G. Rickover, *How the Battleship Maine Was Destroyed* (Washington: Dept. of the Navy, Naval History Division, 1976).

152 "Al-Ahram Al-Arabi: A High-Ranking Yemenite Intelligence Official Blames the US for the Cole Bombing." Middle East Media Research Institute, July 17, 2001. (http://www.memri.org/report/en/print479.htm).

153 Joe Vialls, "Bali Micro Nuke - Lack of Radiation Confuses 'Experts'—'The bomb flashed and exploded like a micro nuke, but our Geiger counters don't show any radiation'." (http://www.angelfire.com/me4/al_fikr/Bali_Nuked.htm).

154 Sidney Jones, "Who are the terrorists in Indonesia? Conspiracy theories over the Bali bombing are rife in Indonesia." *The Observer*, October 27th 2002.

155 "Mossad agent Mike Harari implicated in Bali bombing, 9/11 - check out his false passports!" TruthJihad.com blog, February 18, 2011. (http://truthjihad.blogspot.com/2011/02/mossad-agent-mike-harari-implicated-in.html).

156 Mathieu Miquel, "March 11, 2004. The Madrid 3/11 Bombings: Was it Really an Attack by 'Islamic Terrorists'?" Global Research, November 28, 2009. (http://www.globalresearch.ca/march-11-2004-the-madrid-3-11-bombings-was-it-really-an-attack-by-islamic-terrorists/16424).

157 Nafeez Ahmed, *The London Bombings: An Independent Inquiry* (London: Duckworth, 2006).

158 Nick Kollerstrom, *Terror on the Tube: Behind the Veil of 7/7, an Investigation* (Joshua Tree, CA: Progressive Press, 2011).

159 Nandita Sengupta, "Pak TV channel says 26/11 hatched by Hindu Zionists." The *Times of India*, December 2, 2008. (http://timesofindia.indiatimes.com/india/Pak-TV-channel-says-26-11-hatched-by-Hindu-Zionists/articleshow/3785654.cms?referral=PM).

160 Adrian Levy and Cathy Scott-Clark, "CIA bin Laden hunter David Headley plotted Mumbai massacre." *Sunday Times*, November 3, 2013. (http://www.thesundaytimes.co.uk/sto/news/world_news/Asia/article1335376.ece).

161 Yanira Farray, "US-Indo-Israeli Axis." Veterans Today, July 26, 2010.

162 Webster Tarpley, "Major Hasan Of Fort Hood: A Patsy In A Drill Gone Live?" Infowars, November 15, 2009. (http://www.infowars.com/major-hasan-of-fort-hood-a-patsy-in-a-drill-gone-live/).

163 Kurt Haskell, "The Colossal Deceit Known As The Underwear Bomber Case." (http://haskellfamily.blogspot.com/2011/09/colossal-deceit-known-as-underwear.html).

164 Jason Rynan, "Underwear Bomber Abdulmutallab: 'Proud to Kill in the Name of God'." February 16, 2012. (http://abcnews.go.com/Blotter/underwear-bomber-abdulmutallab-sentenced-life-prison/story?id=15681576).

165 "Gordon Duff: Times Square Bombing Part of CIA False Flag Against Pakistan." *Veterans Today*, May 13, 2010. (http://www.veteranstoday.com/2010/05/13/gordon-duff-time-square-bombing-part-of-cia-false-flag-against-pakistan/).

166 Dave Lindorff, "Craft International Services hired guns at the Boston Marathon: Why Such Secrecy about Private Military Contractor's Men Working the Event?" April 25, 2013. (http://thiscantbehappening.net/node/1718).

167 Sheila Casey, "False flag theater: Boston bombing involves clearly staged carnage." Truth and Shadows, May 8, 2013. (http://truthandshadows.wordpress.com/2013/05/08/false-flag-theatre-boston-bombing-involves-clearly-staged-carnage/).

168 Dave Lindorff, "Did the FBI Snuff Out a Boston Marathon Bombing Witness? Dark Questions About a Deadly FBI Interrogation in Orlando." Counterpunch, March 24, 2014. (http://www.counterpunch.org/2014/03/24/dark-questions-about-a-deadly-fbi-interrogation-in-orlando/).

169 F. William Engdahl, "The Boston Bombings and the CIA Connection. Graham Fuller and Uncle Ruslan Tsarnaev." Global Research, May 17, 2013. (http://www.globalresearch.ca/the-boston-bombings-and-the-cia-connection-graham-fuller-and-uncle-ruslan-tsarnaev/5335416).

170 ibid.

171 James Corbett, "Who Is Graham Fuller?" The Corbett Report, May 8, 2013. (http://www.corbettreport.com/who-is-graham-fuller/).

172 ibid.

173 "CIA trained ISIL in Jordan: Report." Press TV, June 23, 2014. (http://www.presstv.com/detail/2014/06/23/368231/cia-trained-isil-in-jordan-report/).

174 *Miami Herald*, "Who Is Iraq's Abu Bakr al-Baghdadi?" June 13, 2014. (http://http//www.miamiherald.com/2014/06/13/v-print/4176171/who-is-iraqs-abu-bakr-al-baghdadi.html).

175 Kevin Barrett, "Who Is Abu Bakr al-Baghdadi?" Press TV, July 14 2014.

176 Kevin Barrett, *Questioning the War on Terror* (Madison, WI: Khadir Press, 2009) pp. 21-22.

177 "All Terrorists are Muslims…Except the 94% that Aren't." Loonwatch, January 20th, 2010. (http://www.loonwatch.com/2010/01/not-all-terrorists-are-muslims/).

178 Shadia Drury, *Leo Strauss and the American Right*. NY: Palgrave, 1999.

179 Ron Suskind, "Faith, Certainty, and the Presidency of George W. Bush." The *New York Times Magazine*, October 17th, 2004. (http://www.nytimes.com/2004/10/17/magazine/17BUSH.html?_r=3&ex=1255665600&en=890a96189e162076&ei=5090&partner=rssuserland&).

180 Naomi Klein, The Shock Doctrine: The Rise of Disaster Capitalism. NY: Metropolitain, 2007.

181 Gordon Duff, "Paris Terror: The Smell of False Flag." *Veterans Today*, January 15, 2015. (http://www.veteranstoday.com/2015/01/15/neo-paris-terror-the-smell-of-false-flag/).

182 Gordon Duff, "Too Classified to Publish: Bush Nuclear Piracy Exposed." *Veterans Today*, May 20 2014. (http://www.veteranstoday.com/2014/05/20/too-classified-to-publish-bush-nuclear-piracy-exposed/); and Gordon Duff, "Nuclear Roundtable: America's Nuclear Arsenal." *Veterans Today*, June 24 2014. (http://www.veteranstoday.com/2014/06/24/nuclear-roundtable-americas-nuclear-arsenal/).

183 On Bernays, see: *Century of the Self*. DVD. Directed by Adam Curtis, 2002 (http://topdocumentaryfilms.com/the-century-of-the-self/).

184 Mustafa Caglayan, "Norman Finkelstein: Charlie Hebdo is sadism, not satire." (http://www.sott.net/article/291724-Norman-Finkelstein-Charlie-Hebdo-is-sadism-not-satire).

185 "Rupert Murdoch: World Freedom Dependent on Israel's Future." The Algemeiner,

November 8, 2013. (http://www.algemeiner.com/2013/11/08/rupert-murdoch-world-freedom-dependent-on-israel/).

186 Anthony Hall, "Harper, The Ottawa Shooter, and the Selling of War." (http://www.veteranstoday.com/2014/10/31/harper-the-ottawa-shooter-and-the-selling-of-war/); Mark Taliano, "Canada: The Ottawa Shootings and the Derogation of Constitutional Rights. Did Zebaf-Bibeau Act Alone?" (http://www.globalresearch.ca/canada-the-ottawa-shootings-and-the-derogation-of-constitutional-rights-did-zebaf-bibeau-act-alone/5410986); Barrie Zwicker, "Canada's False Flag Terror: Fingerprints of US Involvement." (https://truthandshadows.wordpress.com/2014/11/08/canadas-false-flag-terror-fingerprints-of-u-s-involvement/).

187 Ali Abunimah, "France begins jailing people for ironic comments." (http://electronicintifada.net/blogs/ali-abunimah/france-begins-jailing-people-ironic-comments).

188 Mohammad Tomazy, "French Cartoonist Zeon Arrested for Anti-Zionist Work." The Arab World 360, March 7, 2015. (http://www.arabworld360.info/2015/03/french-cartoonist-zeon-arrested-for.html).

189 http://www.lefigaro.fr/flash-actu/2012/03/30/97001-20120330FILWWW00344-toulouse-la-france-traumatisee-sarkozy.php

190 http://fr.euronews.com/2015/01/13/les-victimes-de-l-attaque-contre-l-epicerie-casher-enterrees-a-jerusalem/

191 http://oumma.com/11936/tuerie-de-toulouse-netanyahu-lecon-a-juppe

192 http://www.lexpress.fr/actualite/monde/proche-moyen-orient/netanyahu-pret-s-il-le-faut-a-declencher-une-attaque-contre-l-iran_1183455.html

193 http://tempsreel.nouvelobs.com/politique/20121031.OBS7687/netanyahou-aux-juifs-de-france-venez-en-israel.htmlhttp://www.ladepeche.fr/article/2012/03/16/1307536-un-temoin-je-voyais-les-flammes-sortir-de-l-arme.html

194 http://obsession.nouvelobs.com/high-tech/20121012.OBS5502/contre-le-terrorisme-un-senateur-ump-veut-surveiller-internet.html

195 http://www.egaliteetreconciliation.fr/Hollande-denonce-theorie-du-complot-et-negationnisme-30589.html

196 http://www.ladepeche.fr/article/2012/03/16/1307536-un-temoin-je-voyais-les-flammes-sortir-de-l-arme.html

197 http://www.egaliteetreconciliation.fr/Montauban-le-temoin-a-vu-le-visage-du-tueur-11082.html

198 http://www.lefigaro.fr/actualite-france/2012/03/18/01016-20120318ARTFIG00055-montauban-le-tueur-porterait-un-tatouage-sur-le-visage.php

199 http://www.leprogres.fr/rhone/2012/03/20/tuerie-de-toulouse-j-ai-vu-le-tueur-il-avait-les-yeux-verts?image=659C4459-9A88-4EB6-BED6-F2406F41F748#galery

200 http://www.lemonde.fr/societe/video/2012/03/19/toulouse-l-emotion-des-familles-devant-l-ecole-juive_1672128_3224.html

201 https://www.youtube.com/watch?v=_qjQztmw3KA

202 http://radiorcj.info/2012/03/20/7376/tuerie-de-toulouse-les-corps-des-victimes-rapatries-en-israel-aujourdhui/

203 These examples and others are reported by Gordon Thomas in his *Histoire secrète du Mossad, de 1951 à nos jours,* Nouveau Monde Editions, 2006.

204 http://www.dailymotion.com/video/x8rwx2_la-fausse-agression-antisemite-du-r_news?start=241#from=embed

205 http://www.alterinfo.net/Les-fausses-agressions-antisemites-delits-crimes-ou-vulgaire-propagande-sioniste_a26038.html

206 http://www.dailymotion.com/video/x99k2q_alex-moise-s-envois-lui-meme-des-me_news#from=embed. Other examples may be seen at: http://cristos.over-

blog.com/pages/Les_coups_montes_et_fausses_affaires_antisemites-1516845.html

207 https://www.youtube.com/watch?v=rugVNJrzJuw

208 Christophe Barbier, in *C dans l'air* (France 5), le 12 mars 2012

209 O. Recassens, D. Hassoux et C. Labbé, L'Espion du Président, Robert Laffont, 2012. Also see http://www.franceinter.fr/emission-dans-le-pretoire-bernard-squarcini-se-defend-dans-l-express

210 http://arthurzbygniew.blogspot.fr/2010/10/france-gare-au-retour-de-manivelle.html

211 https://www.youtube.com/watch?v=-LSkZ7g5Kdc

212 "De toute façon, je devais t'appeler pour te dire que j'avais des tuyaux à te donner, mais en fait j'allais te fumer."

213 http://www.metrofrance.com/info/mohamed-merah-un-indic-de-la-dcri/mlcA!zbO76JImEPU/

214 http://tempsreel.nouvelobs.com/monde/20120328.OBS4777/mohamed-merah-s-est-il-forme-lors-de-ses-voyages-a-l-etranger.html

215 We are considering the scenario of the "hijacked conspiracy," a hypothesis I developed in relation to 9/11: http://www.egaliteetreconciliation.fr/La-double-imposture-du-11-Septembre-29162.html

216 http://www.wat.tv/video/proches-mohamed-merah-sous-choc-4yohl_2i6xp_.html

217 http://www.ledauphine.com/faits-divers/2012/03/22/merah-la-haine

218 http://www.lefigaro.fr/actualite-france/2012/03/29/01016-20120329ARTFIG00361-l-avocat-de-merah-je-ne-l-ai-jamais-connu-religieux.php

219 http://www.agoravox.fr/actualites/politique/article/mohamed-merah-tueur-d-enfants-le-114471

220 http://www.jeanmarcmorandini.com/article-276609-en-2010-une-plainte-contre-mohamed-merah-qui-avait-endoctrine-un-ado-et-l-avait-seque

221 http://www.numerama.com/magazine/22180-mohamed-merah-avait-son-acces-internet-sous-ecoute.html

222 http://videos.tf1.fr/jt-20h/claude-gueant-des-negociations-sont-en-cours-7082494.html

223 http://www.20minutes.fr/societe/906699-20120328-affaire-mohamed-merah-proches-abdelkader-merah-rendus-fresnes

224 http://www.youtube.com/watch?v=-LSkZ7g5Kdc

225 http://videos.tf1.fr/jt-we/les-details-de-l-assaut-vus-par-le-patron-du-raid-7087812.html

226 http://videos.tf1.fr/jt-we/les-details-de-l-assaut-vus-par-le-patron-du-raid-7087812.html

227 http://news.sky.com/home/video/16194180 : vidéo supprimée

228 http://www.europe1.fr/France/Merah-a-bien-filme-sa-cavale-meurtriere-1002467/

229 http://lci.tf1.fr/france/faits-divers/merah-pere-denie-a-tout-francais-le-droit-de-le-faire-taire-7093182.html

230 http://www.ladepeche.fr/article/2012/03/28/1317278-y-a-t-il-un-troisieme-homme.html

231 http://www.sudouest.fr/2012/03/29/affaire-mohamed-merah-une-piece-du-scooter-retrouvee-dans-une-voiture-abandonnee-673090-5215.php

232 "Hunt for Charlie Hebdo Killers Focuses on Brothers, 3rd Suspect in Custody." CNN, posted 12:02 p.m. 1/8/2015. (http://fox40.com/2015/01/08/hunt-for-charlie-hebdo-killers-focuses-on-brothers-3rd-suspect-in-custody/).

233 John Eskow, "The Bizarre Compulsion of Black Men to 'Reach for their Waistbands'." Counterpunch, November 28-30 2014 (http://www.counterpunch.org/2014/11/28/the-bizarre-compulsion-of-black-men-to-reach-for-their-waistbands/).

234 Francesco Cossiga, "Osama-Berlusconi? Trappola giornalistica." *Corriere della Sera*. 30

November 2007.

235 Daniel Hopsicker, *Welcome to Terrorland: Mohamed Atta & the 9-11 Cover-up in Florida* (Walterville, Oregon: Trine Day, 2005).

236 Elias Davidsson, *Hijacking America's Mind on 9/11: Counterfeiting Evidence.* NY: Algora, 2013.

237 "Robert Fisk: Even I question the 'truth' about 9/11." The *Independent,* August 25, 2007. (http://www.independent.co.uk/voices/commentators/fisk/robert-fisk-even-i-question-the-truth-about-911-462904.html).

238 Seymour Hersh, "What Went Wrong: The CIA and the Failure of American Intelligence." The *New Yorker*, October 8, 2001. (http://www.newyorker.com/magazine/2001/10/08/what-went-wrong).

239 "Context of 'After 8:46 a.m. September 11, 2001: Hijacker's Passport Allegedly Found near the World Trade Center'." *History Commons* (http://www.historycommons.org/context.jsp?item=a091201passportfound).

240 Truth Jihad Radio interview with Bruce Lawrence, broadcast February 16, 2007 (http://eddieleaks.org/its-bogus/).

241 Alexander Kouzmin, Matthew T. Witt and Andrew Kakabadse (eds), *State Crimes Against Democracy: Political Forensics in Public Affairs* (NY: Palgrave Macmillan, 2013).

242 "Civil Case: King Family versus Jowers." The King Center (http://www.thekingcenter.org/civil-case-king-family-versus-jowers).

243 Amedy Coulibaly wurde hingerichtet, *Alles Schall und Rauch*, January 12, 2015. (http://alles-schallundrauch.blogspot.co.at/2015/01/amedy-coulibaly-wurde-hingerichtet.html).

244 Ted Thornhill, "Children's worker reveals how mother's suicide helped turn the Kouachi brothers from 'sweet young boys' into infamous Islamist murderers." *Daily Mail,* January 19, 2015. (http://www.dailymail.co.uk/news/article-2916450/Children-s-worker-reveals-mother-s-suicide-helped-turn-Kouachi-brothers-sweet-young-boys-infamous-Islamist-murderers.html).

245 Alasdair MacIntyre, "A Partial Response to my Critics." In *After MacIntyre: Critical Perspectives on the Work of Alasdair MacIntyre*, ed. John Horton and Susan Mendus (Notre Dame: University of Notre Dame Press, 1994), 303.

246 Josef Pieper, *Abuse of Language, Abuse of Power* (San Francisco: Ignatius Press, 1992), 34-35.

247 Edith Stein, quoted by John Paul II in *Homily of John Paul II for the Canonization of Edith Stein* (Oct 11, 1998), available at http://w2.vatican.va/content/john-paul-ii/en/homilies/1998/documents/hf_jp-ii_hom_11101998_stein.html.

248 http://france3-regions.francetvinfo.fr/basse-normandie/2015/02/11/coutances-vincent-reynouard-condamne-deux-ans-de-prison-ferme-pour-negationnisme-653515.html.

249 Daniel Spaulding, "Free Speech Farce." *The Soul of the East,* January 30, 2015. (http://souloftheeast.org/2015/01/30/free-speech-farce/).

250 Stanley Fish, *There's No Such Thing as Free Speech and it's a Good Thing Too* (Oxford: Oxford University Press, 1994), 102.

251 See especially William T. Cavanaugh, "A Fire Strong Enough to Consume the House: The Wars of Religion and the Rise of the State." *Modern Theology* 11, no. 4 (October 1995).

252 William T. Cavanaugh, *Migrations of the Holy: God, State, and the Political Meaning of the Church* (Grand Rapids: Eerdmans, 2011).

253 Rémi Brague, "Are Non-Theocratic Regimes Possible?" *Intercollegiate Review* (Spring, 2006), 11, available at http://www.mmisi.org/ir/41_01/brague.pdf.

254 Tom Breidenbach, *IX*XI/The Wicked Child* (NY: Groundwater Press, 2014).

255 Thomas Molnar, *Twin Powers: Politics and the Sacred* (Grand Rapids: Wm. B. Eerdmans,

1988), 137.

256 Alasdair MacIntyre, *Whose Justice? Which Rationality?* (Notre Dame: University of Notre Dame, 1989), 336.

257 Thaddeus J. Kozinski, "Modernity's Apocalypse." In *The Blueprint: Reflections, Debates and Propositions for a New Catholic Social Action Plan*, ed., Guido Preparata, (forthcoming, 2016).

258 Sheldon Wolin, *Democracy Incorporated* (Princeton: Princeton University Press, 2008) 9.

259 James Alison, "Contemplation in a world of violence: Girard, Merton, Tolle." A talk given at the Thomas Merton Society, Downside Abbey, Bath (November, 2001). (http://girardianlectionary.net/res/alison_contemplation_violence.htm).

260 William T. Cavanaugh, "The Liturgies of Church and State." *Liturgy* 20, No. 1 (2005): 25-30.

261 William T. Cavanaugh, "The Empire of the Empty Shrine: American Imperialism and the Church." *Cultural Encounters* 2, no. 2 (Summer, 2006), 15.

262 Ibid.

263 Neil Kramer, "Invisible Empire." May 22, 2014. (http://neilkramer.com/invisible-empire.html).

264 Edmund Waldstein, "Religious Liberty and Tradition." January, 2015. (http://thejosias.com/2015/01/02/religious-liberty-and-tradition-iii/).

265 CBC News, "Charlie Hebdo newspaper shooting timeline: At least a dozen are dead, and numerous people were injured." January 7, 2015. (http://www.cbc.ca/news/world/charlie-hebdo-newspaper-shooting-timeline-1.2892399). Accessed on January 30, 2015.

266 Shaun Sim, "Paris Attack Video: Gunmen Filmed Shootout with Police Officer." *International Business Times*, January 7, 2015. (http://www.ibtimes.com/paris-attack-video-gunmen-filmed-shooting-wounded-police-officer-1776004).

267 Jonathan Cook, "What Hebdo execution video really shows." January 13, 2015. (http://www.jonathan-cook.net/blog/2015-01-13/what-hebdo-execution-video-really-shows/). Accessed on January 30, 2015.

268 Panamza, "Fuite des terrorists de Charlie Hebdo: un trajet impossible." (http://www.panamza.com/180115-charlie-trajet accessed on January 29, 2015).

269 *Le Parisien*, "Amedi, 27 ans, rencontre Sarkozy cet après-midi." July 15, 2009. (http://www.leparisien.fr/grigny-91350/amedi-27-ans-rencontre-sarkozy-cet-apres-midi-15-07-2009-580211.php).

270 *Complete Transcript of the Martin Luther King, Jr. Assassination Conspiracy Trial*, Testimony of Charles Cabbage, 161 – 162. (http://www.thekingcenter.org/sites/default/files/Assassination%20Trial%20-%20Full%20Transcript.pdf). Accessed on January 30, 2015.

271 *Complete Trial Transcript*, Testimony of Dr. Smith, 141. (http://www.thekingcenter.org/sites/default/files/Assassination%20Trial%20-%20Full%20Transcript.pdf). Accessed on January 30, 2015.

272 Mary Uhl-Bien, Russ Marion, Bill McKelvey, "Complexity Leadership Theory: Shifting leadership from the industrial age to the knowledge era." *The Leadership Quarterly* 18 (2007): 298 – 318.

273 Uhl-Bien, Marion, and McKelvey, "Complexity Leadership Theory," 299.

274 Ibid., 303.

275 Ibid., 303.

276 Nick Allen, "Police marksman who shot Jean Charles de Menezes apologises to family," October 24, 2008. (http://www.telegraph.co.uk/news/uknews/law-and-order/3254455/Police-marksman-who-shot-Jean-Charles-deMenezes-apologises-to-family.html). Accessed on January 30, 2015.

277 Stephen Wright, "Undercover police 'spied on the de menezes family': Secret probe

after Brazilian shot dead in catastrophic blunder," *The Daily Mail*, July 23, 2014. (http://www.dailymail.co.uk/news/article-2703451/Undercoverpolice-spied-Menezes-family-Secret-probe-Brazilian-shot-dead-catastrophic-blunder.html). Accessed on January 30, 2015.

278 Tom Cook, "Press freedom in Britain has been 'sacrificed,'" January 29, 2015 . (http://nsnbc.me/2015/01/29/press-freedom-in-britain-has-been-sacrificed/). Accessed on January 29, 2015.

279 Peter Dale Scott, Ph.D., "The Hidden Government Group Linking JFK, Watergate, Iran-Contra, and 9/11." October 5, 2014. (http://whowhatwhy.com/2014/10/05/the-hidden-government-group-linking-jfk-watergate-iran-contra-and-911/#sthash.pYX3miMH.dpuf). Accessed on January 28, 2014.

280 Ibid.

281 Google Maps provides a breakdown of the official narrative route archived by one citizen observer. (https://www.google.fr/maps/dir/48.8807004,2.3728185/48.8784144,2.374224/@48.8789788,2.3730116,17z). Accessed on January 30, 2015.

282 LePoint.fr, "Mohamed Merah travaillait pour les RG: La DCRI est chargée de L'enquete sur les meurtres commis par le djihadiste. Allors qu'elle est elle-meme mise en cause," June 7, 2012. (http://www.lepoint.fr/societe/merah-une-enquete-a-haut-risque-07-06-2012-1470689_23.php). Accessed on January 30, 2015.

283 Jonathan Cook, "Hebdo video." (http://www.jonathan-cook.net/blog/2015-01-13/what-hebdo-execution-video-really-shows/). Accessed on January 30, 2015.

284 Dean Nelson, "Mumbai suspect is US double agent, India claims." December 16 2009. (http://www.telegraph.co.uk/news/worldnews/northamerica/usa/6826571/Mumbai-suspect-is-US-double-agent-India-claims.html). Accessed on January 30, 2015.

285 For more information on September 11ᵗʰ war games please see http://www.911myths.com/index.php/War_Games and for information on the war games training taking place just before and after the Malaysian airliner went missing see http://www.smh.com.au/entertainment/books/first-book-on-mh370-mystery-blames-us-war-games-20140517-38gmf.html ; for information on exercises taking place at the time of the 7/7 London bombing please see https://www.youtube.com/watch?v=E1HPNpxbfX8 ; and for information on the police exercises that were taking place on the day of the Boston Marathon Bombing please see http://www.dailymotion.com/video/xz3pz1_boston-marathon-bombing-the-fbi-and-bomb-drills-ben-swann-on-reality-check_news all accessed on January 30, 2015.

286 Jonathan Cook, "Hebdo video," located at http://www.jonathan-cook.net/blog/2015-01-13/what-hebdo-execution-video-really-shows/ accessed on January 30, 2015.

287 Eleanor Beardsley, "The French Debate: Free Speech Versus Hate Speech." National Public Radio, Feb. 10 2015. (http://www.npr.org/blogs/parallels/2015/02/10/384959376/the-french-debate-free-speech-versus-hate-speech).

288 *Encyclopedia Britannica* (http://www.britannica.com/EBchecked/topic/27646/anti-Semitism).

289 Dictionary.com. Online Etymology Dictionary. Douglas Harper, Historian. http://dictionary.reference.com/browse/antisemitism (accessed: March 09, 2015).

290 *The Jewish Encyclopedia: A Descriptive Record of the History, Religion, Literature, and Customs of the Jewish People from the Earliest Times to the Present Day*, Volume 1. (www.jewishencyclopedia.com/articles/1603-anti-semitism).

291 Archived at http://noliesradio.org/archives/96091.

292 "Israeli forces caught up in Al Qaeda's complex toils in both Golan and Gaza." (http://www.debka.com/article/24223/).

293 "France: Raids kill 3 suspects, including 2 wanted in Charlie Hebdo attack."

(http://www.cnn.com/2015/01/09/europe/charlie-hebdo-paris-shooting).

294 "These 17 Journalists Were Killed by Israel In Gaza." (http://countercurrentnews.com/2014/08/these-17-journalists-were-killed-by-israel-in-gaza/).

295 "Paris march: TV wide shots reveal a different perspective on world leaders at largest demonstration in France's history." (http://www.independent.co.uk/news/world/europe/paris-march-tv-wide-shots-reveal-a-different-perspective-on-world-leaders-at-largest-demonstration-in-frances-history-9972895.html).

296 "To Call This Threat by Its Name." (http://www.nytimes.com/2015/01/19/opinion/marine-le-pen-france-was-attacked-by-islamic-fundamentalism.html).

297 "Paris attacks aftermath: French police arrest 54 people for defending or glorifying terrorism." (http://www.independent.co.uk/news/world/europe/paris-attacks-aftermath-french-police-arrest-54-people-for-defending-or-glorifying-terrorism-9977434.html).

298 The interviews are archived at http://noliesradio.org/archives/category/archived-shows/kevin-barrett-show.

299 "Copenhagen free speech debate shooting RAW FOOTAGE." (https://www.youtube.com/watch?v=-7j_tnHRst0). Accessed March 17, 2015.

300 Webster Tarpley, *9/11 Synthetic Terror: Made in USA*. 5th ed. (Joshua Tree, CA: Progressive Press, 2011). pp 88–90.

301 Tim Pugmire, "CIA confirms Ventura meeting occurred." MPR News, January 3, 2008. (http://www.mprnews.org/story/2008/01/03/jessecia).

302 Jim Fetzer, "New York Times: All the lies they can fit in print." *Veterans Today*, March 14, 2015. (http://www.veteranstoday.com/2015/03/14/the-new-york-times-all-the-lies-they-can-fit-in-print/).

303 "9/11 Eyewitness - FOX Freelancer Harley Guy Mark Walsh." (https://www.youtube.com/watch?v=-5y8PtfKA14).

304 Webster Tarpley, "The Forty-Six Exercises and Drills of 9/11." In *9/11 Synthetic Terror: Made in USA*. 5th ed. (Joshua Tree, CA: Progressive Press, 2011). pp 275–338.

305 Please note that not all contributors to this book share these suspicions, and that of those who do, opinions differ concerning the likelihood that the shooting was a false flag, and the identity and motive of the suspects. Like all contributions to *We Are Not Charlie Hebdo*, this article represents the views of its author and no-one else's.

306 Hicham Hamza, "Zionists linked to "Charlie Hebdo terrorists' escape." Tr. Kevin Barrett. *Veterans Today,* February 1, 2015. (http://www.veteranstoday.com/2015/02/01/zio-charlie/).

307 "Ex-Muslim politician 'girlfriend' of murdered Charlie Hebdo editor was NOT in a relationship with him, claims his family as they spark a furious row." The *Daily Mail*, January 10, 2015 (http://www.dailymail.co.uk/news/article-2904897/).

308 Hicham Hamza, "Charlie Hebdo bombshell! Suicided officer's family denied access to autopsy." Tr. Kevin Barrett. *Veterans Today*, January 26, 2015. (http://www.veteranstoday.com/2015/01/26/fredou/).

309 "France: 'Charlie Hebdo-Watergate'! Amedy Coulibaly executed with tied hands at grocery store in Vicennes—Uncensored and uncut." LiveLeak, January 20, 2015. (http://www.liveleak.com/view?i=956_1421605884).

310 "Amedi, 27 ans, rencontre Sarkozy cet après-midi." Le Parisien, July 15, 2009. (http://www.leparisien.fr/grigny-91350/amedi-27-ans-rencontre-sarkozy-cet-apres-midi-15-07-2009-580211.php).

311 Hicham Hamza, "'AG extraordinaire'" : Hyper Cacher a bien été vendu la veille de la prise d'otages." Panamza, March 19, 2015. (http://www.panamza.com/190315-

hypercacher-pv).

312 Hicham Hamza, "Charlie Hebdo bombshell! Suicided officer's family denied access to autopsy." Tr. Kevin Barrett. *Veterans Today*, January 26, 2015 (http://www.veteranstoday.com/2015/01/26/fredou/).

313 John Lichfield. "Paris attacks: François Hollande sees his popularity ratings double in wake of strong French response to Charlie Hebdo killings." The *Independent,* January 19, 2015. (http://www.independent.co.uk/news/world/europe/paris-attacks-francois-hollande-sees-his-popularity-ratings-double-in-wake-of-strong-french-response-to-charlie-hebdo-killings-9988775.html).

314 Thierry Meyssan, "The State Against The Republic: What Lies Behind the Anti-'Conspiracy Theorist' Discourse." (http://www.voltairenet.org/article187030.html).

315 Hicham Hamza, "Another Charlie Hebdo bombshell: Video falsified!" Tr. Kevin Barrett. *Veterans Today*, February 9, 2015. (http://www.veteranstoday.com/2015/02/09/charlie-falsified/).

316 "Paris gunmen Cherif Kouachi and Amedy Coulibaly 'used child porn sites for covert communication'." *International Business Times,* January 15, 2015. (http://www.ibtimes.co.uk/paris-gunmen-cherif-kouachi-amedy-coulibaly-used-child-porn-sites-covert-communication-1483554).

317 "According to Charlie Hebdo Journalist, one of the attackers had BLUE EYES." (https://www.youtube.com/watch?v=L3oBd2vxHz0). See also: "http://www.dailymail.co.uk/news/article-2909082/Spared-Charlie-Hebdo-journalist-reveals-stared-killer-s-big-soft-troubled-eyes-wouldn-t-spot-colleague-hiding-table.html

318 Ibid.

319 *Egalité et Réconciliation,* "La visite secrète de Lieberman et du Mossad à Paris deux semaines avant les attentats." March 12, 2015. (http://www.egaliteetreconciliation.fr/La-visite-secrete-de-Lieberman-et-du-Mossad-a-Paris-deux-semaines-avant-les-attentats-31628.html).

320 Ibid.

321 Ibid.

322 James Robertson, "Charlie Hebdo: The Third Man." January 17th, 2015. (http://crimesofempire.com/2015/01/17/the-third-man/).

323 "De Rothschild's Print Charlie Hebdo: 'We Doubted Whether We Should Buy Newspaper Libération.'" *Quote* 13:23. January 22, 2015. (http://www.quotenet.nl/Nieuws/De-Rothschild-s-print-Charlie-Hebdo-We-doubted-whether-we-should-buy-newspaper-Liberation-144350).

324 "Charlie Hebdo printing 7 million copies of first post-massacre issue." *Haaretz,* January 18, 1015. (http://www.haaretz.com/news/world/1.637722).

Made in the USA
San Bernardino, CA
12 April 2015